God & Science

God & Science

How the Bible and Science Work Together to Illuminate God & Explain Our Universe

Thomas G. Fournier

Publisher: TGiF Publishing

ISBN: 978-0-9985446-9-4

For permissions, inquiries, or more information, contact:

Thomas G. Fournier

thomas_4nier@yahoo.com

Printed in USA

This book is dedicated to those who aren't afraid to question conventional wisdom and long-standing beliefs in their pursuit of biblical and scientific truth.

Table of Contents

FOREWORD

"I don't believe in the bible because of science."

I've heard this statement many times over the years and it causes me to cringe every time. It is especially rankling because, when pressed for clarification, so few people can actually explain the scientific evidence that they feel refutes the bible. Worse still, they fall back on the "fact" of Darwinian evolution or blithely say something like, "I just don't see how the bible can be true."

"I don't believe in science because of the bible."

I've heard this statement too, and far too many times, from believers who blindly accept what is being thrown at them from the pulpit or take at face value the heavily skewed anti-science rhetoric that is presented by well-meaning, but mistaken (or perhaps misled) clergy or other figures of authority.

But the reality is that the actual knowledge of the sciences, the bible, or both, for too many on both sides of this fence is too superficial to permit an open and honest assessment of either opposing view. I, too, was once guilty of this. I once viewed the seeming disconnect between biblical and scientific knowledge with discomfort but possessed an inadequate ability to explain it. Although I felt that there *must be* a viable explanation for this disconnect, I never really took action to remedy my ignorance. This is, thankfully, no longer the case.

My journey down the road to find the convergence of biblical and scientific wisdom began decades ago, when I first stumbled upon Dr. Gerald Schroeder's thought-provoking and fascinating book, *The Science of God*. The paperback was sitting on a shelf at the local library at ankle level, yet something drew my eyes to it (thank you, Lord!). I poured through the pages of it ravenously, excited that many of my questions regarding the seeming bible-science disconnect were finally being answered and thrilled to learn for the first time that their true teachings <u>do</u>, in fact, converge. My concerted studies in both areas have since helped me to see how they complement rather than contradict each other in so many ways.

This book has been decades in the making. I've spent the last 20+ years pouring over books in various scientific fields, while concurrently dissecting the biblical text, to gain a more solid understanding of their interplay. I've endeavored to scrutinize scientific findings in a way that separates fact from bias in an effort to form my own conclusions. I've also looked at the biblical text more deeply and with fresh eyes, laying aside any preconceived opinions and relying solely on what the biblical text actually says.

My trek over the last few years has been filled with exciting moments of revelation, as well as lengthy periods where I seemed to make no progress whatsoever. I have no doubt that the latter instances were my own fault – the result of periods of complacency brought on by the cares of life or the consequences of submitting to my own selfish desires. Thankfully, my efforts more recently have resulted in much more of the former, filling me with renewed excitement and a greater appreciation of Him, my Beloved Creator.

The merging of biblical and scientific wisdom has, for me, been liberating. Understanding how the bible and the sciences work together has served to increase my awe of Him. I thank God for the drive that He has placed within me to understand His Word and the natural world that He created. I am truly grateful that He has chosen to reveal things to me as He has, especially since I began this quest in earnest not so long ago. He has also put into my heart a desire to spread this message. The rewards have been both uplifting and humbling.

I am sure that there will be those who disagree with some of my conclusions, as well as those who will stubbornly cling to ingrained teachings and simply refuse to accept them, regardless of the strength of the evidence I may provide. But, in writing this book, I have done all that I can do to present them with the strongest possible collection of evidence. I respectfully challenge any naysayers to prove me otherwise. I am not so set in my own ways that I would be unwilling to change my mind, if presented with good evidence to the contrary.

It has been my experience when reading similar books that I often fail to actually review the key passage(s) of scripture or scientific fact(s) that are presented therein, even when I've found them to be quite compelling or fascinating. It isn't laziness so much (…ok…*sometimes* it is…) as it is making the time and taking the effort later on to locate the other book or source to confirm what I just read.

I read during almost every spare moment that I have, which is often just a few minutes here and there between other daily activities. Consequently, it is usually not convenient for me to follow up on a specific tidbit of knowledge at the exact moment of discovery, even when I very much wish to do so. More often than not, the thought is ultimately purged from my brain by other distractions as the day progresses, taking with it any desire I once had to check further into the juicy morsel of data that once piqued my interest. I have, therefore, chosen to incorporate key scriptural passages within the various appendices to make it as convenient as possible for the reader to immediately see that I am quoting scripture as wholly and as correctly as possible, and within the proper context.

I designed the book's cover to reflect God's hand in everything, from the smallest of things (the atom, discretely represented by the 'dot' in the "i" of "Science" within the title) to the largest (the vast cosmos that so prominently lords over our tiny planet, with the earth positioned amidst the two extremes). Superimposed over the entire scene is a triquetra; a symbol that is commonly accepted among Christians to represent the Trinity. The triquetra is meant to depict God's command over every one of these elements. I am very grateful to AJ Main for skillfully turning my simple verbal description into the resulting work of art.

I look forward to continuing my mission of deepening my own knowledge and wisdom of my Creator and His creation and passing it along to anyone who cares (or dares) to listen. It energizes me to know that, whenever I read His Word, I will see Him and His creation with fresh eyes and that wherever I look in nature, I cannot help but see the hand of God.

Most Sincerely,

Thomas G. Fournier

CHAPTER ONE

Exposing the Deceit

The world is being fed a great lie – a glaring, divisive untruth that is being accepted by most without question. Unfortunately, we are so conditioned to lies, thanks in large part to the reality of partisan politics, that we shrug them off without a second thought or have just plain ceased to listen. In every nation, political parties spew their distorted versions of the "truth" in an attempt to affirm their own narrative or to the place the blame for our ills at the feet of their opposition.

But, unlike the unscrupulous, conflicting tales being woven at any given time by any pair of political rivals, this universally accepted lie is far more damaging. That is because, in *this* particular instance, the very same narrative is being projected at us *from both sides* of the argument. Additionally, its impact is global and far-reaching, threatening the future of billions of people. It is the idea that biblical and scientific wisdom do not and cannot peacefully coexist. It is the untruth that, like the opposing poles of a magnet, these two pieces must reside within their respective realms and must never to be brought together.

So-called experts on both sides of the divide (i.e., scientists and theologians) cling stubbornly to this mantra, refusing to consider any fresh evidence that they believe threatens their beliefs, and continue to teach and preach misinformation. But the truth is that recent scientific discoveries and a deeper understanding of biblical wisdom are pairing like never before; the two areas working together to dispel this falsehood.

The scientific advances of the last two centuries regarding the creation of our universe and the laws that govern its operation, the inner workings of cellular life, genetics, particle physics, and quantum mechanics (to name just a few) have revealed a vast wealth of knowledge, enabling us to perform wonderous feats and to make amazing technological advances. Some, such as the incredible fine tuning of physical laws and the inarguable complexity of information within DNA, have also served to open the door for skeptics to the probability of a Creator.

The scientifically inclined need not look anymore upon the bible with derision as scientific discoveries continue, at a growing pace and with increasing depth, to affirm technical principles that were written into the biblical text thousands of years before their modern confirmation. Similarly, our understanding of biblical wisdom is entering a new era as secrets that have been long buried within the biblical text are finally being revealed. For biblical scholars, this has been expected. We were told that this would happen.

In Daniel 12, as the prophet seeks to understand the things that God had revealed to him, the Lord tells him, "*Go your way, Daniel: for the words are rolled up and sealed until the time of the end.*"[1] It is only recently that some of these prophecies have begun to unfold, providing fresh insight into, and a deeper understanding of other prophetic biblical passages that are awaiting fulfilment in these latter days. For example, details within Daniel 7 reveal five currently-existing nations that will be on the earth when Christ returns as He has promised. These nations include the United States of America, the United Kingdom, Russia, Germany, and France (see Appendix A for a detailed explanation). Although each of these five countries has been around for centuries, the key events to unlocking their associated prophecies have only come together during the last several decades to allow them to be identified more definitively.

The reality is that, when paired, biblical and scientific wisdom form a single, cohesive, and astonishing truth. Anyone who still believes that the two are mutually exclusive quite simply has not been doing their homework.

Science is not the Enemy

The truth is that a bible-believing Christian need not fear science, but can, in fact, embrace it. This can be difficult or uncomfortable for Christians and non-Christians alike because it forces them to challenge the teachings of respected theologians and scientists. Unfortunately, it is commonly these very "experts" who readily dismiss any findings that fall outside of their area of expertise, relying on an inadequate understanding of the facts from the "opposing" side. It is my intention, through the pages of this book, to examine

---

[1] *Although my personal preference is to use the King James Version (KJV) of the bible, most scriptural quotes used herein will be from the New International Version (NIV), unless otherwise noted, as I feel that most find it easier to understand.*

the evidence, expose the error in their one-sided views, and demonstrate the harmony that connects scientific and biblical wisdom.

Scientists these days are generally quick to plant their biases on newly revealed scientific findings in a concerted effort to erase any potential biblical connection. They develop theories that stretch the bounds of credibility (e.g., panspermia, punctuated equilibrium, neo-Darwinism, a "bouncing universe"[2]) or hypotheses that can never be observed or proven (such as the existence of a multiverse). Similarly, theologians often reject firmly grounded scientific findings, distorting the facts to ensure that they cannot possibly jibe with biblical wisdom, such as derisively referring to the Big Bang as an "explosion" or denying that it even happened (see Chapter Two). Resorting to outlandish or unprovable hypotheses or rejecting scientific facts in the face of overwhelming supporting evidence serves only to make naysayers on both sides look either ignorant or inept.

Despite the mental gymnastics being performed by the aforementioned "experts", there is a large (and growing!) number on both sides of the divide who are increasingly willing to view the findings openly, laying out the facts and letting them speak for themselves. This is because such things as the extreme fine-tuning of the universe, the complexity of language within DNA, the intricate and vastly involved

---

[2] Panspermia is the hypothesis that life exists throughout the universe and is distributed by space dust, meteoroids, asteroids, comets, and spacecraft through unintentional contamination. The theory argues that life did not originate on Earth, but instead evolved somewhere else and seeded life as we know it. However, the theory fails to explain the origin of life in the first place.

Punctuated equilibrium is the hypothesis that evolutionary development is marked by isolated episodes of rapid speciation between long periods of little or no change. The theory was proposed following recognition that the Darwinian model of evolution was completely unsupported by the fossil record.

Neo-Darwinism is an updated theory of evolution that represents a synthesis of Charles Darwin's theory in terms of natural selection and modern population genetics. The term was first used after 1896 to describe the theories of August Weismann (1834–1914), who asserted that his germ-plasma theory made impossible the inheritance of acquired characteristics and supported natural selection as the only major process that would account for biological evolution. (1)

Bouncing Universe is a theory that the cosmos evolved through a cycle of expansion and collapse, repeatedly expanding then collapsing in on itself due to gravity. (2) The theory fails to explain, however, the actual origin of the universe nor does it address the loss of energy that would occur with each "bounce," which would naturally occur as the result of the First Law of Thermodynamics. For these and other reasons, this theory has been largely discredited.

The multiverse theory suggests that our universe, with all its hundreds of billions of galaxies and almost countless stars, spanning tens of billions of light-years, may not be the only one. Instead, there may be an entirely different universe, distantly separated from ours — and another, and another. Indeed, there may be an infinity of universes, all with their own laws of physics, their own collections of stars and galaxies (if stars and galaxies can exist in those universes), and maybe even their own intelligent civilizations (3). The problem with this theory is that it can never be proven because any other universes would remain forever outside of our ability to observe them.

structure of living cells, and the implications of a more complete fossil record, coupled with freshly revealed biblical prophecies, protest loudly and with growing intensity against the conventional wisdom. They indicate more firmly each day that our natural world could not possibly have developed by chance, providing the strongest evidence yet for a Creator. Despite misleading claims to the contrary by both scientists and theologians, a careful study of scientific and biblical wisdom, performed in concert, affirms that the two can, *and do*, coexist in a mutually supportive relationship.

If you already believe in a Creator, then this makes perfect sense. After all, if the God that is revealed through the bible truly did create the universe and all that is within it (as I resolutely believe), then there should be no discrepancy between what is recorded within His Word and what we can observe through an honest and open study of the natural world that He created. If God is truly responsible for the creation of the universe, then He is also responsible for creating the laws of physics that govern its operation – laws that were generated by Him within the earliest moments of the universe's existence.

God's Instruction Manuals

We have, in fact, been given by God not one, but two records through which our faith in Him can be affirmed – His written Word, which describes the "who", "what", "why", and (to a limited extent) the "how"; and the natural world, which describes the "when" and the "how" in far greater detail. We are informed in His Word that both sources are useful in obtaining knowledge about Him and His creation (Appendix C). When taken together, these records form a far more complete picture than either provides on its own.

The bible was written by dozens of men over of hundreds of years, yet its various books are remarkably cohesive; their teachings supporting and affirming each other to an uncanny degree. This should not be surprising, however, as the biblical text attests that its writings were inspired by God; that, "*…all scripture is given by inspiration of God*" (2Tim 3:16) and that "*...men wrote as the Spirit gave them utterance.*" (KJV 2Peter 1:20-21, see Appendix B).

Consequently, the bible represents the direct word of God and must reign supreme among any other text or source, religious or otherwise.

Yet, while the Bible reigns supreme, it is not the only source through which we can learn about God and His creation. God tells us within His Word that the natural world is also instructive for this purpose. Among the scriptures provided to us through His Word, the following state this most clearly:

In Romans 1, we are informed, in no uncertain terms, that God intentionally reveals Himself through His creation.

Romans 1:19-20: *...what may be known about God is plain to them,* ***because God has made it plain to them.*** *For since the creation of the world* ***God's invisible qualities*** *– His eternal power and divine nature –* ***have been clearly seen, being understood from what has been made****, so that people are without excuse* (emphasis added by author).

In Psalm 19, we are informed that the heavens announce God's glory and declare His works through non-verbal means in a fully open manner that everyone (people of every nation and language, not just highly trained scientists) can understand.

Ps 19:1-4 (and Ps 97:6): ***The heavens declare the glory of God; the skies proclaim the work of His hands.*** *Day after day they pour forth speech; night after night they reveal knowledge.* ***They have no speech, they use no language; no sound is heard from them. Yet their voice goes out into all the earth, their words to the ends of the world.***

In my opinion, the King James version of the Psalm 19 text states this more clearly and eloquently: *"Day unto day they uttereth speech and night unto night they shewest knowledge.* ***There is no speech or language where their voice is not heard.****"*

In Isaiah 45, we are told that God created the cosmos, that He specifically made the earth to be inhabited, and that He has always intentionally and openly declared this.

Isaiah 45: 18-21: *For this is what the LORD says – He who created the heavens; He is God; He who fashioned* and *made the earth, He founded it; He did not create it to be empty but formed it to be inhabited – He says, "I am the LORD and there is no other.* ***I have not spoken in secret from somewhere in a land of darkness. ...Who foretold this long ago, who declared it from the distant past? Was it not I, the LORD?***

In Hebrews 11, He underscores the fact that the universe was created from things that aren't visible (e.g., molecular matter that is imperceptible to the naked eye and guided by physical forces, such as gravity, magnetism, and the strong and weak nuclear forces, that are equally invisible). In this (and in the Romans 1 passage above), He is telling us that there is more to the physical universe than meets the eye – that, if we take the time to closely scrutinize His creation, we will see His hand in everything…that we will come to understand that our universe, world, and life itself are not the result of cosmic accidents.

Hebrews 11:3: "*By faith, we understand that* ***the universe was formed at God's command, so that what is seen was not made out of what is visible.***"

Through these passages, God makes it quite clear within His Word that He uses nature to reveal Himself. With this being true – if God is using His creation to reveal Himself and express His attributes – then what we observe within the natural world must be *comprehensible, verifiable,* and *consistent*. We wouldn't be able to discern His presence or clearly see His attributes if these things were not so. How could we, if the rules were ambiguous and/or always changing?

Science affirms that the laws of physics in the most distant galaxies operate in the same manner as those that we can study here on earth. Sir Martin Rees, an internationally renowned Cosmologist, affirms that, "…all parts of the universe seem to be evolving in a similar way, as though they shared a common origin." (4)

Reigning in Our Skepticism

With God stating so very clearly that He uses the natural world to manifest Himself, Christians should exercise much more restraint before dismissing the sciences, doing so only after some serious consideration of the facts. Our understanding of nature may not be fully complete, but it is very wide and very deep. It is precisely because we possess a solid understanding of our world that we can use this knowledge on a daily basis to our advantage.

While we certainly do not know everything, and while some scientific theories or tenets that are currently held firm may ultimately be proven to be incorrect, the overwhelming majority of our knowledge of physics, biology, chemistry etc. is pretty well established. Through this understanding, we have made advances that improve our standard of living through the creation of electric power, television, microwave ovens, computers, cellphones, GPS technology, and anything else electronic. Science actually has a pretty good track record when it comes to revising its views on the basis of more complete and accurate information.

Yet, many Christians bend over backwards to dismiss the science, often basing their criticisms on things that they do not properly understand. They disregard so much science that has been proven time and again, such as the beginning of the universe through the Big Bang, a theory that is supported by overwhelming evidence within numerous fields of science. Yet, they insist that all of this science is wrong.

God says through the aforementioned passages that He reveals Himself through the natural world and He has given us the ability to question how and why things work as they do and the intellect to figure it out (see Job 32:8, Prov 2:6-8, James 1:5, Isaiah 11:2, Isaiah 48:6-7, and Psalm 119:66). With these things being true, it seems pretty foolish to so casually dismiss findings within the natural world, especially when many of them have been proven time and again through multiple methods. There are many things that God has chosen to reveal to us through nature rather than describing them directly within the pages of the bible.

The natural laws are not directly observable. We can't physically see gravity, magnetism, or any of the other physical laws. Instead, we learn of them through their impact on the world around us (as stated in Romans 1, Psalm 19, and Hebrews 11) and through the gift of intellect with which He has blessed us. It seems that the "comprehensible" part has been assured. In fact, Albert Einstein once remarked that, "The most incomprehensible thing about the Universe is that it is comprehensible."

For us to be able to observe, study, and understand how they work, the physical laws must operate consistently. Were this not so – if the operation of the physical laws and/or their impact on our world was always changing – it would be impossible for us to learn their patterns, predict behaviors, develop and test hypotheses, cultivate an understanding of how they work, and use this understanding to improve our standard of living. The bible tells us in Gen 1:14 that one purpose of the sun, moon, and stars is to serve as reliable indicators for seasons, days, and years. For this to be so, the laws that govern how they operate must be fixed and regular. How could we rely on them to serve as indicators of times, seasons, days, and years if their "laws" weren't fixed?

Yet many Christian apologists insist that the laws of physics – such as the speed of light and the rates of radioactive decay - operated differently in the past and that we can't rely on their present properties to deduce events in the past. The bible and the sciences plainly tell us otherwise.

Fortunately for us, God has put these laws, including their consistent nature, plainly on display. Throughout history, we have observed their impact on the world around us and have become intrigued enough to wonder why and how things within our world/universe act the way that they do. Through careful and prolonged study, we have determined over time how many of these laws work. History is replete with examples of this very process, such as the efforts of Issac Newton and Albert Einstein to understand gravity and the laws of motion, and efforts by Ben Franklin, Thomas Edison, and Nicoli Tesla to tame magnetism and electromagnetism, just to name a couple.

Even when we do not understand *everything* about a physical law, we can still develop enough of an understanding to be able to predict its effect on objects, enabling us to use it to our advantage. For example, scientists still have questions regarding the nature of gravity. Yet, even with some uncertainties, they have a firm enough understanding of its impact to correctly predict the orbits of heavenly bodies and calculate the trajectory and final destination of rockets, satellites, and man-made probes over great distances and with amazing accuracy.

Evidence and Exhortations

When God created the universe, He intentionally left His fingerprints all over it. He provided us with the clues that we would ultimately need to see His hand in everything from the vastness of the cosmos to the impossible minuteness of the quark.[3] In making man in His image, God also instilled within us the intellect (the Neshama; Strong's 5397[4]. See Gen 2:7) and ability to see and understand these clues through the study of the natural world. Many of the bible's scientific teachings were written thousands of years before mankind learned them to be true through the vehicle of modern scientific discovery. This could only be true if the book had indeed been inspired by a Being that transcends time; a God that fully knows the past, present, and future of the created universe.

[3] A quark is any member of a group of elementary subatomic particles that interact by means of the strong force. The protons and neutrons that comprise the nucleus of an atom are themselves comprised of various combinations of quarks. Quarks appear to be true elementary particles; that is, they have no apparent structure and cannot be further dissected into smaller particles.

[4] Any biblical Hebrew/Chaldee and Greek words that are cited herein will be accompanied periodically, as warranted, by the numerical citation (within parens) as indicated within Strong's Exhaustive Concordance to allow the reader to easily locate and review them.

God & Science

Within the pages of the bible, we are instructed to do the following:

- Educate ourselves on its content; to "study to show thyself approved…rightly dividing the word of truth" (KJV 2Tim 2:15);
- To "…prove all things, holding fast to that which is good" (KJV 1 Thess 5:21, Rom 12:2);
- Study the natural world, seeking evidence of Him through His creation (Rom 1:19-20, Ps 19:1-4, Isa 45:18-21, Heb 11:3);
- Reason together to reach a verdict (Isa 1:17-18, Job 34:2-4); and
- Decide upon a matter only after carefully considering it (Prov 18:13).

Throughout our lives, we are going to experience difficult events or circumstances during which we will be unable see a way out of a given predicament and must lean exclusively on our faith in His ability to carry us through. Yet, when it comes to His existence, it seems that God does not expect us to have blind faith. Instead, He has provided ample, *directly observable* evidence of His presence and given us the intellect and abilities to view and understand the evidence in all of its forms (see Appendix C).

More and more each day, the various fields of science reveal God's unmistakable imprint in everything around us. Recent scientific discoveries increasingly affirm His hand in our creation. They testify to the fact that our universe, our world, indeed our very lives required direction – His direction – in order for any of this to be here. The bible and the sciences both affirm that we are not an accident or the result of some fortuitous, unguided chain of events.

Those who are scientifically minded, Christian and non-Christian alike, will find that an honest and open-minded comparison of scientific observations to the numerous, provable scientific claims within the bible will reveal a great deal of harmony between the two. In every instance where a discrepancy is perceived, it can be attributed to an inadequate understanding or misinterpretation of either the biblical or scientific wisdom. In either case, the solution is simple – learn to scrutinize the data for yourself and do not rely (solely) on the oft-erroneous interpretations of others. Honestly, this isn't nearly as difficult as you may think.

Unfortunately, our knowledge of either the bible or the sciences (or both) is typically superficial, or at least far from complete. Additionally, for many of us the scales of knowledge are heavily weighted to one side. We are bombarded daily with an over-abundance of fresh scientific discoveries and viewpoints resulting from the number and ever-increasing pace of modern technological advances. We take them at face value because they are being proffered by well-educated, super-smart people and because we feel that we lack the expertise to question or refute them. We have faith in our scientists and researchers, expecting that they will present their conclusions without bias, based solely on what is being revealed by the sciences through the implementation of the scientific method.

Most of us have been exposed during our high school years to the scientific method, which is defined as the process of *objectively* establishing facts through testing and experimentation. Through the process, we are instructed to observe, collect background information, form a hypothesis, make a prediction, conduct experiments, and analyze and report the results. Unfortunately, it is often easy during the analysis and reporting phases for scientists to skew the results, either deliberately (i.e., with the intent to mislead in order to present or prevent a specific viewpoint) or inadvertently (i.e., by unintentionally allowing their conclusions to be impacted by preconceived notions or biases). Regrettably, this happens all too often.

It is equally regrettable that similar biases come into play on the "faith" side of the spectrum. However, instead of receiving a constant stream of fresh and/or deeper biblical information, the exact opposite is true; the pool of spiritual knowledge has grown stagnant as too many believers have allowed their biblical knowledge to lapse by failing to continue their studies of His Word. Maybe they grew up going to church, attending Sunday school, and saying a blessing before each meal. However, as they matured and the challenges of life demanded more of their energy, and as the constant bombardment of fresh scientific discoveries increasingly seemed to contradict their religious beliefs, they ceased tending to their spiritual growth. Or maybe they simply felt that they'd learned all that they could from the bible.

Whatever the reason for their lapse in biblical learning, they fail to recognize that the bible is an amazingly complex, deep text. While, they may understand (at least superficially) that it provides a wealth of easily understood knowledge concerning everyday matters, they do not realize that it is also filled with a far deeper wisdom than the human mind can ever fully comprehend. This only becomes obvious as one delves with real purpose into the biblical text. It is only then that its more subtle, hidden wisdom is revealed.

Allow me to illustrate how misunderstanding, misinterpretation, or blind misguided belief can skew one's viewpoint, using an example from each side of the divide.

Example #1: Failure to Objectively Consider Scientific Observation

While you may not understand complex scientific jargon and may have *zero* desire to unravel mind-boggling mathematical equations, you may be surprised to learn that much information that is available through the sciences (or at least the general conclusions thereof) is written in simple enough terms for a layperson to understand, allowing you to draw your own conclusions. Let's use the latest information regarding Darwinian evolution as an example.

Darwinian evolution preaches that life developed spontaneously over billions of years as amino acids randomly formed proteins – broke apart – formed other proteins – etc., continuing this process until they finally (and quite by accident) stumbled upon a workable sequence that resulted in the first simple life form (i.e., bacteria and photosynthetic algae comprised of a single, living biological cell). As the theory goes, once life began, it plodded along for another billion years or so as the proteins continued to randomly modify themselves until they ultimately evolved from single-celled organisms into multi-cellular (i.e., eukaryotic) life.

Following this model, a group of cells would eventually evolve into a fish, which subsequently evolved into a higher form of life by growing appendages and moving onto land, where it further evolved into other creatures having features that were adapted to the local environment. However, simply breaking down the key components of the theory in the light of current scientific knowledge reveals the fallacy of Darwinian evolution. The first part of the Darwinian equation (i.e., the random assemblage of amino acids into proteins that support life) provides the first significant challenge to the theory.

All living things are made of cells, with a typical person being comprised of over one hundred trillion of them (that's 100,000,000,000,000 cells). A collection of cells forms the various tissues throughout your body, like organs, bones, and blood vessels, and they are anything but simple. Each cell is comprised of thousands of individual parts that allow the cell in its entirety to function much like a factory. Cells are made of proteins, tiny molecular machines that are themselves comprised of hundreds of amino acids. Proteins come in hundreds of shapes, but they must be in the correct form at each place within your body in order to function properly.

Think of it this way… if you were building a car, amino acids would be the most basic parts, like the nuts, bolts, wire, and other small, individual pieces that comprise each of the larger components. The amino acids must be assembled in multiple correct combinations to form the wide variety of larger components (i.e., the proteins) that are necessary for creating a fully functioning automobile. Proteins would be the individual, larger components, like the starter, alternator, radiator etc.; each component working together to create a smoothly running, fully functioning automobile (i.e., or each cell of a living organism).

A wide variety of basic parts (i.e., the amino acids) and components (i.e., the proteins) must be manufactured, and in the correct quantities and types, to provide you with a fully functioning automobile. This is the function of DNA, which serves as a blueprint. DNA tells the cell how to correctly assemble the amino acids into functioning proteins, specifying the proper sequence of construction and indicating the quantity of each part that is needed to obtain the desired result. Steve Jobs (co-founder of Apple and trailblazer of the modern computer industry) once stated that, "DNA is like a computer program but far, far more advanced than any software ever created." [5]

What are the Odds?

Of the approximately 500 amino acids that exists naturally, only 20 are actually useful in supporting life. These 20 amino acids are like a 20-character alphabet, with each character required to be in a very specific sequence within the protein chain in order to form a life-supporting protein. An incorrect sequence results in no life. The odds are astronomically against this occurring by chance, naturalistic processes.

According to Tim Barnett of the organization Stands to Reason [6], if you take a protein that is comprised of only 150 amino acids (a pretty low number), then there are approximately 10^{195} possible ways that the amino acids could be arranged within it. That's a "1" followed by 195 zeros! Given this, and various other conditions that are required to build a functional protein, there is only *a single chance* out of 10^{164} possible combinations of a life-supporting protein being assembled through random, unguided processes!

That's not 1 chance out of a
million (1,000,000);
billion (1,000,000,000); or
trillion (1,000,000,000,000)...
but only ***1*** chance out of

***100,000,000,000,000,000,000,000,000,000,000,
000,000,000,000,000,000,000,000,000,000,000,
000,000,000,000,000,000,000,000,000,000,000,
000,000,000,000,000,000,000,000,000,000,000,
000,000,000,000,000,000,000,000,000,000,000***

combinations that a functional protein could form by random processes!!

Those are pretty long odds, long enough to be considered statistically impossible. A statistical impossibility is a probability that is so low as to not be worthy of mentioning. Sometimes it is quoted as 10^{50}, although the cutoff is inherently arbitrary. Although not truly impossible, the probability in this case is low enough so as to not bear mentioning in a rational, reasonable argument. (7)

And remember...this is just for the random assembly of a *single* life-supporting protein!! The odds of this happening hundreds of times *and* in the correct, life-supporting sequence grow more and more implausible at each step along the way.

For life to have spontaneously arisen via random point mutations within DNA is, for all intents and purposes, impossible. According to renowned physicist Dr. Gerald Schroeder, "...it would be as if nature chose by random from a bag containing a billion billion billion (repeated 40 times) proteins *the one* that worked, and then repeated the trick a trillion times!" (8)

To put it another way, for every single functional sequence of amino acids (i.e., a sequence that is suitable for life), there are 10^{77} non-viable combinations [(6)]. Quite simply, the number of unworkable combinations (i.e., the number of combinations that would NOT result in life) far exceeds the number of workable combinations. Sir Martin Rees states, "The challenge of fully elucidating how atoms assembled themselves...into living beings intricate enough to ponder their origin is more daunting than anything in cosmology." (9)

In his book, Darwin's Doubt, Dr. Stephen Meyer, renowned geophysicist and outspoken proponent for the convergence of biblical and scientific wisdom, uses the following analogy (10).

If a thief was attempting to steal a bicycle that was secured to a post via a 4-dial lock, there is a reasonable chance that he could do so, if given a 24-hour day to find the correct combination. A 4-dial lock has 10^4 (i.e., 10,000) combinations (i.e., 0000 – 9999). There are 86,400 seconds in a 24-hour day. If the thief could flip through one combination every second, he could cover 3,600 combinations in one hour and all 10,000 combinations in less than 3 hours.

However, if the combination lock had 10 dials, then the number of possible combinations would be 10^{10} (i.e., 10,000,000,000). Given the same 24-hour day, and allowing for the thief to work through one combination every second, he would only be able to get through 0.00000864% of the total available combinations before the day came to an end. It would take him almost 115,741 days (or over 317 years) to run through every single combination (at the rate of one combination per second).

In the case of DNA, trying to hit upon a single viable solution would be like trying to crack the combination of a lock that is comprised of 10^{77} possible combinations (i.e., 100,000,000,000,000,000,000,000,000,000, 000,000,000,000,000,000,000,000,000,000,000,000,000,000,000,000); a vastly greater number of dials.

It is precisely because the chances of this happening are so remote that Darwinian evolution provides for billions of years for this process to have occurred spontaneously. After all, with so few workable combinations available within so vast a number of possible combinations, adherents to Darwinian evolution recognize that it would have had to take a significant amount of time – billions of years – for amino acids to "stumble" upon a viable sequence. Is it then possible that this is how life truly began? Unfortunately for Darwinists, the answer is "no."

Was There Enough Time?

The paleontological record unambiguously demonstrates *exactly the opposite* of what evolutionists expected to find – that simple life appeared on earth *as soon as the planet was cool enough for life to exist.* Microfossils, in the form of single-celled bacteria and photosynthetic algae, appear within the fossils record as soon as the earth had cooled sufficiently from its initial molten state approximately 3.8 billion years ago, when the earth was still less than a billion years old. There were no billions of years available for this process to have occurred spontaneously. In fact, there wasn't enough time for randomness to have processed even a miniscule fraction of the potential combinations.

> If you are a proponent of the Young Earth theory and do not believe that the world/universe is billions of years old, I urge you to simply disregard for now any references to these lengthy time frames and continue reading. I will provide ample evidence for them later on, for your consideration. Regardless of whether or not you ultimately agree on the time frames involved, I think that you will still find plenty of accurate, reliable, and fascinating content herein.

The fossil record shows that the initial appearance of simple life on earth was abrupt and that it existed as *the only life form* on the earth for three billion years. Then, multi-celled organisms suddenly burst onto the scene within the seas *all at once, fully formed and functional*, during what has been labeled as the Cambrian Explosion. We are not talking here about a single celled organism becoming a mildly larger organism, the number of cells doubling or tripling along a trajectory that would eventually form vastly more complex creatures. We are talking here about how life went *instantly* from creatures comprised of *one cell* to creatures comprised of *billions and trillions of cells* overnight! Then, about 100 million years later, land animals suddenly appeared with the very same abruptness.

Contrary to naturalistic evolution, there are no fossils that show the transition from sea animals to land animals. Evolutionists will toss around an example or two of a fossil that they say represents this transition, but this is purely speculation. There is no real confirmed evidence of this anywhere in the fossil record. Yet, if sea animals actually *had* evolved during the million years preceding land animals, there should be a plethora of fossilized remains showing this transition. Such is not the case. Land animals appear just as abruptly on the scene as sea life did millions of years before.

A vast array of completely formed sea creatures – crustaceans, fishes, aquatic mammals – swiftly and unexpectedly emerged within the oceans approximately 530 million years ago. There was no hint in the preceding fossil record of single-celled organisms that this dramatic event was about to occur. Just as astounding is the brevity of the event, when compared to the totality of time that has elapsed since the Big Bang. Were we to compress the entirety of time since the initial Big Bang into a single 24-hour day, the Cambrian explosion would not have occurred until the 21st hour and would have lasted for only 2 minutes of the available 1,440 minutes within this notional 24-hour day.

Since the theory was first proposed, Darwinists (in their belief that life arose gradually and morphed from simple to complex over long periods of time) have expected that this sequence of events would have been captured within the earth itself. They were certain that the fossil record, which was still in the earliest stages of development during Darwin's time, would ultimately provide a host of transitionary fossils – remnants of creatures that were captured in mid-transition from one form to another. Over a century and a half later, Darwinists stand rebuked – the earth has provided no such evidence despite a vastly more complete fossil record from sites across the globe. The transitional fossils that Darwin was sure would ultimately be revealed simply do not exist.

Let's summarize the very basic facts that have been presented so far:

1. Rather than taking billions of years, life arose on earth *as soon as it was possible* for it to exist (strike one!);
2. After 3 billion years of existing on earth solely as single-celled organisms, life instantaneously made the leap from single-celled organisms to a whole host of complex, multi-cellular aquatic animals (strike two!); and
3. No mid-transitional fossils have been found within the fossil record, which has grown vastly more complete during the almost two centuries that have elapsed since the theory was proffered (strike three!).

These are some of the very basic scientific facts surrounding Darwinian evolution and *you do not need advanced scientific knowledge or a college degree to understand their implications*! Anyone viewing these facts with an open mind must reach the conclusion that Darwinian evolution cannot possibly be true. The fact that the self-organization of life also runs in direct opposition to the Second Law of Thermodynamics provides another significant chink in the armor of Darwinism (see the discussion Flying in the Face of the Second Law, pg. 25).

Individually, each of these facts provide a direct and significant challenge to Darwinian evolution. Taken together, they provide the theory with an insurmountable obstacle. And, when combined with evidence from other fields of science, such as molecular biology, microbiology, genetics, and chemistry, the theory becomes indefensible. Yet incredibly, scientists and laypeople continue to cling stubbornly to the dead horse of Darwinian evolution, devising modified versions of the theory that grow increasing more improbable and smack of desperation.

They seem incapable of examining the evidence objectively and continue to view each new finding through a jaded and rigid prism.

The Darwinian Evolution Propaganda Machine

Despite its many obstacles, Darwinian evolution is typically cited as a "fact" rather than as the theory that it is (and a largely disproven one at that). It is difficult to find a documentary that has been produced by such media giants as The Discovery Channel, History Channel, PBS, National Geographic or dozens of other such organizations where there isn't at least one subtle nod to Darwinian evolution. It may be in the form of a single spoken line – something along the lines of, "Millions of years of evolution have equipped the tortoise with the ability to…" – but it is always there and it is always presented as a forgone conclusion. The covers of such prominent magazines as Scientific American and Time provide perfect examples of this, unabashedly attributing the explosion of life to "evolution" with such feature stories as:

- Uncovering the Origins of Evolution's Big Bang (Scientific American, June 2019)
- Evolution's Big Bang (Time, December 4, 1995)
- The Puzzling Big Bang of Animal Evolution (Scientific American, November 1992)

Even seemingly unbiased books written on topics other than evolution tout it all too often as a reality (some, perhaps unintentionally). One such book, which otherwise contains a treasure trove of helpful information regarding the fine tuning of the universe, states, "*Humans are the result of billions of years of evolution, built out of a myriad of complex molecules and structures*." [(11)] Another, while speaking of the intricacies of a living cell's ability to transform an embryo into blood, bone, and flesh, states, "…*our life is just one generation in humankind's evolution, an episode that is itself just one stage in the emergence of the totality of life*.", and, "*We are the outcome of time and chance: if evolution were rerun, the outcome would be different*." [(12)]

Both of the aforementioned books convey a wealth of helpful and fascinating information and I would recommend them highly to anyone who is interested in the mechanics of how our universe is constructed and the forces through which it operates. But their authors, like so many others, seem incapable of relegating Darwinian evolution into the realm of theory, where its status as a viable hypothesis remains tenuous, at best.

As recently as November of 2024, a Popular Mechanics article claims to have captured evolution in progress [(13)]. The title of this particular article seems to be aimed at deliberately misleading the reader into believing that it is speaking of an example of macro-evolution (i.e., the evolution of one body plan into another) rather than micro-evolution (i.e., a gradual change in a single trait, such as the color of an animal's fur or a change in the size of its tail).

Unfortunately, this evolutionary bias permeates the one area that, more so than any other, touches the lives of almost everyone on the planet – the entertainment industry. Countless movies speak of Darwinian evolution as an established fact, some even going so far as to make it a central theme. For example, in the first few minutes of the movie *Prometheus,* one "scientist" derides the protagonist for her religious beliefs, chastising her for brushing aside "millions of years of evolution" while rolling his eyes and scoffing aloud, as if this were the most ridiculous thing in the world. The "fact" of Darwinian evolution is also a central theme to the entire Jurassic Park franchise. Framing the theory in this way (i.e., continually citing it as a fact rather than the theory that it is) is bound to have a significant impact on the large segment of the population whose only source of such information is the *deliberate misinformation* being spewed by Hollywood and the general media.

This Hollywood mindset is pervasive, with countless films either building up evolution or mocking belief in God. It's no small wonder, given the fact that most schools today – even college-level institutions – still teach Darwinian evolution as the only viable option, despite the growing skepticism within scientific circles as to its veracity. School teachers and college professors are prohibited from discussing any other possibility – especially one that mentions God – at the risk of losing their jobs!

The threat of being openly ridiculed or potentially losing a job, combined with an inability to provide a substantive counter-argument, engenders a meekness among many Christians that is not only wholly unnecessary, but detrimental to the cause of spreading the "Good News." Christians need to arms themselves, spending just a few minutes each week studying both biblical and scientific matters with the goal of both defending and promoting one's faith.

Darwinian evolution is just one example within a single scientific field where the science is intentionally skewed world-wide. Other glaring examples include the farce of human induced global warming and the "science" behind the global response to COVID-19 prior to 2023, much of which has since been debunked. However, in the interest not going off on a tangent, I will refrain from addressing these things here. (If you would like to better understand the fallacy of the global warming agenda, see Appendix D.)

The "science" behind Darwinian evolution and human induced global warming is intentionally misrepresented and almost universally misunderstood by those preaching these myths as well as by the general public. Unfortunately, this is also commonly the case on the theological side of the house. We'll examine an example of this next.

Example #2: Inadequate Understanding of Biblical Wisdom

The present English bible has been translated from Latin (Vulgate), which was translated from Greek (Septuagint), which originated in Hebrew. While the central messages and themes of the bible have certainly been retained, there are some minor points that have gotten lost in translation at each step. For example, there were four words within the original Hebrew and Greek texts for "hell," each of which had a distinctly different meaning. They include, "sheol" (Strong's 7585) and "hades" (Strong's 0086), both of which mean "the grave" or the "realm of the dead/departed," "tartaros" (Strong's 5020) which is the netherworld – the place reserved for demons and fallen angels, and "ghehennah" (Strong's 1067), the fire and brimstone hell of everlasting punishment for those who have rejected Christ. Yet, every time the word appears in the English bible, it is rendered simply as "hell," which can lead to confusion.

For example, in Acts 2:31-32, Peter is recounting the words of David, who said, "*He (David) seeing this before spake of the resurrection of Christ, that His soul was not left in hell…*" I've heard people ask, "Why would Jesus go to hell?" with their thoughts being on the "hell" of fire and brimstone. I asked the question once myself a while back, with the very same mindset. It wasn't until many years later that I realized my error. The word used in Acts 2:31 for "hell" is "hades" – the abode of the dead. It was not "ghehennah" – the place of everlasting torment where, according to Jesus, both the body and soul can be destroyed (Matt 10:28).

Other things that were lost in the translation were not actually words or phrases, but points of grammar. For example, within the original Hebrew text of Gen 1:1-2, the nouns and verbs are in reverse order in comparison to the remaining 29 verses in the chapter, which is meant to indicate that the actions of the first two verses had already been completed prior to the action of Gen 1:3. This fact was not captured within the subsequent Greek text, meaning that those who later translated it into Latin and English were oblivious to it. This inadvertent omission has had a significant impact on how some perceive the age of the universe/earth (more on this in Chapter Three). The 1917 Schofield Reference Bible recognized this and added a footnote for Gen 1:1 that read, "The first creative act refers to the dateless past and gives scope for all the geologic ages." Unfortunately, this footnote has since been removed from more recent renderings of the bible, leaving modern students unaware.

People (at least, those who give it any thought) operate under the assumption that God *instantaneously* created the heavens and the earth and everything therein – that the very second that He uttered the words, these things came to be. While this may be true for some things, the bible clearly informs us that this was the exception rather than the rule. For example, Genesis 1:1 says the following, "*In the beginning, God created* (bara; Strong's 1254) *the heavens and the earth",* giving the impression that this was an instantaneous event." Yet later, in Exodus 20:11 (and Exod 31:17) we are given a slightly different version of this, stating, "*For (in) six 'days' the LORD made* (asah: Strong's 6213) *the heaven and the earth, the sea, and all that is in them."* Similarly, Nehemiah 9:6 states, "*Thou, even Thou, art LORD alone; Thou has made* (asah) *the heaven, the heaven of heavens with all their host, the earth and all things that are therein, the seas and all that is therein, and Thou preservest them all…*"

The distinct difference in the verbiage within these passages is instructive. It is telling us that God first instantly created the raw materials (i.e., matter and energy), *then*, over a period of time of unknown duration, He fashioned those materials into the heavens and earth with which we are currently familiar. Further proof of this is provided through closer analysis of some related biblical language.

Creating, then Making

The Hebrew word that is used for "created" in Genesis 1 is "bara", and is generally understood to mean "to create something new – something that didn't exist before – creation ex nihilo" (14). (There are those who suggest that "bara" does not necessarily mean "creation from nothing; a viewpoint with which I completely disagree based on the evidence provided herein.) Conversely, the Hebrew word for "made" in Exodus 20 is "asah", which means "to do" or "to make" in the broadest sense." Some suggest that the words used within the bible for "created" and "made" are interchangeable. This is certainly not true. The two words have vastly different connotations, as evidenced by the following:

- The word "bara" is used as a verb 55 times in the Old Testament, *with God being the initiator of the action in each and every instance* (see Appendix E). By contrast, the word "*asah*" is used hundreds of times in the Old Testament, with either God or man being the initiator of the act. From this alone, we can deduce that the action that occurs when "bara" is used is a very special event that can only be initiated by God. Were "bara" used only a handful of times, we would not be able to state so dogmatically that this is so.

  Incidentally, the same is true of the Greek equivalent, "ktizo (Strong's 2936)," in the New Testament, which is used 15 times by the Apostles, each time to describe things that were newly created (not formed) by God. Tellingly, the meaning of the Greek word is, "to fabricate, *form originally; through the idea of the proprietorship of the manufacturer*."

- In every instance where the terms "bara" or "ktizo" are used, it is in reference to one of the special things that God created as something completely new, namely; the heavens, the earth, light and darkness, wind, animal life, human life, (cloud, smoke, and fire as a canopy over Mt Zion), the angels, and (euphemistically) a clean heart (within man) (see Appendix E).

- In Genesis 2:3, we are told that the LORD rested on the seventh day, "…from all His work that God *created and made*." The immediate, consecutive use of the two words within the very same sentence provides, by itself, concrete evidence that the two words have completely different meanings. This is solidified by a closer look at the biblical Hebrew.

  According to Dr. Rodney Whitfield, physicist, biblical Hebrew scholar, and author, this passage would more accurately be translated as, "…created for making," indicating that the "making" is intentionally being described as having occurred *after* the "creating." [(15)] Several older versions of the bible actually stated this within a footnote, although it has been removed from more recent copies.

- Isaiah 43:6-7, uses both of these terms and adds a third term, yatsar (Strong's 3335), to indicate a progression in God's development of man, affirming that God first "formed" (yatsar) him from the dust of the earth then made (asah) man in His own image by breathing into man His spirit (Neshama), creating (bara) man as a new creature. (This will be covered further in Chapter Four – The Making and Creating of Man.)

Bringing Order to a Disorderly World

In addition to the distinct differences in the wording for "created" and "made," the six-fold use of the phraseology "and there was evening, and there was morning" within Genesis 1 is unique. This phrase occurs only in the bible's very first chapter, at the end of Creation Days One through Six. It is not used to conclude Creation Day Seven, nor is it used to mark the passage of time in any other place within the bible. [5]This should signal to us that there is more meaning to the text here than we can get from a cursory reading. An explanation for this was provided to us almost a thousand years ago by the respected biblical commentator Nahmanides.

Nahmanides (also commonly known as Ramban), was a leading Jewish scholar, rabbi, and philosopher who lived between 1194 and 1270 A.D. He is known and respected among the Jews for his commentaries on the Torah (i.e., the first five books of the Old Testament), Mishnah, and Talmud (the latter two are a written collection of Jewish oral traditions and laws). Some of his observations are so deeply insightful that they could be mistaken as excerpts from a modern science textbook.

Almost a thousand years ago, he spoke incredibly accurately of the state of energy, matter, and time during the first moments of creation using terms and concepts that we have only begun to understand during the last century. This strongly suggests supernational (i.e., divine) inspiration.

Nahmanides is one of two highly respected Jewish biblical commentators that I will cite frequently herein, the other being Moses Maimonides. Maimonides is considered to have been the greatest Jewish philosopher of the medieval period. He lived between 1135 and 1204 A.D. and wrote several commentaries on Jewish law that are still widely revered within the Jewish community, where he is considered to be one of the leading rabbinic authorities of all time. His *Guide for the Perplexed*, which dissects the Torah in an effort to resolve conflicts between biblical and secular knowledge, is considered by the Jewish people to be a masterpiece.

---

[5] The bible tells us that God rested on Creation Day Seven and did not create or make anything further. It also tells us in Exodus that God made everything for six, not seven days This means that Day Seven was not actually a "creation" day. However, in the interest of clarity and consistency, I will continue to refer to it herein as Creation Day Seven as this is how it is widely known.

Nahmanides and Maimonides provided commentary on Genesis almost a thousand years ago based on the biblical Hebrew in which the Torah was written. I cite them frequently for the purposes of this book because their astute observations were written long before modern scientific discoveries and were, therefore, not influenced by them. In other words, they were not trying to force the biblical narrative to agree with modern scientific discoveries.

In explaining the use of the phrase "evening and morning" in Genesis 1, Nahmanides states that the Hebrew words for evening (i.e., erev; Strong's 6153) and morning (i.e., boker; Strong's 1242) also carry the root meanings of "mixed up" (i.e., disorder) and "distinguishable" (i.e., order), respectively. He suggests that, through these words, the bible is describing the flow of each Creation Day from a state of initial disorder to one of order, rather than marking the passage of time. In his analysis, it is God's way of saying that He took what was in a state of disorder (erev) at the beginning of each day and made order (boker) out of it.

For example, the matter/energy that resulted from the Big Bang initially existed as a gigantic cloud of superheated gases (commonly referred to as a plasma). From that cloud, matter began to cool and accrete (i.e., come together due to gravitational attraction) into galaxies, stars and planets. This was God's "making" (asah) of celestial objects following His "creation" (bara) of matter that initially existed at the atomic level. God took what was in a state of disorder (erev) and made order (boker) out of it. The phrase is not meant solely to indicate a passage of time, and certainly does not indicate a 24-hour day (see The six references within Genesis 1 to "evening and morning", pg. 62). Interestingly, the phrase "*and there was evening, and there was morning*" is not uttered to mark the end of Creation Day Seven, likely because God rested on that day and did not create or make anything else (Gen 2:1-3).[6] There was no more "disorder" that He wished to put into "order."

The use of these very specific words (i.e., created and made, evening/disorder to morning/order) within Genesis 1 is no accident. They are intentionally being used to describe a creation event during which God first created the raw materials, then subsequently fashioned those materials into the elements of the universe that we see today in the form of galaxies, stars, planets, moons, and the innumerable other celestial

---

[6] The creation of Eve is the sole exception to this in that God made her at some point following (Creation) 7. Although this may seem to contradict the statement of Genesis 2:3, where God is said to have "*...rested from all His work which God created and made*," closer scrutiny of the Hebrew text tells a different story. See The "Building" or "Bearing" of Eve, pg. 123.

objects, transitioning them from a state of disorder (erev) into "order" (boker). When viewed in this way, the Genesis account, written thousands of years ago, accords very well with what we have only fairly recently learned (since the mid-20th Century) through study of the physical sciences, such as cosmology.

Amazing Insight from Long Ago

The laws of physics teach us that everything in the universe appeared abruptly from nothing (i.e., the Big Bang), that the initial matter/energy existed in a highly disordered state (i.e., a super dense chaotic plasma from which not even light could escape), that light eventually separated from darkness (i.e., during a period shortly after the Big Bang that is known as "Recombination), and that the galaxies, stars, and planets were ultimately assembled over time from the accretion (i.e., collection or assemblage due to gravity) of this newly created matter. We have a solid enough grasp of the laws of physics to determine the length of time that it took for each of these events to unfold.

It is interesting to note that the biblical commentator Nahmanides stated these very same things in his commentary on Genesis, which was written long before our modern understanding of the laws of physics.

Nahmanides wrote, "*All that exists under the sun or above it was not made 'ex nihilo', as a first beginning, but He brought forth from the complete and absolute nought a very subtle substance devoid of real existence, but which had the potency to produce, fitted to assume a shape and emerge from potentiality into reality. …After this, He did not create anything but formed and made from it…clothing things with form and putting them into shape. Now, with this creation, which was like a small fine point(!) and had no substance, were created all things in the heaven and the earth.*" [16]

What Nahmanides is saying here is that God first created, from absolutely nothing, invisible matter that He then used to form everything within the physical universe that we can see, feel, and experience. What's more, he stated that the initial creation started from a single, miniscule point long before this was realized by modern cosmologists. His description, written almost a thousand years ago, is in such perfect accord with modern cosmology that it could have been extracted from a modern-day textbook (…with just a little tweaking of the language into modern English, of course).

In his "Guide for the Perplexed", Moses ben Maimon (more commonly known as Maimonides) also provides several fascinating aspects of creation that are strikingly much aligned with modern-day scientific knowledge. He states: (17)

- That time itself was formed as part of creation.
- That all things were initially created together (i.e., as unformed matter) and later molded separately and in succession.
- That the laws of nature were not permanently fixed until after the close of Creation Day Six, with nothing new being created after the close of Creation Day Six (at which time the Second Law of Thermodynamics gained governance).
- That the "waters" that the God separated on Creation Day Two were of a "mysterious" nature that was distinctly different from the vaporous or liquid water that exists upon the planet earth and that the portion of the waters being described within this text was "water by name only, not in reality" (see Chapter Three, pgs. 47-48, for a more complete discussion on this).

Nahmanides and Maimonides demonstrated astounding perception over a thousand years ago, hitting on several key facts about the beginning of the universe that we have only fairly recently confirmed. Not only did they state that the universe had a beginning, but they affirmed that time itself was formed as part of creation, that the universe started out as a small, fine point, and that it was comprised of invisible matter that was mysterious in nature (i.e., plasma). I find it very hard to believe that they could have had this understanding and made these incredibly accurate claims without God's inspiration, especially given the prevailing wisdom and attitudes that existed during their time.

Flying in the Face of the Second Law

One final point of interest with respect to the biblical account of the creation epoch…

The Second Law of Thermodynamics indicates that the state of entropy (i.e., disorder) of the entire universe, *as an isolated system*, will always *increase* over time and that the changes in the entropy in the universe can never be negative (meaning that any change will always be toward *more* disorder, not less). This will always be true unless this "isolated system" is acted upon by an outside force.

However, the organization of the universe and the development of life *are examples of exactly the opposite*. In both instances, order developed from disorder. These events actually run counter to the Second Law of Thermodynamics (or the Law of Entropy). This means that both of these creation events had to have been influenced by an outside force (i.e., God), who completed their original arrangement *contrary* to this physical law.

We are informed through Gen 2:3 that God rested on Day 7 from all that He had created (bara) and made (asah). Additionally, the organization of disorder into order (the erev/evening and boker/morning that was described at the conclusion of each of the first six Creation Days) is no longer explicitly specified after Creation Day Six, further indicating that the creation and making of things by God (*counter to the Second Law of Thermodynamics)* was completed on that day. Since the creation event was completed, the universe has begun to act *in accordance with the law of entropy,* and has been steadily devolving from a state of higher order to a state of higher entropy (i.e., disorder) through cosmic expansion and heat loss.

The bible actually mentions this entropy, referring to it as the "bondage of corruption" under which the "…*whole creation groaneth and travaileth in pain together*…." (Rom 8:19-20, Ps 102:25-26, Isa 51:6).

The Evidence Mounts

The aforementioned examples are just two among many that illustrate how a superficial examination of the evidence, whether scientific or biblical, can jade our understanding of the truth. Anyone wishing to know the whole truth must dig a little further, examining and reexamining the evidence as fresh findings come to light. We must be willing to admit when the evidence runs counter to our current beliefs and be prepared to change our stance when required. We must not cling so tenaciously to any particular paradigm that it skews our interpretation of the facts. We must be willing to lean on what the facts are actually telling us and not rely so heavily on the *interpretation* of the facts by scientists and theologians. In doing so, we will see that these facts are jointly demonstrating complete agreement among scientific and biblical wisdom in many areas, including, but certainly not limited to the following:

- The instantaneous creation/appearance of the universe from absolutely nothing
- The creation of the laws of physics and their consistency since their inception
- The extreme fine tuning of these physical laws throughout the universe, which is required for life to exist
- The expansion of the cosmos
- The specific sequence of events that occurred within the earliest moments of the universe's creation (i.e., the Big Bang)
- The instantaneous appearance of simple life on earth
- The sudden appearance of complex animal life in the seas
- The sudden appearance of complex land animals
- The abrupt change in man's quality approximately 6,000 years ago, when man was created in God's own image

While the bible is not meant to be a science textbook, it does contain a number of scientific facts that were far ahead of their time. [(18)] Evidence that supports these biblical details can be found in every major field of scientific study, including cosmology, paleontology, microbiology, archeology, meteorology, molecular biology, chemistry, and others.

"Ah," says the skeptic, "but doesn't the bible teach the absurd notion that the universe and everything in it is less than 10,000 years old?! How do you reconcile that with the overwhelming scientific evidence to the contrary?!"

The answer is simple – there is no need to reconcile this perceived discrepancy because the bible, itself, actually states no such thing. In spite of the dogmatic pronouncements of biblical scholars and theologians on the subject, and despite the wide-spread belief among Christians in a young universe, the bible does not directly say anything about the age of the universe. It does, however, provide significant evidence that attests to the universe's great age (see Chapter Three).

The assessment of 6,500 or so years for the existence of the universe/earth is a man-made estimate that is based on an analysis of biblical genealogies, the duration of key events that are provided within the bible, and reliance on an English translation of two biblical verses that differ slightly in the English translation from what is stated in the original Hebrew text. Although the English translation is off only slightly, the inaccuracy carries with it significant implications. Moreover, there is significant biblical evidence that contradicts this assessment of a Young Earth (see Chapter Three). Finally, when combined with the overwhelming physical evidence that God has provided for us within the natural world – evidence that attests to the universe's great age – it becomes very difficult to cling to an age of 6,500 years for the universe.

It has already been demonstrated that God reveals Himself through His creation. With that being the case, it begs the question, "Would He allow the existence of so much evidence that attests to the great age of His creation if the universe were truly young?" I *suppose* He could... But, doing so would be duplicitous, which would be in contradiction to His true and faithful nature. Either God's creation truly testifies that it is much older than 6,500 years, or God is deceiving us, which is something that He cannot do.

Considering a Matter Before Offering a Response

For those Christians whose feathers have been ruffled by the preceding revelation regarding the age of the universe, I urge you to read on. The *biblical* evidence for it will be subsequently provided in great detail herein (see Chapter Three). For now, I would urge you – in accordance with God's direction – to lay aside your skepticism, continue reading, and ultimately make up your mind on the subject after you have weighed all of the facts. We are cautioned in Proverbs 18:13 (KJV) that, "*He that answereth a matter before he heareth it, it is folly and shame unto him*". According to this passage, it is in our best interests to fully consider a matter before making up our minds on it. Prov 1:7 further states that anyone who despises wisdom and instruction is a fool, implying that we should actively seek it.

The age of the world is just one of several points upon which there is disagreement among Christians worldwide. Other significant points of contention include such things as the acceptability of homosexuality, the role of women in the church, speaking in tongues and other spiritual gifts, and even such monumental events as the length of the great tribulation period and the timing of the rapture.

Fortunately, not a single one of these points of contention is a salvation issue. Regardless of how opinions may differ on some aspects of faith, the bible is perfectly clear as to how and through Whom one is saved (John 14:6, Acts 4:12, Acts 16:30-31, Romans 10:9-13, Ephesians 2:8-9, Titus 3:5, and many others), and it has nothing to do with what one believes regarding the age of the world or any of the other aforementioned points of disagreement.

No matter what you currently believe regarding the age of the world or any other issue, your beliefs must be built upon a solid foundation; one that has been constructed through thoughtful, careful study of God's Word and His World. Any belief that rests solely on the opinions or interpretations of others resides on pretty shaky ground. God's Word warns us against this, exhorting us to "prove all things", to not blindly stand on the word of anyone else (1Thess 5:21, Rom 12:2, 1 Tim 15).

I urge you to take up God's challenge and examine the evidence for yourself, in accordance with Prov 18:13, before making up your mind. You may ultimately still disagree with some of my conclusions, but you will at least have made an *informed* decision. There is no harm in a little disagreement among Christians so long as both parties treat each other with mutual respect.

Choosing Wisely

Contrary to the opinions of many theologians, forming a belief in any one specific scientific area does not require you to accept all other scientific theory. For example, some theologians tie belief in the Big Bang to belief in Darwinian evolution, stating that belief in one necessitates belief in the other. This is nonsense! In this instance, the two theories cover distinctly different topics that would be governed through completely separate natural processes, were they both true. Also in this instance, there is significant scientific and biblical support for one (i.e., the Big Bang) and zero support in either realm for the other (i.e., Darwinism).

I believe in the infallibility of God's Word. I am a firm believer in the Big Bang based on its *actual* scientific description *precisely because* it perfectly matches the biblical description of the Genesis creation event. Conversely, I certainly *do not* believe in Darwinian evolution as a viable theory based on both biblical teachings and the overwhelming scientific evidence against it. Additionally, although I believe in an old world, there is good reason to believe that the Grand Canyon may not have been formed by millions of years of erosion, as is the conventional wisdom, but that it was carved, at least in part, through a single, sudden catastrophic event (i.e., a great flood), as is indicated by the geological evidence. (19)

For the scientifically minded skeptic, who may be quietly cheering at my seeming rebuke of some Christian views, I must point out that the scientific community, too, has its own, equally numerous points of contention. There is dissention within the ranks regarding such things as:

- The origin of life
- The viability of Darwinian evolution (although its demise seems pretty well settled to me)
- Whether or not the complexity of cellular organisms, the arrangement of information with DNA, and the extreme fine tuning of the universe does or does not indicate design
- The cause of the Big Bang singularity (A singularity is a point in space-time where the laws of physics cease to operate, such as in a black hole.) [(20)]
- The cause of the Inflationary Epoch singularity (that initiated the expansion of the universe). (Something (or someone) had to both initiate it *and* turn it off at precisely the right times in order for our universe to possess the perfect expansion rate that it currently has.)
- That nature of the laws of physics prior to Plankt Time (i.e., 10^{-43} seconds after the Big Bang)
- The nature and cause of consciousness
- The nature of gravity
- The nature of Dark Matter/Dark Energy (which comprises over 95% of our universe)

A rapidly growing number of scientists are refusing, often times much to their detriment, to go along with the conventional wisdom and are throwing down the gauntlet, insisting that the facts within their respective disciplines be allowed to speak for themselves.

It is not my intention here (nor anywhere else within this book) to mock or disparage either scientists or theologians. My goal is to demonstrate through these examples, and others herein, that there is ample blame to go around, with "experts" on both sides being equally culpable in pushing a faulty narrative. Neither side is viewing the evidence in a truly objective fashion. I appeal to those on both sides for a joint study of the natural sciences and biblical wisdom through the very same lens, letting the evidence speak for itself. It is my belief that, upon doing so, the divide between scientific and biblical knowledge will be exposed for what it is: an inappropriate and wholly man-made chasm.

The Demarcation of Recorded Human History

The life, death, and resurrection of Christ are such established facts in world history, through both biblical and plentiful non-biblical sources, that the timeline of human history has long been divided into "B.C." (Before Christ) and "A.D." (Anno Domini – The Year of Our Lord). There can be no question that, for the past 2,000 years, the entire world has recognized the significance of Christ's time here on earth, going so far as to distinguish between the time periods before and after His appearance on the earth.

The fact that these designations have in recent years been replaced with B.C.E. (Before Common Era) and C.E. (Common Era), in yet another attempt to erase God from the equation of history, is inconsequential. Changing the terms cannot hide the fact that the entire world has, for over two thousand years, viewed Christ's life on this earth as the dividing line of human history.

Like Christ's life, death, and resurrection, many of the physical laws have been well established during the last few centuries. These natural laws have been operating since the earliest moments of the Big Bang and we have a very solid understanding of many of them. Even in instances where our understanding remains incomplete, such as the nature of gravity, we understand enough to successfully predict how these laws will impact our surroundings.

We have come to learn a great deal over the last few centuries regarding these laws and how they govern everything from the behavior of sub-atomic particles to the nature and composition of the universe as a whole. Concerted study of them has allowed us to verify that they are, and always have been, remarkably consistent. Were it not so – if there were any significant variability within these laws (as many Christians who are skeptical of science suggest) – our world could not exist or, at the very least, would be devoid of life. It is noteworthy that the bible makes this very specific point, telling us that the laws of physics that were initiated by our Creator are fixed and reliable (Jer 33:20-25, Rom 8:19-22, Psalm 104:19-20, see Appendix F).

A slight deviation in the values for <u>any single one</u> of these laws would likely have resulted in a universe that is incapable of supporting life (see Chapter Six). Yet, here we are!

It is precisely because of the consistency of these laws that mankind has been able to make such significant technological leaps as our understanding of them has grown deeper and more complete. If these laws were constantly changing, not only would we have been unable to develop many of the things that we take for granted today, like electricity, cell phones, computers, GPS technology, or any electronic device, but life itself would not be possible. The reliability of these laws is absolutely necessary if we are to "prove all things" (1Thess 5:21, Rom 12:2) and to "consider a matter before responding" (Prov 18:13), as He has instructed us. Indeed, it would be impossible for us to prove anything at all if the evidence was always changing.

Through the following chapters, we'll delve deeper into many of the aforementioned topics, using both of the tools that God has provided to us (i.e., His Word and His World) to gain a more complete understanding of Him and His creation. I hope you will find the information presented herein to be fascinating and enlightening, regardless of your current views. If nothing else, I hope you will ultimately develop a deeper understanding of, and appreciation for, both His Word and His World as you carefully and objectively consider the facts. For me, gaining this knowledge and understanding – that is, seeing the harmony between His Word and His physical creation – has been liberating, instilling within me an ever-increasing awe of the power, wisdom, and love of our Creator.

CHAPTER TWO

The Bible Said It; Science Now Agrees

For thousands of years, the bible has taught that there was a beginning to our universe. Although the time period for the writing of the book of Genesis cannot be stated dogmatically, the first book of the bible precedes the present date by at least 2,500 years, and maybe by as much as 3,500 years. The book's text accurately describes not only the initial creation of the universe from nothing, but the specific sequence of events that subsequently occurred, resulting in the development of galaxies and stars, the formation of the earth, and the emergence of life.

The bible taught these things first, and thousands of years prior to their confirmation through modern scientific discovery. Moreover, the book of Genesis *is the only religious text in the entire world* that accurately describes these events, attesting to its divine origin and to its supremacy over the "gospel" of any other of the world's religions. By contrast:

- Hinduism teaches that, in the beginning, there existed a mighty cobra that lived in the vast cosmic ocean. And in the hands of this cobra lay the sleeping Vishnu, the creator god. A lotus flower grew from Lord Vishnu's navel with Brahma sitting on it. Brahma separated the flower into three parts - the heavens, the Earth and the sky.
- The Mayan Popol Vu states that Tepeu (the maker) and Gucumatz (the feathered spirit) joined their thoughts together to create the universe. They proceeded to create man, first out of wet clay, then out of wood; with both attempts failing. In their third attempt, they successfully created man out of maize dough. Subsequently, they created four kinds of animals – a parrot, a coyote, a fox, and a crow.

- The Babylonians believed that two primordial gods – Aspu and Tiamet (or Tiamat) – mated and gave birth to a new crop of gods. However, Tiamet hated the new gods and set out to destroy them. While attempting to do so, Tiamet became trapped in a net. The other gods beat Tiamet to a pulp, cracked her skull, then dismembered her; using one half of her body to create the sky and the other half to create human beings, plants, animals, and the creatures that occupy the land today.

- In Greek mythology, the world was endlessly empty and full of a being known as Nyx – the deity of darkness. The goddess Nyx is believed to have laid a golden egg. After sitting on the egg for eons, the egg hatched, producing the deity of love Eros, with the broken shells of the egg becoming the sky and the earth.

- According to Incan legend, the great creator deity, Viracocha either rose from Lake Titicaca or emerged from the cave of Paqariq Tampu during the time of darkness to bring forth light by making the sun, moon, and the stars. He later made mankind by breathing into stones, but his first creation were brainless giants. So, he destroyed them with a flood and made humans, beings who were better than the giants, from smaller stones. After creating them, they were scattered all over the world.

- One Chinese creation story states that the universe began as a chaotic soup without any structure, within which lay a black egg that housed a gargantuan being known as Pangu – a hairy giant with two horns and two tusks. While Pangu slept, the universe was kept in perfect balance, with equal amounts of darkness (yin) and light (yang). Upon waking up from his deep sleep, Pangu proceeded to escape from the egg. By so doing, he broke the force that kept the universe in perfect balance. The top half of the egg shell, which represented *yang*, turned into the sky; while the bottom half, which represented *yin*, became the earth. Upon his death, Pangu's body fell to the earth and turned into several earthly things, such as:

    - His breath turned into the wind and clouds;
    - His eyes became the sun and the moon;
    - Pangu's limbs and head turned into the mountains;

- His muscles turned into the fertile land;
- Pangu's thick facial hair became the stars and the galaxy; and his voice became thunder.
- From the parasites that feasted on his body came forth the first human beings.

➢ Islam offers no detailed description of the creation epoch but does state some aspects of it that generally mimic the book of Genesis.

It is only within the last 60 years (i.e., since the late 1960's) that the sciences have confirmed that there was, in fact, a beginning to our universe and that the specific sequence of events occurred in precisely the order that is described within Genesis. Yet, while science has confirmed that these events did occur, there are several key events that science *cannot* explain, such as the sudden appearance of the universe itself from absolutely nothing. The equally sudden emergence of life (not just once, but twice) also continues to baffle those who seek to understand these events solely through the lens of the natural sciences. In fact, the further scientists dissect the evidence, the more amazed they are at the incredible fine tuning of the natural laws, with more of them reluctantly admitting that the existence of our universe and the life within it could not possibly have come about by random chance.

One of the most obvious points of convergence has already been mentioned: the sudden appearance of the universe from absolutely nothing. As we have already covered the biblical description of this in the previous chapter, I won't rehash it here other than to reiterate that the bible tells us through the use of the words "bara" and "asah" that, in the beginning, God created matter from nothing and then made or fashioned the heavens and the earth from this material, transforming it from an initial state of disorder (erev/evening; 6153) to order (boker/morning; 1242). Other biblical passages tell us that, since its creation, God has stretched out the heavens. But, what does cosmology say about these things?

Let's take a closer look at how exactly the biblical and scientific wisdom converge with respect to the creation of the universe and our world.

Big Bang Cosmology in a Nutshell

The following is a simplified explanation of the origin of the Big Bang theory. The actual story is much more complex and involves many other significant players. However, the intent of this book is not to provide a thorough treatise for any one area of scientific study, but to demonstrate how biblical and scientific knowledge are in complete agreement. There is ample information freely available online and through literally thousands of books to anyone who wishes to learn about the Big Bang in greater detail. For the purposes of this writing, I urge that you accept this explanation in the spirit in which it is provided – as a broad overview for the uninitiated rather than as a fully detailed description.

Prior to the 1900's, our Milky Way galaxy was thought to comprise the totality of the universe. Everything that is visible in our night sky was thought to be a star, planet, comet, or nebula that existed within the boundary of our own galaxy. Although telescopes had been around for 300 years, they had not been developed sufficiently to allow scientists the ability to search deep enough or clearly enough into the cosmos to reveal its true extent. This changed in the early 1900's with the building of the 100-inch telescope at the Mount Wilson Observatory.

Using this telescope, Edwin Hubble discovered (in 1924) that what was originally thought to be a nebula (i.e., a cloud of interstellar gas) within the Milky Way galaxy was actually a totally separate galaxy (i.e., Andromeda) that existed outside of and far beyond the perimeter of our own. For the first time, we began to realize that the universe is much larger than we thought. [7]

A few years later (in 1929), Hubble realized, through studying the light that is being emitted by other galaxies, that all of them were moving away from each other, leading to the profound conclusion that our universe is expanding. (The idea that our universe was expanding was actually introduced two years earlier by a Belgian priest named Georges Lemaitre, who theorized that the universe began at a single point with the "explosion" of a single primordial atom.) The expansion of the universe led to the inference that, at one time, the universe must have started out from a single focal point, as Lemaitre had suggested. After all, if the expansion were to be reversed, the galaxies would move closer together until they ultimately merged at a single location.

---

[7] It is truly sobering to realize, as one looks up at the innumerable points of light in the night sky, that many of these points are not individual stars, but entire galaxies; each itself composed of billions of stars.

For the next several decades, scientists hotly debated whether or not the universe had a beginning, with multiple competing theories being bantered about. Fred Hoyle, a renowned astronomer who did not subscribe to the idea of an expanding universe (and the implication of a beginning), is accredited with having coined the term "Big Bang" during a radio broadcast in 1949. Hoyle had a competing theory, called the "Steady State", in which he suggested that the universe has always existed in the very same condition, with new matter continually being created to fill in the void between the galaxies as they moved away from each other. He derisively called the "expanding universe" theory the "Big Bang", a moniker that stuck and is still used today. It wasn't until the mid-1960's, with the discovery of the cosmic microwave background radiation (CMB), that the Big Bang theory became the dominant hypothesis for the universe's origin.

CMB (also commonly referred to as the cosmic microwave background radiation, or CMBR, and cosmic background radiation, or CBR) is essentially a fossil of electromagnetic energy – a remnant of the oldest light in the universe. The existence of CMB was predicted by Ralph Alpherin in 1948 during a study that he was conducting on Big Bang Nucleosynthesis. Using the laws of physics, he surmised that, if the universe had started out from a single point, then it would have had an incredibly high temperature (i.e., billions of degrees Fahrenheit) due to the density of matter at that point (because matter gets more energetic the more tightly it is compressed, resulting in extremely rapid energies and exceedingly hot temperatures).

With the expansion of the universe, the CMB temperature would have cooled as the matter/energies became more dilute within the ever-growing space of the universe. Picture, for example, how the boiling water within a ceramic coffee cup would cool if you were to toss it into a swimming pool. The heat that was once concentrated within the small space of the cup would dissipate and dilute, spreading throughout the hundreds or thousands of gallons of pool water. Similarly, any radiation that was created within the initial high temperature of the universe would have become more dilute as it expanded with space itself, cooling as the initial heat dispersed throughout the ever-growing volume.

Alpherin predicted that the current universe should be awash with the remnant of the initial, immensely hot radiation, which would now exist in the microwave frequency band as CMB. As this radiation was emitted during the earliest epoch of the universe's emergence, its detection and measurement would provide scientists with significant insight into the conditions of the early universe.

This CMB was discovered quite by accident almost 20 years later when, in 1964, American radio astronomers Robert Wilson and Arno Penzias, who were using the Holmdel Horn Antenna in New Jersey to search for neutral hydrogen, picked up a persistent, odd buzzing sound that appeared to be emanating from everywhere. It wasn't until they had conferred with researchers at nearby Princeton University that they realized the significance of their discovery. Confirmation of the expansion of space and the discovery of CMB propelled the Big Bang theory to the forefront of cosmology, where further discoveries have since firmly cemented it as the leading theory of the universe's origin.

What the Big Bang *IS*….and *ISN'T*

NASA defines the Big Bang theory as, "…the idea that the universe began from absolutely nothing as just a single point, then expanded and stretched to grow to its current size." [(1)] This theory has only recently (since the mid-1960's) been widely accepted by scientists and its supporters continue to grow in number as multiple, more current discoveries have served to strengthen its viability. Yet, the bible has been saying this very same thing for thousands of years within its very first sentence! *The Big Bang theory and the bible both state that the universe had a beginning from absolutely nothing, and that is has since been continually expanding*!

Despite its name, the Big Bang was not actually an explosion. An explosion is defined as, "a *violent and destructive* shattering or blowing apart *of something* (emphasis added by author), as is caused by a bomb." According to this definition, in order for something to explode, (1) that "something" must first *exist* (i.e., it must already be a thing); and (2) the process is violent and destructive. In fact, the Big Bang, as proffered by NASA, describes *the exact opposite* of these criteria!

The Big Bang was not an explosion in space, but an explosion *of* space. The Big Bang is the idea that, "…all the matter and energy of the Universe was once crushed into a single point, a single infinitesimal granule of everything. The Big Bang itself is the moment when everything began. …Immeasurably hot and dense, that which would ultimately become our Universe was initially crammed into a volume just a tiny fraction the size of a proton" [(2)]

Under NASA's definition of the Big Bang, the process is one through which time, space, and energy/matter *suddenly came into existence out of nothing*. According to the science, these elements emerged all at once (i.e., they were *created*, not destroyed) from nothing; they did not previously exist. This is exactly what the bible tells us in its very first sentence, that, "In the beginning, God *created* from nothing (bara) the entirety of the physical universe (i.e., the heavens and the earth).

Once one understands the *true scientific definition* of the Big Bang theory and considers it within a biblical frame of reference, the convergence of biblical and scientific wisdom, with respect to the initial creation event, is undeniable.

Incredibly, Christian apologists and scientists alike still bristle at the thought and insist on denying this obvious convergence of truth. Some very influential Christian apologist organizations commonly scoff at the idea of the Big Bang, either rejecting altogether the viability of the theory or derisively saying such things as "when was the last time that an "explosion" created anything?" (3)(4) I've heard other theologians mock the theory with the statement, "First, there was nothing. And then, it exploded!", a statement that is met by outbursts of derisive laughter from unwitting church congregations.

Such statements, especially in the face of the *overwhelming* scientific evidence that supports the Big Bang, expose a superficial understanding of the science and/or the biblical text and creates division among Christians that is wholly unwarranted. These utterances turn Christians away from scientific fact that is actually in perfect harmony with the bible and which might otherwise serve to bolster their confidence in the reliability of the biblical text. Accepting the science would also enable them to share God's Word in the language that non-believers accept (i.e., the language of science).

Trying to sway the opinion of a non-believer using just the bible is usually an exercise in futility simply because they don't believe it to be true. But if a Christian were able to demonstrate how the sciences clearly indicate a Creator while simultaneously showing how this is in direct accord with the biblical text, this would present the non-believer with some serious food for thought.

As we shall see, the agreement between scientific and biblical wisdom with respect to the Big Bang creation event is, by itself, stunning. But when we also view each individual Creation Day event through *both* lenses as an orderly, day by day advancement from disorder to order, the convergence is too incredible to be relegated to coincidence. This will be discussed much more thoroughly in Chapter Four. However, before we can delve further into this, we must address the following, very impactful creation era question: How old is the universe?

Is the cosmos young or old? Should its age be measured in billions of years or only thousands? Can *both* be correct? (The latter option may sound ridiculous, but there is actually a plausible theory for it.) One's belief in this area is bound to have an impact on one's understanding of the entire creation period. Consequently, this will be the subject of the very next chapter.

CHAPTER THREE

The Age of the Universe

There are places within the bible where a detailed timeline is provided regarding certain events; chronologies that summarize how long it took for certain things to occur or that summarize the total number of years of an event or a person's life. A partial list of these chronologies includes the following:

- The specific duration of Noah's flood (Gen 7 and 8)
- A summation of the number of years (i.e., 430) that Israel spent in captivity in Egypt (Exod 12:40)
- The 480-year time period between Israel's exodus from Egypt and the building of the temple (1Kings 6:1)
- The timetable for Christ's appearance and death following the rebuilding of Jerusalem, the subsequent destruction of Israel as a nation, and the ultimate desecration of the temple by the antichrist (Dan 9:24-27)
- And complete durations of the lives of many key and minor personages within the Old Testament, including Adam, Seth, Enos, Cainan, Mahalaleel, Jared, Enoch, Methuselah, Noah, and Lamech (Gen 5:5-29, Gen 11:10-11, and Gen 25:7).[8]

These summaries are provided because, for various reasons, they are important to the bigger picture. However, it is important to note that no such timeline or summation is provided within the bible when it comes to the creation epoch. *The bible itself makes no claim for the age of the earth/universe.* Any current estimations for the age of the universe and

---

[8] Although the bible says that Enoch lived 365, years, God ultimately took Enoch from the earth before he died (Gen 5:23-24). While there is disagreement as to when, specifically, Enoch was born, he never died. Consequently, he is, technically, the longest living man!

earth that are based solely on the biblical text are man-made assessments that rely on various, sometimes erroneous interpretations of scripture.

The description of the creation account within Genesis 1 is summarized in very general terms by a mere 426 words that are arranged in just 31 verses. With such an abbreviated chain of events, it is unreasonable to expect that what we are told within Genesis 1 comprises the totality of everything that happened. By the time that Adam had lived only 130 years of his 930-year long life, the fall of man had already occurred, he and Eve had been banished from the Garden of Eden, Cain had murdered Able, and their third son, Seth, was born. Additionally, somewhere very early on within (or prior to) those 130 years, the serpent who tempted Eve in the Garden of Eden had already fallen and had encouraged other angels to rebel against God. Clearly, we are not informed of everything that happened.

Consider the following…

By Gen 4:13-14, as God is sending Cain away for the murder of Abel, Cain expresses fear about being slain by "others" that were on the earth. Who were these others? How could this have caused Cain concern so early in human history? Remember – this is less than 130 years after Adam was created. If Adam and Eve were truly the very first humans, as the biblical text indicates, then how many other people could even have existed at this point? Yet, by Gen 4: 17-18, sometime after God banished Cain but before the birth of Seth, the earth's population was sufficient enough that people began to cluster into cities (Gen 4:17). Where did all of these people come from?

If Adam and Eve were truly the first people on the earth, the population would have been quite small by the time Cain was banished. Even with Eve baring one child every year, there would have been less than 140 people on the earth at the time (280 maybe, if she had twins every single time following the birth of Seth). Cain was the first offspring of the "first couple" and was born sometime during the first 130 years of Adam's life. We know this because Eve bore Seth, their third child, when Adam was 130 years old (Gen 5:3) and after Cain had been banished for killing his brother (Gen 4:16-25). Yet, seemingly as soon as Cain was driven from the presence of the LORD, Cain "knew his wife" and bare Enoch. Where did Cain's wife come from? Clearly, the bible does not provide the full story here.

There are two main views with respect to the age of the world; one of a Young Earth, with the earth and the entire universe believed to be between 6,500 and 10,000 years old, and one of an Ancient Earth, with adherents accepting the age of the universe and earth as approximately 13.8 billion years old and 4.6 billion years old, respectively, based on both the biblical and scientific evidence. There are also multiple variations of the latter scenario, some of which will be briefly described below, and yet another theory, which I refer to as the Duality Model, that suggests that the 13.8 billion years of the Ancient Earth model and the 6,500 years of the Young Earth model are both correct. This theory has been proffered by world-renowned physicist Dr. Gerald Schroeder, and it is not nearly as far-fetched as it may initially appear.

The Young Earth View

It may come as a surprise to you to learn that the idea that the world/universe is young is a relatively new one. Prior to the middle of the 20th century, people had no problem accepting the thought that the world was ancient and saw no conflict between an ancient universe and biblical teachings. In fact, the idea of a young universe is a fairly recent development, having arisen during the 1950s and 1960s. [(1)(2)] From the very first century following Christ's time on this earth, scholars, both Christian and non-Christian, have casually debated the nature and length of the six creation days, but the idea of an ancient universe was widely regarded as a distinct possibility.

The Young Earth model is based primarily on the following:

- A belief that the creation events that span Genesis 1 were completed within a single period of six 24-hour days. This is based on the English text of Exodus 20:11 and 31:17, both of which state, "*For in six days the LORD made the heavens and the earth, the sea, and all that is in them...*".
- A tallying of the genealogies and duration of key events as described within the bible from the time of Adam, who was created on Creation Day Six. This leads them to conclude that Adam is just a single day younger than the oldest land animals and is less than a week younger than the entire universe.
- A fully literal translation of the biblical text. (see "A Caution Regarding Biblical Literalism", pg. 46)
- A belief that most, if not all scientific conclusions are either erroneous or have been deliberately skewed to present a case for a world that is significantly older than 10,000 years.

The Ancient Earth View

The Ancient Earth model is based on some or all of the following:

- Belief that God unambiguously reveals Himself through his creation (see God's Instruction Manuals, pg. 4, and Appendix C) and that what we observe in nature, as He reveals Himself, is trustworthy.
- Belief that the overwhelming physical evidence through which He is revealing Himself affirms an ancient earth and confirms several scientific principles that were revealed long ago through the biblical text, such as the creation of the universe from nothing, the expansion of the universe, and the sudden appearance of life.
- Subtle grammatical differences in the biblical Hebrew between Gen 1:1-2 and the rest of Genesis 1 that indicate that there was a span of time of unknown duration prior to the first creation "command" in Gen 1:3.
- A belief, based on several elements within the biblical texts, that either the days within Genesis 1 are not literally six, 24-hour days OR that they ***are*** six 24-hour days, but that there is a span of time of unknown duration that occurs between them.

Which View is Most Likely Correct?

A close look at these views reveals several problems with the Young Earth view, including:

- A reliance solely on the English interpretation of the biblical text. The English version inadvertently modifies the meaning of some passages, such as Exod 20:11 and Exod 31:17, such that they are not fully in accord with the original Hebrew.
- The fact that there are gaps within several biblical genealogies. It is also not unusual for scripture to pass over very long periods of time with little or no remarks. For example, Gen 5:25-27 states that Methuselah lived 969 years and begat sons and daughters, yet Lamech is the only offspring that is mentioned by name. Lamech, too, living a total of 777 years, is said to have begat sons and daughters, yet Noah is the sole offspring of his that is mentioned (Gen 5:28-31). Additionally,

there is no summation within scripture of the genealogies that are mentioned within Gen 5 and Gen 11, as there is for other events such as in Exod 12:40 and 1Kings 6:1.

- Young Earth creationism interprets the words "day", "evening", and "morning" without symbolism, as plain terms meant to be understood literally, despite significant biblical evidence in many instances to the contrary. A fully literal translation of Gen 1:14-19 would place the creation of the sun on day four, meaning that early plant life existed without the benefit of the sun's warmth and nourishment (through photosynthesis) for at least one day. This would not be physically possible unless God used supernatural means to keep it alive, something that is neither stated nor implied within the biblical text. (See "A Caution Regarding Biblical Literalism," pg. 46, for additional considerations.)
- An erroneous belief that accepting an Ancient Earth requires one to accept that life evolved through naturalistic processes alone (i.e., Darwinian evolution).
- Claims, contrary to biblical teachings and solid scientific verification, that the laws of physics have not always operated as they do today.
- Belief that the majority of scientific observations and assessments are erroneous.

Conversely, when looking at the biblical text for what it *actually* says, as opposed to what we are *told* that it says, there appear to be far fewer problems with an Ancient Earth view.

Those who believe in an Ancient Earth accept that the scientific evidence supporting billions of years is overwhelming and true, especially when paired with the significant *biblical* evidence that they believe also supports this view. While some scientists may stand accused of skewing facts, when it comes to the age of the universe there is just too much empirical physical evidence, verifiable through multiple means, that attest to its great age. As we shall see, the bible also supports this ancient age. To disregard it all is foolish and irresponsible.

I believe that God provides a factual revelation of Himself through nature – just as He very clearly says that He does (see God's Instruction Manuals, pg. 4, and Appendix C) and that His revelations indicate an ancient earth. I also believe that there is significant evidence within the bible itself of an ancient earth; that the biblical text speaks to a universe that is far older than a mere 6,500 years.

I am not one who lightly questions God's motives for doing things as He has. He is omnipotent and omniscient and can accomplish things whenever or however He deems best. But I do have to wonder why, if the universe is truly young, He would allow there to be such a mountain of evidence attesting to its ancient age. He tells us that He continually uses the natural world to reveal Himself and that natural world attests to an ancient earth. Either this ancient age is actually correct, we are intentionally being deceived by God (which is impossible, given His nature), or all of our observations and assessments are wrong.

Although the Young Earth and Ancient Earth models are predominant, and while there are differing opinions even among the two schools of thought [9], there is another option that actually marries the two. I call this the Duality Model, which states that the 13.8 billion years of the Ancient Earth model and the 6,500 years of the Young Earth model are both correct. This theory, proffered by renowned physicist Dr. Gerald Schroeder in his book *The Science of God*, is most certainly intriguing and quite plausible.

Dr. Schroeder describes how time dilation and the expansion of the universe make both timelines possible, depending upon the viewpoint of the observer. It was initially my intent to synopsize his theory herein, but I could find no way to do so concisely without omitting aspects of it, and I did not wish to lessen its impact by a feeble attempt to do so. I highly recommend that anyone interested in this hypothesis read chapters three and four of Dr. Schroeder's book. (Actually, I recommend reading the whole thing, but these two chapters will suffice for anyone seeking to understand how both timelines can be correct.)

A Caution Regarding Biblical Literalism

The bible is both simple and complex. In most instances, the meaning of a passage is immediately obvious to the reader, requiring no interpretation. In these instances, the text can be taken literally. At the same time, less obvious meanings are commonly buried within the text,

---

[9] Some Ancient Earth Creationists believe that the creation days of Genesis 1 are not six literal 24-hour days but represent creation epochs. Others believe that the six creation days of Genesis 1 are, in fact, literally six 24-hour days, but that each creation day was separated by a long period of time. In either case, the biblical evidence indicates a far more ancient universe than one would glean through a casual reading of the biblical text.

manifesting themselves only after considerable study and reflection and/or becoming clear as a result of one's life experiences. Then there are times when both of these criteria can be true within the very same passage, with both the literal and figurative meanings being equally applicable. Let's look at some examples of scripture that clearly should not be taken literally.

- Several scriptures tell us that the earth is fixed and immovable (1 Chronicles 16:30, Psalm 93:1, Psalm 96:10, Psalm 104:5, and others). Were we to take this literally, we would state resolutely that the earth does not rotate, nor does it revolve around the sun. However, we know that the earth does, in fact, rotate and move through space in its orbit around the sun. What these biblical texts are implying is that when God made the earth, He established its patterns – its rotation and orbit, weather patterns, the water cycle, etc. – fixing or setting them in such a way that they would continually operate exactly how He "fixed" them until He declares otherwise.
- The first three creation days end with the phrase, "…and there was evening, and there was morning, the nth day." Yet, the sun does not appear on the scene until Creation Day Four. How could there have been evening and morning without the sun? This is actually a very good example of a scripture that has multiple meanings (For an explanation of this, see Chapters Three and Four)
- In the Garden of Eden, God warns Adam against eating from the Tree of the Knowledge of Good and Evil, with the consequences being that Adam would "surely die" were he to do so. To emphasize the He meant business, God didn't just say that Adam would die, but that he would "surely die." Yet after eating of the forbidden tree, Adam lives another 900+ years. How was this possible in light of God's admonishment? (See Physical vs Spiritual Death, pg. 119)
- The KJV version of the bible mentions the existence of unicorns in several places (Num 23:22, Num 24:8, Deut 33:17, Job 39:9-10, Ps 22:21, Ps 29:6, Ps 92:10, Isa 34:7). The Hebrew word that is translated as "unicorn" is "reym", which better translates to "wild ox or bull." Indeed, in most instances

where the word is used (114 instances in the Old Testament), the latter is exactly how it is translated.

- 2Peter 3:5 says that, long ago and by God's word, the heavens came into being and the earth was formed out of the water and by water. This verse is consistently translated across various bible versions, such as:
    - NIV: "*......by God's word the heavens come into being and the earth was formed out of water and by water.*"
    - NASB: "*...by the word of God the heavens existed long ago and the earth was formed out of the water and by water.*"
    - CSB: "*...By the word of God the heavens came into being long ago and the earth was brought about from water and through water.*
    - NLT: "*...that God made the heavens long ago by the word of His command, and He brought the earth out from the water and surrounded it with water.*
    - ESV: "*...that the heavens existed long ago, and the earth was formed out of water and by water.*"
    - KJV: "*...that by the word of God the heavens were of old, and the earth standing out of the water and in the water.*"

The term used in 2Peter 3:5 for water is "mayim" (Strong's 4325), which is used throughout the bible to describe water in various forms. Even in Genesis 1 it is evident that the word "waters" is being used to describe different things. In Gen 1:9, it is clearly being used to describe the seas. Yet, in Gen 1:6-7 God divides the waters above, in the midst of, and below the firmament/sky. Deut 4:18 and 5:8, which speak of "*...fish that is in the waters beneath the earth,*" tell us that the waters below the firmament equates to physical bodies of waters, like oceans, lakes, and rivers. It is safe to assume that the waters in the midst of the firmament/sky would equate to clouds and precipitation. So, what are the waters *above* the firmament/sky? They are *above* the sky/atmosphere, so this must be referring to the "waters" out in the cosmos.

There are those who attempt to make the case that 2Peter 3:5 is referring to the floodwaters of Noah's time based on the verse that immediately follows (2Peter 3:6). However, the Greek word that is translated in 2Peter 3:5 as "standing/formed" is "*sunistao*" (Strong's 4921 with the meaning of being comprised of (i.e., constituted or consisting of). The verse is stating that the earth was *comprised of,* not covered with water. This word is being used here, as well as in Col 1:14-17, to describe the physical composition of the universe and earth. The laws of physics teach us that the earth is comprised of more than just molecules of water, so there must be another meaning here.

As the physical evidence – evidence that has been provided by God Himself – suggests that the earth was never *comprised* solely of water, there must be more to the story here. In Gen 1:6-7 and 2Peter, I suggest that the "waters" that God separated, or which He formed, were not all comprised of literal liquid water – actual H_2O as we know it. It is my belief that, in some instances, the bible is describing matter that was in a plasma state. In this form, matter flows or behaves in a manner similar to water.

In his *Guide for the Perplexed*, the biblical commentator Moses Maimonides seems to agree with the idea that the term "waters" refers to more than just liquid H_2O. He states the following (almost a thousand years ago, long before anyone knew about plasma):

"*...the phrase, 'And He divided between the waters' does not describe a division in space, as if the one part were merely above the other, while the nature of both remained the same, but a distinction as regards their nature or form. One portion of that which was first called "water" was made one thing by certain properties that it received, and another portion received a different form, and this latter portion is that which is commonly called "water". The division of the waters refers to ...a distinction by a separate form. It is therefore clear that there has been one common element called water, which has been afterward distinguished by three different forms; one part forms the seas, another the "firmament" (i.e., the earth's sky), and a third part is over the firmament, and all this is separate from the earth. ...It has been declared here by our Sages that the portion above the firmament is only water by name, not in reality. ...The account of the firmament, with that which is above it and is called water, is...of a very mysterious character.*" (3)

The bible is written in the language of man, and was composed in such a way as to be comprehensible to Jews living in ancient times as well as to those of us living in the modern era. There was no Hebrew word for "plasma" back in the days of Moses, so the author used the closest facsimile – water, because plasma behaves much like a fluid. Had the term "plasma" been used in the text of Gen 1:6-7 (if such a word had existed back then), people living in ancient times would have had been clueless as to the nature of the substance. As the earth is (and always has been) comprised of much more than water (in any of its forms), I suggest here that the term "waters" is referring to matter that existed in a state of plasma in the earliest ages of our universe.

These are just a few of the many instances where a fully literal reading of the biblical text can lead to an improper understanding of its meaning. This is especially true when reading a *translation* of the original biblical Hebrew. For instances where the literal meaning seems to make poor sense or where one passage seems to contradict another, the reader must exercise caution and not jump to conclusions. To extract the proper meaning from any scriptural passages where a contradiction seems to exist, it is best to compare the text with other, similar biblical passages to gain a correct understanding. There are also many instances where the use of a bible concordance is necessary to view the language and its meaning within its proper context.

Significant Biblical Evidence for an Old World

My belief in our Creator formed within me at a very early age. By the time I was nine, I felt absolutely certain that God must exist. As the years moved along and I was bombarded by Darwinian evolution and other scientific "facts", I realized that there was a discrepancy between my biblical and scientific learnings. Yet, my faith never wavered. I felt certain that these discrepancies would ultimately vanish were I to keep studying. I placed my questions into His hands and waited for Him to reveal the answers to me.

In 2004, He finally gave me the first clues, directing my eyes to a copy of Dr. Gerald Schroeder's book, *The Science of God.* (To be fair to My Creator, it wasn't His fault that it took so long for Him to reveal the answers…for too long I didn't actively seek His face.)

As I began to realize that biblical and scientific wisdom were actually far more in sync than I had been led to believe, I developed a passion for learning even more. I've since read *The Science of God* over a dozen times, trying to poke holes in Dr Schroeder's theories and memorizing several key points. Since my initial reading, I have purchased dozens of copies of the book, providing a copy for free to anyone whom I felt had a similar, genuine interest in finding the truth.

God & Science

Reading "*The Science of God*" started a continuing quest of reading similar, faith-based books, as well as secular science books, in an effort to personally scrutinize and compare biblical and scientific knowledge. In the past two decades of concerted study, I have been awed by what I have learned and by the harmony that exists among His Word and His World.

Most recently, my studies have been focused on gleaning the biblical evidence for an ancient earth. As the scientific evidence for it is so abundant and overwhelming, and as I knew (because He says so – see God's Instruction Manuals, pg. 4, and Appendix C) that there should be no discrepancy between what He reveals to us through His Word and His World, I was absolutely certain that this evidence *must* exist and that He would reveal it to me – that, if I sought, I would find (Matt 7:7-8).

While many Young Earth proponents suggest that God created the universe and earth with the "appearance" of antiquity, I could not accept this line of reasoning because it would be deceitful, which is something that God cannot be. So, I began a concerted effort to uncover the biblical evidence for an ancient earth. I was not disappointed. Ultimately, the following facts were revealed to me through the biblical text:

- The grammar of the biblical Hebrew within Gen 1:1-2 indicates a passage of time of unknown duration prior to God's first formative command within Genesis 1:3
- God first "created" (bara) then made (asah), over an unknown period of time, the various components of our universe
- The earth already existed in a barren state before God began to prepare it for habitation beginning in verse 3 of Genesis 1
- Evidence affirming that the term "yom", which is consistently translated in the bible as "day", is rarely used to indicate a 24-hour time period (with a single exception)
- The phrase "evening and morning" is used within Genesis 1 in a way that indicates a flow from a state of disorder to one of order, rather than marking the passage of 24-hour days
- The bible does not describe in detail the occurrence of some very significant events before the creation of Adam/Eve, such as the fall of Lucifer
- The fact that the specific sequence of creation events, as described within Genesis 1, aligns perfectly with what is being

revealed through nature regarding the formation of the universe over a vast period of time

- Use of language that indicates a passage of time prior to key biblical creation events, such as "now, at last" (happa'am) and "it came to pass"

Each of these facets will subsequently be discussed herein in greater detail.

"Creation" First – "Making" Second

The current English language version of the bible has been translated from no fewer than three previous versions, including the original Hebrew/Chaldee, Greek, and Latin. While God has seen to it that the key messages and themes of His Word have been retained, some minor points have gotten lost during each step of translation. This is, unfortunately, true of the bible's very first two verses, the original text of which indicates that *there was a passage of time of unknown duration between Gen 1:1-2 and God's first formative command of Gen 1:3.*

That's right! The biblical Hebrew of Gen 1:1-2 is written in such a way as to indicate that God created parts of the physical universe, including the earth, in their entirety *prior to* His first creative utterance in Gen 1:3 that kicked off Creation Day One.

There are many who cite Exod 20:11 and Exod 31:17, and the six "evening and morning" references within Genesis 1, as "proof" that God created every single thing within a sole period of six 24-hour time periods. But there is ample biblical evidence to the contrary. Let's examine this further.

Biblical Hebrew does not specify the tense of an action (i.e., past, present, or future) nor the duration of an event (i.e., how long it took to complete) in the same way as other languages. (4)(5)(6) Instead, tense is commonly indicated in biblical Hebrew based on the *sequence* of the wording.[10] For example, an *ongoing* activity would be indicated by placing the verb first and the subject of the verb second (4). This is the case for the sentence structure within Gen 1:3-31, where the six creation days are being described. Conversely, *an activity that has been concluded* would be indicated by placing the noun first and the verb in the second position within the sentence, as is the case for Gen 1:1-2.

---

[10] With respect to Hebrew verbs, Dr. R. Whitfield says the following, "Verbs in biblical Hebrew only indicate that an action is complete (finished) or incomplete (not finished). In biblical Hebrew, the verb itself does not specify the duration of verbal actions, and does not convey the time ordering of verbal actions. (However,) biblical Hebrew does sometimes indicate the ordering of past actions. It does this not by verb forms, but by (i.e., through) word order, and several other means." (7)

The Hebrew that comprises the first two verses of Genesis 1 is grammatically different from the following 29 verses of the very same chapter. This fact, by itself, would have signaled to the reader of the biblical Hebrew that the first two verses are meant to be viewed in a different light than the rest of the chapter. This grammatical idiosyncrasy, which is not apparent when reading the English language version of the bible, would have indicated that the actions of Gen 1:1-2 *had already been completed* prior to God's first creative command in Gen 1:3. It would further have implied the passage of an unspecified period of time between Gen 1:2 and Gen 1:3, the latter verse being where God utters His first recorded creative command.

The reversed word order of Gen 1:1-2 causes the first two sentences of Genesis 1 to serve essentially as a prologue, providing background information for the events that are subsequently going to be described. This method is commonly used throughout the bible, when some background information is deemed necessary, prior to providing a description of subsequent events, to aid the reader in fully understanding the context of the text that follows. For example, the temptation of Eve by the serpent starts with background information about the tempter. Gen 3:1 states, "*Now the serpent was more subtle than any beast of the field, which the LORD had made...<u>and he said</u> unto the woman...*" This background info tells us two things; that the serpent was devious; and that the serpent had been made (asah – Strong's 6213) by God at some point, just as the beasts of the field had been.

The first part of Gen 3:1 provides background info that helps the reader to understand how the serpent was able to trick Eve, being more subtle and cunning. The grammar in the wording, "*...and he said unto the woman...*" in the second part of Gen 3:1, which differs from the grammar in first part, signals the end of the background info and the beginning of a new narrative, just like each, "*...and God said...*" does at the beginning of every creation day within Genesis 1. Unfortunately, the two parts of Gen 3:1 appear within the same scriptural passage within our English translation.

The numbering of the verses in this instance fails to provide the proper, more logical break, inadvertently merging two completely separate aspects (i.e., the background information and the subsequent, active attempt by the serpent to trick Eve).

> It is important to remember that the scriptural passages were not numbered within the Hebrew text as it was originally written. This did not occur until 1227 A.D. when the bible was divided into chapters and verses to make it easier for people to locate specific passages. The system was refined over the next couple of centuries until the current numbering system was officially adopted, in 1555 A.D. As this system of dividing the biblical text was completed by man, it is not without its shortcomings, such as combining the background information of Gen 3:1 with the active, ongoing attempt of the serpent to trick Eve.

Job 1:1-5 is another example of the bible providing background information. These verses speak to the righteousness of Job, the blessings of his family, and the extent of his riches prior to the events of Job 1:6 that completely turn his life upside down. The opening narrative of Job is meant to demonstrate that Job was prosperous and considered righteous by God and that God was confident that Job would remain faithful to Him regardless of any tragic challenges that Satan would throw at him.

Through the specific word order of Gen 1:1-2, we are being told that God *concluded* the creation of the physical universe (i.e., the heavens and the earth) at the very beginning *prior to* the events that begin in Genesis 1:3. Then, starting with the first, "*…and God said….*" of Gen 1:3, the text goes on to explain how God prepared the earth for habitation, in accordance with His original plan (Isaiah 45:18-21), starting on it from an uninhabitable but *preexisting* condition (see Existence of the Earth Prior to Gen 1:3, pg. 55). Each of the subsequent six creation days is then bracketed by "…and God said" (to mark the beginning) and "…there was evening and there was morning, the nth day" (to mark the end of each creative act). Both of these nuances (i.e., the differing grammar of Gen 1 verses 1 through 2 and the bracketing of days that occurs in verses 3 through 31) clearly indicate that Creation Day One begins in verse three, not in verse one, and that other events were completed prior to verse three.

In his book, *Seven Days that Divide the World,* Oxford University Professor of Mathematics John Lennox makes the following, very astute observation regarding the differing grammar of Gen 1:1-2, "The initial creation took place before day 1, but Genesis does not tell us how long before. This means that the question of the age of the earth (and of the universe) is a separate question from the interpretation of (the length of the six creation) days. In other words, ...the text of Genesis 1, in separating the beginning from day 1, leaves the age of the universe indeterminate. It would therefore be logically possible to believe that the days of Genesis are twenty-four-hour days...and to believe that the universe is very ancient." (8)

Existence of the Sun and Earth Prior to Gen 1:3

Genesis 1:2 tells us specifically that the earth was "without form, and void" prior to God's first creative command in Gen 1:3. The Hebrew words for these two terms are, respectively, "tohuw' and "bohuw" and, according to *Strong's Exhaustive Concordance of the Bible*, have the following meanings (9):

- tohuw (8414) – to lie waste, a desolation (of surface), confusion, empty place, without form, nothing, vanity, waste, wilderness
- bohuw (922) – to be empty, a vacuity, an indistinguishable ruin, emptiness, a void

In describing the earth as "tohuw and bohuw" within Gen 1:2, we are either being told that the earth did not yet exist *or* that it did exist, but in a chaotic, uninhabitable condition. Use of the phrase "tohuw and bohuw" in other places within the biblical text (Jeremiah 4 and Isaiah 34) strongly indicates that it is meant to describe the latter condition – an existing, but uninhabitable wasteland.

In Jeremiah 4 and Isaiah 34, "tohuw and bohuw" are used to describe the condition of the earth following a catastrophic event (i.e., erets; 0776), with the resulting landscape specifically stated as being uninhabitable by man. Yet, in these same instances, geographic features, such as mountains, hills, stream beds, "fruitful places", palaces, fortresses, and the ruins of cities still exist, but in a desolate state. In both passages, this "tohuw and bohuw" land is specifically described as being uninhabited by man, although some wildlife (cormorants, bitterns, owls, ravens, wild beasts of the dessert) is said to be present within the Isaiah passages. These things could certainly not be if "tohuw and bohuw" were meant to indicate a state of nonexistence. Additionally, the reference to "broken down cities", the overgrowth of palaces and fortresses by thorns, nettles, and brambles, and the existence solely of certain types of wildlife indicates that these places once thrived before becoming decimated.

Based on the Jeremiah and Isaiah passages, the translation "uninhabitable wasteland" seems to most accurately describe the meaning of the phrase "tohuw and bohuw." This is further supported through other chapters within the books of Jeremiah and Ezekiel, which are filled with references to the destruction of Israel in much the same way due to the peoples' transgressions. Jeremiah 51:29-43, in particular, also describes a land that is in such a state of desolation as to be uninhabitable by man, with wild beasts being the sole living creatures therein (see also Jer 34:22 and Jer 44:2). Although the words "tohuw" and "bohuw" are not used within these passages, the description is exactly the same as for those verses where these words *are* used.

So, based on the wording of Gen 1:1-2 in the biblical Hebrew, the physical universe and the earth both existed – with the latter in a desolate, uninhabitable state – prior to Gen 1:3. However, the biblical text provides no indication as to how much time had elapsed between Gen 1:2 and Gen 1:3.

This opens the door for the passage of millions or even billions of years prior to the preparation of the earth for habitation that begins in Gen 1:3.

The Hebrew wording provides yet another very important clue to this in that Gen 1:2 would more accurately be translated as "*and the earth had become a wilderness*" (i.e., tohuw and bohuw) rather than "*…the earth was a wilderness*." The verb in Gen 1:2 is "hay'eta" and it is written in the same grammatical way as Gen 1:1, indicating that this is already a fully completed action. [10]

According to some very distinguished biblical scholars [11], either "had become" or "it came to pass" are more accurate translations for "hay'eta." In either case, such a translation indicates that a time interval of unstated length had passed. The wording indicates a condition that had already been achieved at some point in the past, with no indication as to the length of time that had passed with the earth existing in this condition prior to Gen 1:3. This makes perfect sense because, according to the biblical text, God did not create (bara) these celestial objects from nothing but used the primordial matter that He created at the initial Big Bang creation event to "make" (asah) or "form" (yatsar) them over a period of time (see "Creation" First – "Making" Second, pg. 52.).

If you consider the wording of the biblical text carefully, you will realize that there is actually no specific command given by God for the creation of the earth. We are simply informed in Gen 1:2 that the earth existed in an uninhabitable state. The first instance of the Genesis creation account where the earth is definitively referenced occurs on Creation Day Three (Gen 1:9-13), at which time God is described as separating the waters from the dry land, clearly indicating that the planet had already formed by this time.

Never in Genesis 1, nor anywhere else within the bible for that matter, does God utter the command "let there be earth", in a manner similar to other creative acts that are described therein. The same is true of the sun, moon, and stars, which God "forms" (asah) <u>*prior to*</u> Creation Day Four and sets them into place <u>*by*</u> Creation Day Four. The bible does not tell us that He created (bara) them on that day, but that they would, from that point on, be "visible" such that they could now be used for determining seasons and times (see also Exod 20:11 and 31:17, pg. 68).

Gen 1:16 and Gen 1:17 state that God "*had made*" the two great lights (i.e., the sun and moon) to rule the daytime and the night and "*had set*" them in the sky of the heavens. In both instances, the form of the verb that is used within the biblical Hebrew text indicates that these actions *had already been completed*. In these verses, the word "made" (asah) is used, not the word "created" (bara). That is because the creation (of space, time, matter, and energy) had already occurred, as stated in Gen 1:1-2, so that the creation period being described within Exodus 20:11/31:17 is referring to the preparation of the earth from the materials that God previously created (bara).

<u>Meaning of the Hebrew Word "Yom" (day)</u>

The Hebrew word that is translated as "day" throughout the bible is "yom" (3117 and 3118). The word is used over 2,300 times within the bible, with it being used most often to describe only the hours of daylight. The word typically does not include the nighttime hours. [(12)] In fact, with the very first use of the term in Gen 1:5, God specifically labels the term "yom" (3117) as "light" and differentiates it from darkness, which God labels as "night."

This distinction is underscored further within Gen 1:14, 16, and 18, each of which clearly distinguishes the day (i.e., light) from the night (i.e., darkness). *In every instance* where "yom" is used within Genesis 1 outside of the "evening and morning" references that conclude each creative "day," it refers solely to daylight hours. At no time is the term clearly used within

Genesis 1, and rarely is it used by itself within other biblical passages, to indicate a 24-hour day. According to physicist and Hebrew scholar Dr. Whitefield, in those rare instances within the bible where the word "yom" does refer to a 24-hour period, that 24-hour period is not established solely by the word "yom" itself. Instead, it acquires the meaning of a 24-hour period due to an associated modifying word, such as the Sabbath Day. When "yom" does refer to 24 hours, the use is almost exclusively connected with the Sabbath, a festival, or a ceremony. [(13)]

In John 11:9, Jesus specifically makes an unambiguous distinction between day and night, stating, "Are there not twelve hours of daylight? Anyone who walks in the daytime will not stumble, for they see by this world's light. It is when a person walks at night that they stumble, for they have no light." Although the Greek word used here for "day" is "hemera" (Strong's 2250, which can be used to describe both the hours between dawn and dark and a whole 24-hour period) and not the Hebrew word "yom", a clear distinction is being drawn between daylight and nighttime. Other passages where "day" is specifically distinguished from night include, but are certainly not limited to Deut 9:25, Gen 7:4, Gen 7:12, Gen 7:17, and Exod 34:28.

The second most common use of the term "yom" is to refer to long periods of time such as in Num 3:1, which refers to "the Day (yom; 3117) of the LORD." This phrase (i.e., the day of the LORD) appears almost three dozen times within the bible and clearly refers to a period of time that is longer in duration than 24 hours. Additionally, there are at least two places within the bible where multiple "generations" are said to have occurred within a single "yom". If one were to insist on the term "yom" equating to a single 24-hour day, the passage of several generations could not possibly have occurred during such a brief time span when viewing these passages in context.

- Gen 2:4; These are the *generations* of the heavens and of the earth when they were created (bara), *in the day (yom) that the LORD God made (asah) the earth and the heavens*

  In this verse, the word day (yom) seems to be used to cover the initial creation event (Gen 1:1-2), a period of time potentially comprised of millions or billions of years plus all six of the days (yom) where God prepared the earth (Gen 1:3-31).

Alternatively, it could be meant to cover just the 6-day period where God prepared the earth for habitation. In either case, generations are said to have occurred within a single day.

- Gen 5:1-2; This is the book of the *generations* of Adam. *In the day that God created man*, in the likeness of God made (asah) He him; male and female created (bara) He them and blessed them, and called their name Adam, *in the day* when they were created (bara).

  Gen 5 goes on to list all the generations from Adam through Noah; at least nine generations of offspring that clearly were not "begat" during a single 24-hour day.

Some other scriptural verses where the word "day" (yom) is used to indicate a long period of time, or to distinguish between the hours of light and darkness, include (this list is not all-inclusive, but highlights just a few):

- In Gen 2:17; God warns Adam against eating of the tree of the knowledge of good and evil, warning him that, "…in the day (yom) that thou eatest of it thereof thou shalt surely die." So, what happens? Adam eats of the tree and lives for several hundred more years, to the ripe old age of 930!! How could this be if he was supposed to "surely die" on the "day" that he committed the trespass? Shouldn't he have died within 24 hours, if the term "day" actually meant 24 hours? (See Physical vs Spiritual Death, pg. 119)
- Exod 34:28 describes Moses receiving the Ten Commandments from God on Mount Sinai, stating that he (Moses) was, "…there with the LORD forty days (yom) and forty nights…"
- Num 3:1 states, "These are the generations of Aaron and Moses in the day (yom) that the LORD spake with Moses in Mount Sinai. As with Genesis 5 above, there are clearly more generations of offspring than could have been conceived within a single 24-hour day. Also, according to Exod 34:28, Moses spoke with the LORD for forty days and forty nights; clearly more than a single 24-hour day.

- Ps 90:4 and 2Peter 3:8; These passages compare a thousand years in the sight of God to a single day (the "yom" in Ps 90:4 is translated as "yesterday"). This should not be taken literally as 1,000 years, but should be taken to mean that time means nothing to God. He exists outside of space and time and is, therefore, not bound by either.
- Isaiah 11:10; "...in that "day," the Lord shall set His hand again to recover the remnant of His people..." This is referring to the re-assembly of the Jewish people from the various place spanning the globe to which they have been scattered, a period spanning over 2,000 years. The Jews have, since May 1948, been returning to Israel in large numbers.
- Isa 23:15 – "...in that "day," Tyre shall be forgotten seventy years." Here, a day is unambiguously equated with seventy years.

Within the biblical text, the term "yom" is not used by itself specifically to describe a 24-hour time period. *In the few places where a 24-hour day is indicated in the bible, it is not described as being from "evening to morning", as is the case in Genesis 1, but from "evening to evening"*, such as in Leviticus 23:32. This is a practice that is still followed today by modern Jewish communities.

Gen 7:17 is one of the rare instances where a 24-hour period *seems to be* indicated solely through the use of "yom." However, this verse reiterates what was already stated in Gen 7:12, where it was specifically said that the rain (of Noah's flood) would fall "day" and "night." Here, again, the term "day" (yom; 3117) is clearly being distinguished from the night.

It is often suggested by Young Earth advocates that the word "day" (yom) must be taken to mean a literal 24-hour day when the word is prefixed with a number. They go on to suggest that this is the case for the days in Genesis 1. However, both of these assertions are actually incorrect.

According to Gleason Archer, formerly an Associate Editor of the *Theological Wordbook of the Old Testament*, "There were six major stages in this work of formation, and these stages are represented by successive days of a week. In this connection it is important to observe that none of the six creative days bears a definite article (i.e., the word "the") in the Hebrew text. Therefore, the translations "*the* first day," "*the* second day," etc., are in error.

The Hebrew says, "And the evening took place, and the morning took place, day one" (Gen 1:5). Hebrew expresses "the first day" by *hayyom harison*, but Gen 1:5 says simply "*yom ehad*" (day one). Again, in v. 8 we read "*yom seni*" ("a second day") not *hayyom hasseni* ("the second day"). (14)

So, each of the days of Genesis 1 are actually referred to in the biblical Hebrew as "a" first day, "a" second day, "a" third day, and not "*the*" first day, "*the*" second day", "*the*" third day, etc. This indicates that these days may not have been directly connected, meaning that a period of time may have elapsed between each of them. When combined with the evidence that has already been provided herein (i.e., where not a single instance of the use of the word "yom" in Genesis 1 refers to a 24-hour period) see "Meaning of the Hebrew Word "Yom", pg. 57), it seems likely that the days were, in fact, separated by periods of time.

In discussing how the days are numbered in Genesis 1 and the missing indefinite article "the", Professor Lennox (*Seven Days that Divide the World*) suggests the following, "…(there is the possibility that) the writer did not intend us to think of the first six days as days of a single earth week, but rather as a sequence of six creation days; that is, days of normal length…in which God created something new, but days that might well have been separated by long periods of time. We have already seen that Genesis separates the initial creation, "the beginning," from the (six day) sequence of (creation) days…therefore, the six creation days themselves could well have been days of normal length, spaced out at intervals over the entire period of time that God took to complete His work. The outworking of the potential of each creative fiat (meaning, the outcome of each of the expressions of "and God said") would occupy an unspecified period of time that God took to complete His work." (15)

What Professor Lennox is saying here is that each creation day could very well have been a normal 24-hour day as we know them, but that each of the days could have been separated by a significant length of time. This means that stuff *began* to happen at God's command but that the event(s) took a much longer period of time to reach their completion. God said, "Let there be…" and the event began. But, once begun, the unfolding of the event took a long period of time to complete.

As Professor Lennox points out, "One consequence of this is that we would expect to find what geologists tell us that we actually <u>do</u> find – fossil evidence revealing the sudden appearance of new levels of complexity, followed by periods during which there was no more creation (in the sense of God speaking to inaugurate something radically new). (…there is the possibility that) each of the creation days inaugurates a period of outworking but is not coterminous (i.e., having the same boundaries within space and time) within that period." (parenthetical information added by author for clarity) (15) The days, therefore, could very well comprise six 24-hour periods, but each day could be separated by a lengthy time period.

The six references within Genesis 1 to "evening and morning" do not indicate a 24-hour time period.

For the majority of the world's people, a day is defined as, "the interval of light between two successive nights", "the time between sunrise and sunset," or as "a division of time equal to 24 hours and representing the average length of the period during which the earth makes one rotation on its axis." (16) However, a "day" has always been marked differently by the Jewish people, who have always used "evening to evening" to mark the passing of individual, 24-hour days.

The description of time in this way (i.e., the evening and morning references within Genesis 1) is unorthodox and signals something unique. Given that this six-fold reference to evening and morning appears solely within Genesis 1, and the fact that other passages within the biblical text indicate that the Israelites did not mark the passage of time in this manner, the use of this phrasing is perplexing. How do we reconcile this?

Each creation day of Genesis 1 begins with the phrase, "*…and God said….*" and ends with the phrase, "*…and there was evening, and there was morning, the* n^{th} *day*." Many suggest that the distinctive verbiage of "evening" and "morning" within Genesis 1 is a clear indication that each Creation Day was comprised of a 24-hour day having a night and a day. But there is certainly evidence to the contrary.

Firstly, this phrase occurs at the end of Creation Days 1 through 6 but it is missing from Creation Day 7. This is a curious and glaring omission, if the phrase were meant to be used as a daily marker for the seven days that make up the 7-day week of creation.

Secondly, this phrase is also not used in any other place throughout the bible to mark the passage of time. In other places within the bible, a 24-hour day is described as being from "evening to evening", as the Israelites started each new day at sunset. For example, the Sabbath was (and still is) described as starting at sunset on Friday and ending at sunset on Saturday (Lev 23:32)[11]. Additionally, there are numerous instances

[11] Further evidence of the evening starting a new day can be found within Exod 12:18, Neh 13:19, Lev 11:24, Deut 23:11, Mark 1:29-33, Mark 16:1, Luke 4:40, and John 20:1.

where significant events are said to have occurred "at even" (i.e., at the start of a new day). Some examples include:

- Angels appearing to Lot in Sodom (Gen 19:1),
- God's provision of quail as meat for the complaining Israelites (Exod 16:13),
- The continual burnt offering of a lamb (Exod 29:39-42, Num 28:4),
- God's direction to the Israelites to begin every Passover celebration (Lev 23:5, Num 9:3, Josh 5:10),
- The disciples of Jesus waiting until the even at the close of the Sabbath (i.e., the start of the next new non-Sabbath day) to bring the diseased and possessed to Him for curing so that they did not defile the Sabbath, when no work was supposed to be done (Mark 1:32)
- Insistence of removing Jesus from the cross 'at even' so that He did not remain there for the duration of the Sabbath, when physical work was prohibited
- Jesus' first appearance to His disciples at even on the first day of the week, following His resurrection (John 20:19)
- The arrival of the Holy Ghost (Acts 2:1)
- Many instances where those who are "unclean" are required to cleanse themselves and remain outside of the camp until the beginning of the new day "at even" (Num 19:19)

Still, there are those who feel that the six evening and the morning references of Genesis 1 establish the parameters that make up a day. I do not agree with this for the reasons already provided. The Israelites strictly followed the dictates of God (when they weren't misbehaving) with respect to observing times and seasons. If God had meant evening and morning to comprise a day, then this is how the Israelites would have observed it. However, the Israelites have for millennia considered a single 24-hour day to be comprised of one evening to the next, a pattern that is still in use by modern day Jews.

We have already seen that the biblical commentator Nahmanides has provided us with an explanation, in his commentary written almost 800 years ago [(17)], for the six "evening and morning" references of Genesis 1 that is fascinating and provides a glimpse into the some of the bible's less obvious, deeper wisdom. He suggests that the wording is God's way of saying that He took what was originally in a state of disorder, following the initial creation, and put things into order (see Bringing Order to a Disorderly World, pg. 22).

Use of the phrase "…and it was so / and it came to pass"

The phrase "and it was so/and it came to pass" appears over 300 times within the biblical text, six of which occur within Genesis 1 to indicate the completion of God's formative commands. While it could be argued that the phrase indicates the immediate completion of the action, the preponderance of the biblical evidence suggests otherwise.

It is interesting to note that the English translation of the phrase for each of the six times that it occurs within Genesis 1 differs from the hundreds of other times that the phrase appears elsewhere within the bible. Within Genesis 1, the phrase is translated as "…and it was so," giving the impression that the stated action was completed immediately. However, in the hundreds of *other* places where the phrase appears, it is translated as "…and it came to pass…," and is used to indicate a passage of time between what is being stated and the actual conclusion of the event. 2Kings 15:12 provides a perfect example of this.

The 2Kings verse states, "*This was the word of the LORD which He spake unto Jehu, saying, Thy sons shall sit on the throne of Israel unto the fourth generation. And so it came to pass*." Clearly, for this to have "come to pass", these events would have had to occur over the duration of the four generations of progeny that followed God's statement. The "…and so it came to pass…" in the 2Kings verse uses the very same biblical Hebrew as the "…and it was so…" within Genesis 1.

Amos 5:14 is another good example. This passage speaks to God being or remaining with His people "*so long as they seek good and not evil*." This speaks to a potentially indefinite period of time, lasting for as long (or short) a period of time as the people elect to do good over evil. In many other places where the phrase is used, the passage of a period of time, sometimes lengthy, is implied.

Within Genesis 1, the phrase, "…and it was so…" is stated on Creation Days 2, 3, 4, and 6, occurring twice on days 3 and 6. Use of this phrase was not needed on the Creation Day One because the ignition of the sun would have been instantaneous. According to Gen 1:1-2, the sun and earth would already have been formed[12], but it wasn't until Creation Day One, as stated in Gen 1:3, that the sun was ignited at God's first (recorded) command.

The phrase was also not needed on Creation Day Five because God was instantaneously creating something completely new (bara), namely, the forms of life that would inhabit the waters. We know that this was an instantaneous act because the term "bara" was used rather than "asah.". The fossil record bears witness to the fact that aquatic life appears suddenly, fully formed, and in an amazing variety about 530 million years ago in what is often referred to as the Cambrian Explosion (see Was There Enough Time?, pg. 14).

With His initial creation, God originated all of the physical laws that govern how our universe operates. It is, therefore, not unreasonable to expect that He would make or fashion things in accordance with the laws that *He* designed so that our world would always appear as "natural." I believe this to be the case, based on the biblical evidence.

If you look closely at the creation days where the phrase "…and it was so…" is used in Genesis 1, you will note that its use is restricted either to those events that would have occurred over a lengthy period of time by scientific reckoning (i.e., using natural physical processes) or for events that describe processes that were meant to continue from that point forward (i.e., the earth producing vegetation, a life-sustaining atmosphere, human and animal life). These include:

- Creation Day Two: The development of the earth's oxygen-rich atmosphere, which took billions of years to reach the point where life could be supported; a process that continues.
- Creation Day Three: The emergence of land masses (by slow moving geologic processes) and the beginning of plant life, with God directing the earth to bring forth grass. (The emergence of plant life began on this day, but continued for the duration of the creation epoch and on into the present day. Initially, and for a long period thereafter, the only plant life was photosynthetic algae, which worked to bring the level of atmospheric oxygen to its present level.)

---

[12] Gen 1:1-2 state that God initially created the heavens and the earth. We have already seen that these things occurred prior to Gen 1:3. The laws of physics tell us that the sun formed prior to the earth, so the sun must also have been included within the first two verses of Genesis 1.

- Creation Day Four: The visible appearance of the sun, moon, and stars as the earth's atmosphere transitions from translucent to transparent due to the rise in atmospheric oxygen. From this point forward, the sun, moon, and stars have been used to mark times and seasons.
- Creation Day Six: The making (asah) of land animals and hominids. Like the emergence of plant life on Creation Day Three, this was done in a way to ensure that these would remain as continual processes.

Further details for each of these events are provided in Chapter Five – Preparing the Earth for Habitation.

Of special note here should be the text of Genesis 1:14-15, which states, "*And God said, let there be lights in the firmament of the heaven to divide the day (yom) from the night and let them be for signs, and for seasons, and for days and years. And let them be for lights in the firmament of heaven to give light upon the earth, and it was so/and it came to pass*." According to Dr. Whitefield [(18)], the phrase "…and it was so" was written in the pluperfect form in the biblical Hebrew, indicating a *completed* action. This indicates that the sun, moon, and stars had completed at least one evolution of God's command, *having already served their function of indicating seasons, days, and years for at least one cycle*. How could this have "come to pass" if the "day" here was referring to a 24-hour time period?

On Creation Day Three, God directs *the earth* to bring forth grass, herb yielding seed, and fruit bearing trees rather than directly speaking them into existence. Although I cannot be dogmatic as to why He directed this of the earth rather than creating them directly, I would suggest that He started the growth of plant life in the soil in such a way as to guarantee that the production of plant life would continue as a natural course of things; a process that would endure to the present day. This also occurs on Creation Day Six, when God directs the earth to bring forth land animals and creeping things. (See Creation Day Three and Creation Day Six in Chapter Five for a more thorough description of these events.)

One could argue that with God nothing is impossible and that He could have easily created or made everything instantaneously. This is certainly true. However, this is neither stated nor implied within the biblical text. In fact, the opposite is true. The bible clearly describes a creation event (bara) that is followed by periods of making (asah).

2 Peter 3:5 and Psalm 90:4 describe how a thousand years to God is the same as a day. This is meant to illustrate that time is of no consequence to God as He exists outside of space and time and is therefore not limited by either. A creation epoch that spanned billions of years would have required no more or less of His effort than one that occurred within 7 nanoseconds. He is eternal and could have taken as much – or as little – time as He wished. Doing so through the natural physical processes that He created would have had the lasting benefit of ensuring that the natural world would always appear as natural to us.

A naturally occurring world is important because it allows every person on earth to retain their free will, deciding for themselves whether to accept that the world has evolved through natural processes or to recognize and accept God's part in its creation. If the existence of the universe were so obviously miraculous, people would be forced to accept God's hand in its creation and free will would be compromised.

As further evidence that some Genesis 1 events took a significant amount of time is the use of the phrase "happa'am" (Strong's 1945 and 6471) by Adam within Gen 2:23 upon seeing Eve for the first time. This phrase is used 13 times within the Old Testament and routinely carries the connotation of "at last" or "finally." [13] Its usage in Gen 2:23 strongly suggests that a lengthy period of time had elapsed between the creation of Adam and the creation of his mate. (19)(20) According to Gen 2:23, upon seeing Eve for the first time, Adam states, "*This is now/finally/at last* (happa'am) *bone of my bones and flesh of my flesh…*"

A casual reading of Genesis 2 seems to indicate that God created Adam, placed him in the Garden of Eden to dress it and keep it, that God formed the beasts of the field and birds of the air and had Adam name them all, then created Eve, all within the same day. However, the use of this phrase by Adam indicates that a significant amount of time had elapsed since God created him. Otherwise, we are forced to accept that Adam could not get through a single 24-our day without needing a mate. With all of the events of that day (i.e., the day that Adam was created), and with God as his companion, this hardly seems plausible.

The organization *Reasons to Believe* affirms the following: "According to the text, the exclamation that came from Adam's lips when he first saw Eve was, in Hebrew, "*happa'am*." This expression is translated in Genesis 30:20 as "now at last" and in Genesis 46:30 as "now

[13] Other verses where "happa'am" is used include Gen 18:32, 29:34, 29:35, 30:20, 46:30, Exod 9:27 and 10:17, Judges 6:39, 15:3, and 16:28

finally." The Theological Wordbook of the Old Testament translates this term in Genesis 2:23 as "at last." The Brown-Driver-Briggs Hebrew and English Lexicon translates it in the same passage as "now at length." [(21)] In any case, the phrase indicates that a period of time has elapsed.

In the original Hebrew, Exod 20:11 and Exod 31:17 do not state that God created everything within a single contiguous period of six 24-hour days

These Exodus verses are used as a key piece of evidence by those who support a Young Earth to prove their case. However, closer scrutiny of the biblical Hebrew indicates that the six creation days being described within them do not comprise the totality of the creation epoch.

In the English translation, the Exodus 20:11 and Exod 31:17 passages read, "*For in six days the LORD made the heavens and the earth, the sea, and all that is in them, but He rested on the seventh day*." On the surface, there seems to be no margin for error – no wiggle room built into the text. It says it right there… "for *in* six days…". Shouldn't we take that to mean that God created everything within a single, six-day period, just like the text says? The answer would, of course, be "yes", ***IF*** that were what the biblical Hebrew text actually says. The problem is that the biblical Hebrew differs slightly from the English translation. The difference is minor, but the implications are not.

The original Hebrew text reads, "*For six days the LORD made …*" The word "in" that appears within the English translation does not actually appear within the original Hebrew text [(22)]. The addition of this single, two-letter word in the English translation adds meaning that suggests that God completed every single creative act *within* (i.e., ***in***) this six-day time period. But this is not what is stated within the original Hebrew text nor is this indicated in any other biblical verse.

Removal of the word "in" does not refute or dispute the fact that God commanded things during six separate days. However, it *does* support the idea that these six days occurred at some point *after* God's initial creation. In fact, when viewed through the lens of the events of Gen 1:1-2 *having already been completed prior to* Gen 1:3, where the first of God's formative commands is recorded, this seems to be the case. It also opens up the possibility that these were not six *consecutive* days, but that there may have been long periods of time between each of the six days.

Based on the wording here, the creative commands could well have been uttered on six individual days, with the results ultimately taking a much longer period of time to complete. In other words, the entire creation period need not have occurred during a single period of time. Let me use an analogy…

Let's say that I built a garden shed in my backyard during three consecutive weekends. The first weekend, I poured a concrete foundation on Friday, letting it set on Saturday before constructing the frame on Sunday. The second weekend, I finished the framing and added a roof on Saturday and built the walls on Sunday. On the final weekend, I rigged the electrical wiring, installed the doors and windows, and put up drywall on Friday, sanded and re-mudded the drywall on Saturday, then finished the drywall sanding and painting on Sunday. The actual build took six days to complete but the whole project spanned 16 days, with periods of lag time needed in between for the concrete to set and to finish at least two rounds of drywall taping and sanding.

If the two Exodus verses are referring to the six days (yom) during which God prepared the earth for habitation (which appears to be the case), then they do not incorporate *all* creative acts because the Hebrew grammar has already informed us that the original creation (Gen 1:1-2) occurred *before* these six days (yom). Moreover, the creation of Eve happened *after* these six days (yom)."

The biblical text very clearly states that God rested on the Seventh Day, ending His (creative) work (Gen 2:1-3, Heb 4:3-4). Yet, several verses later – seemingly on the same day – God makes Eve as a helper for Adam (Gen 2:22). Either the biblical text is in error – which I do not believe is the case – or God fashioned Eve sometime after Creation Day Seven (see The "Building" or "Bearing" of Eve, pg.123). If the latter is the case, then this, too, would indicate that not all creation events occurred during the sole six-day period that is seemingly indicated by the Exodus verses. This is a very sticky point for those that insist, based on Exod 20:11/31:17, that God created everything within single contiguous period of six 24-hour days.

God's first recorded formative command appears in Gen 1:3, where He begins to prepare the earth for habitation in accordance with His plan (Isaiah 45:18-21). However, this command reflects His efforts to "make" (asah), not "create" (bara). We are clearly informed by the grammar of Genesis 1:1-2 that the creation (bara) of the heavens and the earth occurred *before* Gen 1:3. Yet, the bible does not record God's creative commands as the initial creation of Gen 1:1-2 unfolded. We are simply told in general terms that He did so. God's direct commands are not recorded until He begins to prepare the earth (Gen 1:3).

Genesis 1:3-31 reflects God's efforts to prepare the earth, actions that are *initiated* by His command on six individual days or "periods" but which were likely completed over a much longer period of time. Exod 20:11 and 31:17 speak of this very same six day creation period, which could not have included the initial creation, as stated in Gen 1:1-2, because the Hebrew grammar tells us that the initial creation happened prior to Gen 1:3. If God created the heavens and the earth before His first utterance within Gen 1:3 to prepare the earth, then any claim that *everything* was created within a single period of six 24-hour days cannot be supported.

As part of the Ten Commandments, the Israelites are instructed to "*...remember the sabbath and keep it holy.*" The people were instructed to work for six days, then to rest on the seventh day, performing no manner of work. God states that, as He Himself rested on Creation Day Seven, the people are to mimic His example (Gen 20:8-11). However, Exod 20:8-11 is being used as a simile rather than as a direct correlation simply because God's efforts during the six days of creation were vastly different from man's.

God's six-day work week established the pattern, but it was also very different from ours in several important ways so a direct, one-for-one correlation cannot really be made. For example, God's days are not like our days as He is unbound by time. His six-day creation period occurred only once whereas ours repeats every seven days. Nor is He saddled with limited physical stamina, periodically requiring rest. The same is certainly not true of human beings.

In Exod 20:8-11, God's direction is for the Israelites to emulate His example, working for six periods – which would be the six 24-hour days to which they were accustomed – and resting on the seventh because it is healthy for human beings and animals to do so.

Let's summarize some key facts so far from this discussion:

- The term "yom" (3117) is most commonly used within the biblical text to indicate the hours of daylight, not a 24-hour period. Most notably, in every instance where "yom" is used in Genesis 1, it is used to describe the daylight hours ***only*** and does not include the nighttime hours.

- The second most common use of the term "yom" is to indicate a long period of time.

- "Yom" is not used by itself within the bible to indicate a 24-hour time period. In the instances within the bible where the word "yom" does refer to a 24-hour period, it acquires the meaning of a 24-hour period due to an associated modifying word, such as the Sabbath Day or the Day of Atonement.
- The six-fold references to "evening and morning" in Genesis 1 are likely not being used to indicate the passage of 24-hour days as this phraseology for measuring time is not used anywhere else in the bible and using it to do so would contradict other biblical passages where the passage of days is specified.
- A 24-hour day in the bible is described as being from evening to evening (Lev 23:32).
- Use of phrases such as "…and it came to pass/…and it was so" and "happa'am" indicate a passage of time. In many instances, the Hebrew grammar indicates *completed* rather than ongoing actions.

<u>The Creation Scenario</u>

Given the facts that have thus far been presented, the sequence of events being described within Genesis 1:1-31 appears to be:

- <u>First</u>, God *instantaneously* created (bara) *from nothing* all the matter/energy that was ever going to exist within the entirety of the physical universe during the very first moment of creation (Gen 1:1).
- <u>Secondly</u>, Following the initial creation, God made (asah), through the natural physical processes that He created (bara) and during a period of time that is unspecified within the biblical text, the physical structures of the heavens (i.e., galaxies, suns, and planet earth) into corporeal structures using the matter/energy that He initially created (Gen 1:1-2). At some unknown point during this process, the sun and earth are formed, with the earth existing in an uninhabitable state (the "tohuw and bohuw" of Gen 1:2).

These first two actions occurred prior to Gen 1:3 based on the Hebrew grammar within Gen 1:1-2. The inversion of the noun and verb in the first two verses of Genesis clearly indicate that these actions had already been concluded at an unknown point prior to Gen 1:3. There is no way to determine, based on the biblical text, the duration of these events nor how long before the rest of Genesis 1 (i.e., starting with Gen 1:3) they occurred.

- Thirdly, at some undisclosed point after the earth had been made (asah), God began to prepare it for habitation (Gen 1:3-31, Isaiah 45:18-21). It is at this point that the first of His direct commands (i.e., the first, "and God said" that begins the six creation days) is recorded in the bible. Starting in Gen 1:3, we are given the details – the sequence of God's commands through which He rearranged the earth over six days, much like a potter turning a lump of clay into a more ornate vessel, over time, by first shaping it, then adding ornamentation and design, then baking and glazing it.[14]

The biblical evidence presented so far certainly (and strongly) indicates an Ancient Earth. I was actually quite surprised at the volume of this evidence once I began to earnestly scrutinize the text. I had been reading the bible for decades and none of these things ever before jumped off the pages at me. But, of course, I had never before truly delved deeply into the meaning of the Hebrew text in my quest to gain some answers. Additionally, my recent studies were accompanied by fervent prayer asking God to provide me with insight and wisdom into both His Word and His World. I am sure that He recognized the genuineness of my desire to know – that I truly wanted to understand any perceived discrepancies between biblical and scientific wisdom – for He opened my eyes almost daily with a fresh revelation. This book is the result of those revelations and the deeper wisdom that He provided to me as the result of my prayers.

As I gained this knowledge and wisdom regarding His creation through rigorous study of the bible in concert with the latest scientific advances, I was so pleased and excited to learn that there is, in reality, no discrepancy between them. There is plenty of evidence within the bible that the universe and the world upon which we live are ancient – a fact to which nature speaks quite loudly – rather than being merely thousands of years old. As I merged the biblical evidence with the teachings of nature, so that I was considering both God's Word and God's World in

---

[14] There is another view that the earth previously existed (i.e., prior to the creation events that are described within Genesis 1, and was being re-formed after "becoming" formless and void in gen 1:1-2 following Lucifer's corruption of the previous version. This is based on a belief that the wording of Genesis 1:2 indicates that the earth *became* formless and void (from a preexisting state where this wasn't so).

accordance with His instruction, I found that the preponderance of the evidence from both sources overwhelmingly indicated a universe/earth that is of considerable age.

Now that we have reviewed the biblical evidence for an Ancient Earth, let's take a look at the scientific evidence for it and examine how closely it matches the story of creation as it is provided to us through Genesis 1.

The Scientific Evidence for an Ancient Earth

Having occurred almost 14 billion years ago, the Big Bang is, of course, the poster child for an Ancient Universe. Although some specific questions remain regarding the Big Bang, much of physics is very well understood. According to theoretical physicist and astrobiologist Paul Davies, "...pretty much all of the basic physics pertaining to the time between just a millionth of a second and several minutes after the Big Bang is now regarded as routine. ...the physics of the early universe can be directly tested in the laboratory." On Long Island, New York, a large machine called a heavy ion collider proves his point. The collider is designed to slam the nuclei of gold and other heavy atoms together head-on, with enough force to recreate the conditions of the early universe as they were one millionth of a second after the beginning, when the temperature was over a trillion degrees." (23)

But, other than Big Bang nucleosynthesis, what evidence is there within the scientific world that our universe and earth are ancient?

Here are just some of the many directly observable indicators for an Ancient Universe in nature, according to Dr. Hugh Ross (24):

- A star such as our sun takes millions of years to form and millions of more years from the point of its ignition (i.e., birth) to become stable. Through the laws of physics, we understand that the luminosity and intensity of our sun were unstable for the first 100 million years of its life, during which life could not have survived on the earth. This means that our sun was at the very least 100 million years old before life could have been sustained on the earth.

- The existence of dead stars. According to Sky and Telescope, "a star's life expectancy depends on its mass. Generally, the more massive the star, the faster it burns up its fuel supply, and the shorter its life. The most massive stars can burn out and explode in a supernova after only a few million years of fusion. A star with a mass like the Sun, on the other hand, can continue fusing hydrogen for about 10 billion years. And if the star is very small, with a mass only a tenth that of the Sun, it can keep fusing hydrogen for up to a trillion years, longer than the current age of the universe." (25)

The fact that we can observe white dwarf stars, neutron stars, red giant stars, and black holes means that there are stars out there that have completed their life cycle, meaning that they have already existed for anywhere between a few million years to billions of years. While God could have created these star remnants in various stages of their life cycle, this would provide us with an inaccurate picture of stellar life and would be duplicitous – something that God cannot be.

- The age of lunar rocks and other extraterrestrial material. In Genesis One and the Origin of the Earth, the authors state, "Lunar rocks have been dated to between 3.5 and 4.2 billion years. Ages older than 4.6 billion years have not been found in any extraterrestrial materials, so one can reasonably conclude that the solar system is about 4.6 billion years old. This agrees with the sun's estimated age of 5 billion years… The importance of dating extraterrestrial materials is that they were not subject to the effects of weathering that one finds on earth. Hence, one cannot argue that their ages are spurious because of weathering, erosion, plate tectonics, or Noah's flood." (26)

- The existence of fossilized remains. The process of fossilization typically takes millions of years, during which the original organic matter of the dead organism or creature is gradually replaced by mineral deposits from groundwater, creating a rock-like replica of the original organism through a process known as permineralization. The existence of dinosaur fossils means that these dead creatures have been buried for millions of years.

- Lack of radionuclides with long half-lives. Earth's crust is devoid of all short-lived radionuclides. According to Dr. Hugh Ross, "Geologists and geophysicists find no neptunium-237 (half-life 2.14 million years), no aluminum-26 (half-life 720,000 years), no calcium-41 (half-life 103,000 years), no iodine-129 (half-life 17 million years), no technetium-98 (half-life 4.2 million years), and no plutonium-244 (half-life 82 million years). …the present-day lack of short-lived radionuclides in earth, on the sun, or within meteorites convinces scientists that the solar system must be older than a billion years." (27)

- Ice Core Samples, the layers of which provide a continuous record of sediment deposits going back almost a million years. These samples also contain radioactive isotopes through which scientists can verify that the rate of radiometric decay has been constant – without any variation – for at least that far back. While there are those who are skeptical that the layers represent annual events, the correlation of layers to years can be verified through the study of dust deposits from known events such as the eruptions of Krakatoa in 1883 and the multiple eruptions of Vesuvius since the first century, as well as through other means. Ice cores taken from Greenland demonstrate that dramatic global climate changes have been the rule over the past 100,000 years. (28)

- Coral growth rates. The rate at which coral reefs grow is well known, with the record of coral reef layers dating back over 400,000,000 years. Like the ice core samples, the layers of growth contain radiometric isotopes that serve as a reliable form of measurement that, together with the coral growth rate itself, clearly indicate that the earth is at least a half million years old.

- Varves (annually deposited lake sediments). Not only do these sediments capture the dust signatures of global events like Krakatoa and Vesuvius and radioactive decay rates, they also capture other atmospheric conditions, such as pollen types and counts, that provide confirmation of various changes to earth's environment – changes that can be compared and verified through other means.

Additionally, the K-Pg Boundary, a geological marker within the earth's crust, contains a high concentration of the element iridium, which is rare on the Earth but abundant in asteroids. This layer of iridium indicates the impact of an asteroid on the earth approximately 66 million years ago, which is believed to have triggered a mass extinction leading to the disappearance of non-avian dinosaurs and many other species.

These are just a few examples among many where the scientific evidence indicates an Ancient Earth. Entire books have been written regarding each of these factors. Not only is there much more evidence than what is presented here, but the evidence within many of these areas is mutually supportive, with the findings in one area bolstering similar findings in others.

The preponderance of the evidence through His Word and His World via naturally occurring physical markers certainly indicates an ancient age for the universe. Moreover, there is significant man-made (i.e., archeological) evidence that human civilization is much older than the conventional wisdom teaches it to be. This will be the subject of the next chapter.

CHAPTER FOUR

Megalithic Structures and Worldwide Amnesia

There are literally thousands of megalithic sites scattered around the world that defy explanation. Archaeologists frequently try to pigeonhole these sites into the realm of known past civilizations and time periods, but their explanations commonly stretch the bounds of credibility. Take the Great Pyramid of Giza for example…

The claims of Archeologists/Egyptologists regarding when and how the Great Pyramid was built are inconsistent (and are clearly impacted by bias, in my opinion). Most, however, generally agree that the structure was built during the 23-year reign of Pharoah Khufu (a.k.a. Cheops), which is generally accepted to have been from 2589 to 2566 B.C. [(1)]. According to the British Broadcasting Corporation (BBC), "…The entire project took about 23 years to complete, during which time 2,300,000 building blocks, weighing an average of 2.5 tons each, were moved." [(2)]

So, the Great Pyramid is comprised of more than two million individual stone blocks, with an average weight of 5,000 lbs. and a total estimated weight of 6.5 million tons (that's 13,000,000,000 lbs.). Some blocks at the center of the pyramid weigh up to 80 tons (160,000 lbs.!) and were placed at a height of hundreds of feet in altitude within the pyramid's center and in perfect alignment with adjoining interior features. *In order for this feat to have been accomplished in the cited 23-year span, the Egyptian builders would have had to put one block in place every five or six minutes, working around the clock!* Does this seem even remotely plausible?

Just transporting the stone blocks from the quarry to the construction site would have been a herculean task, especially given the fact that some granite blocks were quarried over 500 miles away from the construction site. Compounding the difficulty of this task, it is widely believed that the ancient Egyptians did not use the wheel during the pyramids construction, which means they couldn't have devised a pulley system to aid them in lifting these heavy stones, nor used carts to aid in their transportation over ground. (3)

Just doing the math raises some serious questions that mainstream archeologists consistently ignore. For example, if the Egyptian builders could put even ten blocks in place every day (still a significant feat, which would have gotten harder each day as the pyramid rose in height), it would have taken them more than 630 years to build the structure. Even if they'd had multiple crews working on each of the four sides of the structure and each was putting 10 stones in place every day, it still would have taken over 150 years to build, especially without the benefit of modern machinery or even something as basic as the wheel.

One website focusing on the incredible precision of the Great Pyramid's construction states, "According to archaeologist Rainer Stadelmann, …Khufu most likely ruled more than the 23 years given to him in the Turin Papyrus. Even with a reign of 30 to 32 years, the estimated combined mass (exceeded) 2,700,000 cu. meters (95,350,000 cu. ft) for his Pyramid, causeway, temples, satellite pyramid, three queens' pyramids, and officials' mastabas, which means that Khufu's architects and builders had to put in place a mind-boggling 230 cu. meters (8,122 cu. ft) of stone each day *a rate of one average-size block every two minutes* in a ten-hour day." (4) (emphasis added by author) That's one of the most impossibly rapid rates that I have yet to come across throughout my research into the subject.

In addition to the sheer number of stones, there are other considerations, such as the extreme level of precision in their placement, that make such a feat impossible within the stated timeframe. For example:

- The sides of the pyramid are remarkably straight and are aligned to the cardinal points of the compass to an accuracy of 1/15 of one degree.
- The Great Pyramid's base is level to within just 2.1 centimeters (under 1 in) and the average deviation of the sides from the cardinal directions is 3' 6" of arc.
- The greatest difference in the length of the sides is no more than 4.4 centimeters (1.7 in). (4)

- The 90-degree angles at the corners of the Great Pyramid are accurate to one part in ten-thousand. (5)
- The outer mantle of the Great Pyramid was once composed of 144,000 casing stones, and it is believed that all of them were highly polished and flat to an accuracy of 1/100th of an inch. (6)
- The Great Pyramid of Giza is the most accurately aligned ancient megalithic structure on the planet's surface, facing true north with only 3/60th of a degree of error. Its alignment is mind-boggling. Experts have determined that the Great Pyramid of Giza was located at the exact center of the earth's landmass upon its completion.
- This precision also carried over to the pyramid's interior, where each block had to be precisely fitted to accommodate the various and complex geometries of the internal hallways and chambers (Figure 1), with perfectly square interior angles.

All this means that the blocks comprising the structure couldn't have been just thrown together haphazardly. Each had to have been carefully and meticulously placed. Does it seem even remotely possible to you that the pyramid's construction, with all of its exacting specifications and logistical challenges, could have been completed in a 23-year period? Yet, Egyptologists/archeologists seem to have no trouble accepting and preaching it.

The artist's rendering of Figure 1, showing the various chambers and passages within the Great Pyramid, cannot possibly do them justice with respect to their incredible overall alignment and precise angles, especially given the size, weight, and positioning of the interior stones. I recommend that anyone interested further in these aspects spend some time researching them on their own to gain an adequate appreciation for these achievements.

For those seeking insight into the true purpose of the Great Pyramid, I would also highly recommend Christopher Dunn's thought-provoking books, "*The Giza Power Plant*" and "*Giza: The Tesla Connection.*" Mr. Dunn is a Master Craftsman, machinist, and engineer with extensive knowledge and personal experience in toolmaking in high-tech manufacturing industries and has personally studied the construction of the Great Pyramid using modern tools and equipment.

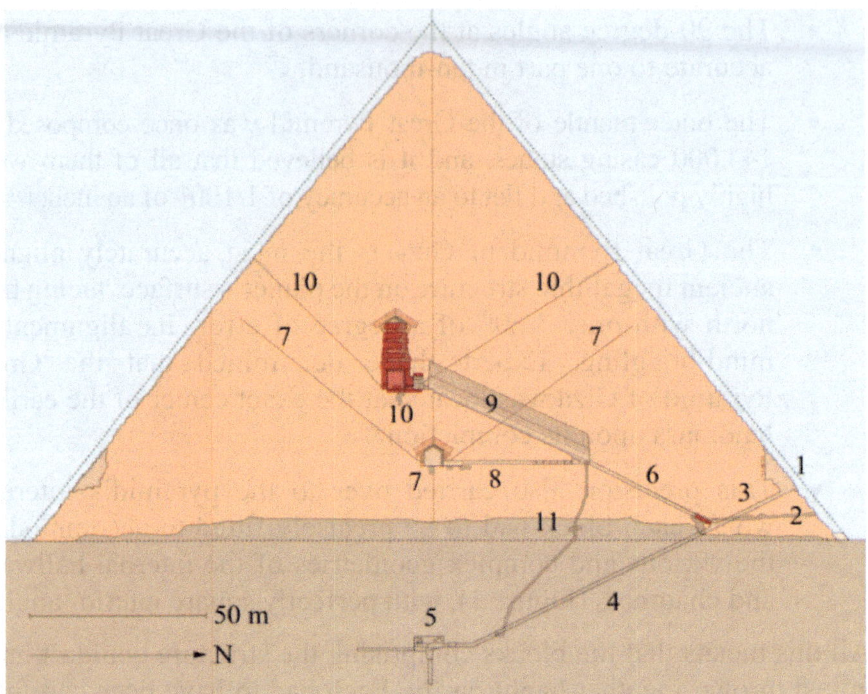

Figure 1: Depiction of the Interior Configuration within the Great Pyramid Schematic section of the Great Pyramid. Note that these are the known voids and chambers—more have since been identified by muon scanning, the nature of which is unknown. 1. Original entrance. 2. New entrance ("tourist" entrance, a forced tunnel by the ninth-century Caliph Al-Ma'mun). 3. Descending corridor. 4. Descending tunnel. 5. Lower chamber. 6. Ascending corridor. 7. Intermediate chamber (or "of the Queen") and relative ventilation ducts. 8. Horizontal corridor. 9. Great Gallery. 10. Upper chamber (or "of the King") and relative ventilation ducts. 11. Vertical tunnel. (Wikipedia; By Flanker, CC BY-SA 3.0, https://commons.wikimedia.org/w/index.php?curid=41041394) [(7)]

Ask the following question on line; "How is the Great Pyramid linked to Khufu?" You will get a variety of answers, the majority of which will skirt the question and simply tell you that the pyramid was built as a tomb for Khufu without actually answering the question of *how* or *why* the structure is linked to him. Those few sites that are brave enough to attempt an actual answer to the question reveal that it is based on a single piece of handwritten graffiti within the pyramid and the mention of Khufu's name in a papyrus fragment in association with an unnamed construction project at the location.

Another preposterous claim by archaeologists/Egyptologists is that the exceedingly high number of hieroglyphs, statues, and monuments across Egypt were carved into granite using such basic tools as copper chisels and stone hammers. Given the comparative hardness of the stone and relative softness of copper, this is quite difficult to believe.

The Mohs hardness scale, developed in 1812 by German mineralogist Friedrich Mohs, provides a straightforward method for determining a mineral's resistance to scratching or abrasion. The scale ranges from 1 (represented by soft talc) to 10 (represented by diamond, the hardest natural substance) and operates on the principle that a harder mineral will scratch a softer one, but not vice versa.

According to the Mohs hardness scale, granite, which was commonly used by the Egyptians when carving statues and stella, ranks between 6 and 7. Copper, on the other hand, has a hardness of 3.0, making is a poor choice for sculpting hard stone. While it *can* be done, it is a very poor choice as a stone carving tool, especially given the vast number of their carvings and the level of precision they consistently achieved.

In *The Giza Power Plant*, *Technologies of Ancient Egypt*, Master Craftsman Christopher Dunn, who has personally worked with copper tools on numerous occasions, states, "You can certainly work-harden copper…However, after a specific hardness has been reached, the copper will begin to split and break apart. …Even after being hardened…, the copper is not capable of cutting granite." [(8)] Yet, time and again, Egyptologists try to sell us on the idea that this was how it was done.

Figures 2.a through 2.c demonstrate the incredibly clean, sharp lines, smoothly curved contouring, and almost perfect alignment and symmetry that the ancient Egyptians were able to achieve. No chipping or cracking is evident where the carvings involve very fine detailing. This will likely not impress those who have never attempted such a feat but will certainly amaze anyone who has worked to sculpt stone. Additionally, repeated hieroglyphic images are nearly perfect carbon copies of each other. It is difficult to accept that this was all done with stone hammers and soft (by comparison with the hardness of the stone) copper chisels.

Figure 2.a: Example obelisk carving #1. Note the exquisitely clean, sharp lines and smooth contouring of the female figure, as well as the perfect symmetry of the orbs and feathers (red boxes). (Photo by M Abnodey on Unsplash)

Figure 2.b: Example obelisk carving #2. Note the fine detail within the swan's wing. One would expect to see chipped, unclean lines in some places if crude stone hammers and copper chisels had been used to create this exacting level of detail. (Photo by M Abnodey on Unsplash)

Figure 2.c: Example obelisk carving #3. Note the perfect alignment and symmetry of the four orbs and how the images on the left are near perfect copies of their counterparts on the right. Every image that is replicated is a near perfect replica, as though they were made with a cookie-cutter type mold. Note also the clean, sharp lines of every single carving. (Photo by Courtney Cook on Unsplash)

The pyramids of Giza are perhaps the most widely known example of ancient megalithic structures. Yet, there is evidence everywhere on this planet of other civilizations that have been lost to time, with many associated sites containing equally complex megalithic structures (Figure 4). Tens of thousands of these structures and sites have been identified around the globe, with many exhibiting a staggering degree of precision that would be difficult for modern man to replicate, even with the benefit of modern machinery. Many are also precisely aligned with cosmological features.

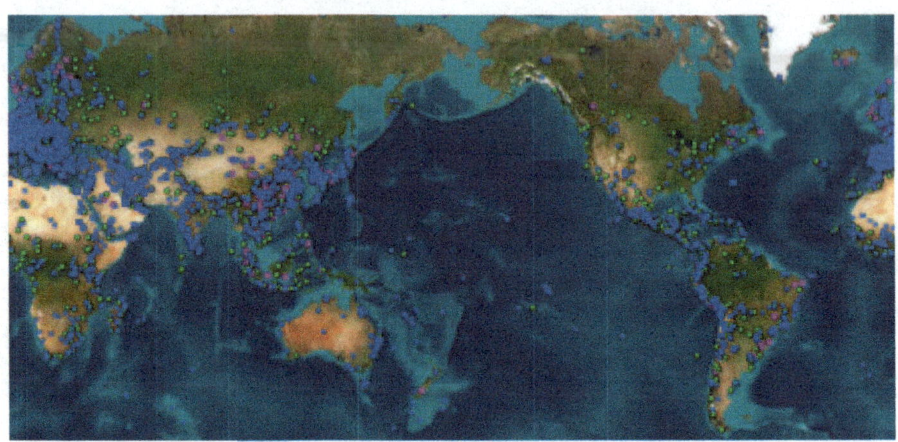

Figure 4: Map of UNESCO World Heritage Sites (as of 12/8/2025)

© (9)

Despite being separated by thousands of miles and by vast oceans, many of the structures are also remarkably similar in appearance, form, and function. How can this be when conventional wisdom tells us that sea faring people did not yet exist during the time that these structures were supposedly built? For all these civilizations to have elected to do things in such similar fashion without any interaction with each other would have been a pretty incredible coincidence.

It is interesting to note that pyramids are the most prevalent structure among these supposedly disjointed ancient cultures, existing in such diverse countries as Egypt, Sudan, Cambodia, Indonesia, France, Italy, Germany, Holland, England, Scotland, Ireland, Mexico, Guatamala, Belize, Honduras, Libya, Lebanon, Peru, Bolivia, Japan, Poland, South Korea, China, South Africa, United States, Nigeria, French Polynesia, Tenerife, Mali, Mauritius, and Pakistan. (10)

Egyptologists try to sell us on the idea that the pyramids were built as tombs for the great pharaohs, yet no mummified remains have ever been found within them. (11) In fact, pharaohs of the early dynasties were buried at Abydos and Memphis, while most prominent later pharaohs, from Thutmose I through Ramesses X or XI, have been found within the Valley of the Kings or at nearby Deir el-Bahri. According to History Cooperative, "The Valley of the Kings is the burial place for almost all pharaohs from the Eighteenth, Nineteenth, and Twentieth dynasties of ancient Egypt. The valley can be divided into the East and West Valleys, with the Eastern Valley hosting the most graves of deceased pharaohs.

Among the most famous pharaohs found there are Tutankhamun, Seti I, and Ramses I." (12)

So, if they weren't built to serve as tombs, as seems to be the case, what was their purpose? Nobody truly knows. However, in his book, *The Giza Power Plant*, Master Craftsman and engineer Christopher Dunn provides a convincing case for how the Great Pyramid of Giza was used as an electrical power generating plant. (13) While this may strike you as absurd, Mr. Dunn uses his training, experience, and field research efforts within the Great Pyramid to paint a seriously compelling case for how the various elements within the pyramid were used to capture the earth's natural energy and convert it, with the aid of chemical solutions such as hydrated zinc chloride and hydrochloric acid, to generate electrical power. I have read the book multiple times now and am convinced, based on the evidence that Mr. Dunn presents, that he is right.

I am not suggesting that all pyramids were used for generating electrical power. I think that this was unique to the Great Pyramid which, with its strange combination of interior chambers, passageways, and other unusual interior features, is unlike any other. I believe that they worked as Mr. Dunn suggests to generate power. The discovery in Iraq of Baghdad batteries, estimated to have been created over 2,000 years ago, is clear evidence that some Middle Eastern civilizations were aware of the existence of electricity and worked to harness it long before its more modern "invention." The lack of soot on the ceilings and wall within the pyramid further suggests that a form of lighting other than flaming torches was used to illuminate its interior.

While many of the aforementioned facts are specific to the ancient Egyptians, there are plenty of examples of advanced technologies from ancient civilizations across the globe. In many cases, the structures erected by these civilizations involve the carving of some of the earth's hardest stone, such as andesite, and the preparation, transportation, and placement of some of the largest stones in the world. Some of the finest examples of this can be found at Puma Punku, in Bolivia and Sacsayhuaman in neighboring Peru (see Appendix G). Examples of these huge stones include:

- At Tiahuanaco, Bolivia, 13,000 feet above sea level, stands the elaborately carved Gate of the Sun, which weighs an estimated 10 tons (9072 kg); an arch carved into a single block of andesite stone. (Appendix G, Figure G1)

- The Stone of the Pregnant Woman lies abandoned in a Baalbek, Lebanon quarry (Appendix G, Figures G2 and G3). It is one of the largest stones ever cut by human (?) hands, weighing an incredible 1,200 tons.
- Three of the largest stone blocks ever used in a man-made structure form part of the Temple of Jupiter at Baalbek, Lebanon. Its foundation contains three massive stones, each estimated to weigh 1,000 tons (that's over 2,200,000 lbs.!). There are few cranes in the world today that can handle such a load (Appendix G, Figure G4).
- The amazing terraces of Ollantaytambo, some containing stones of up to 150 tons (Appendix G, Figures G5 and G6). The quarries for these stones are situated on another mountaintop seven miles distant, meaning that the stones had to be lowered down one mountain, transported over a river canyon with 1000 ft sheer rock walls, then raised up the mountain to their current location.
- Some of the largest granite stones within the Great Pyramid of Giza are found in the King's Chamber, weighing in at up to 80 tons each. Not only have they been somehow raised to approximately 150 feet above ground level, but they were quarried in, and transported from Aswan, almost 600 miles (900 km) away.

Archaeologists insist that these ancient megalithic ruins were built by the Maya, Inca, Aztec, Tolmec, and other such peoples when the reality is that there is significant evidence that these peoples inhabited these ruins after they had already been built and had long since been abandoned. Many of the sites demonstrate an effort to repair damaged architecture, using methods that are clearly more primitive than the original, suggesting a lesser degree of engineering finesse (Appendix G, Figure G9).

In addition to the impressive aesthetic appearance of the sites and the size of the stones used in their construction, the joints of adjoining stones fit perfectly together, each block interlocking seamlessly with the next like the pieces of a puzzle. (Appendix G, Figures G7 – G11). Each massive stone (see Appendix G, Figures G2, G3, and G11 to get an idea of their scale) is unique and seems to have been intentionally molded to fit perfectly amongst its neighbors. Some corners feature stones that have been perfectly rounded (Appendix G, Figure G12). Other surfaces display carvings that are cut with incredible accuracy, having precise right angles, clean and consistent edges and cuts, perfectly aligned drill holes, and other detailing that would be difficult to achieve using modern technologies (Appendix G, Figures G13 – G15). It's almost as if they were done by laser. The surfaces of some stones have been polished to a glass-like finish; again, something that would be difficult to accomplish without the use of modern tooling.

Several of these ancient civilizations have left behind writings that attest to a staggering level of mathematical and scientific prowess. For example, the Mahabharata of India is a text that details time down to millionths of a second, provides detailed schematics for building a flying machine that uses mercury as a power source, and describes such things as time dilation and cloning. The Dogon tribe of Mali seem to have possessed knowledge of Sirius "B" as a dual star system several centuries before it was finally confirmed through modern methods in 1862.

Many of these ancient writings (such as the Epic of Gilgamesh in Mesopotamia, and writings by the Aztecs, Greeks, Hindus, Chinese, the Norwegians, and ancient Native Americans) also contain stories of a global flood, giant beings, flying machines, and the use of weapons of mass destruction. They describe "gods" and "demigods" in much the same way; as beings who arrived suddenly from the sea to impart knowledge; appearing as white, bearded men dressed in robes or as feathered serpents. Some ancient writings also describe the use of levitation in a way that suggests that this was how they were able to lift these gargantuan stones and/or transport them vast distances.

The television series "Ancient Aliens" has dedicated over 20 seasons (over 300 programs) to covering these megalithic sites, with the idea that it was extraterrestrial space creatures who were responsible for building them. It is a truly captivating show that highlights the amazing achievements of the unknown ancient builders, the extent to which this earth is covered by these structures, and the world-wide amnesia regarding their origin. If you can set aside any skepticism you may have regarding the "space aliens" aspect of their explanations (as I do…see my alternative explanation below), the show is really quite fascinating, offering eye-opening, in-depth examinations of hundreds of these megalithic sites and the mysteries surrounding them.

Archeologist Graham Hancock is one who boldly challenges the conventional wisdom regarding these sites in an earnest quest to uncover the truth. Mr. Hancock has authored such books as *Fingerprints of the Gods*, *Forbidden History*, and *Mysteries of the Ancient Past* (just to name a few of his monumental works) and has hosted the series *Ancient*

Apocalypse; all of which deeply probe into the physical construction and purpose of these enigmatic places. As one of the world's foremost authorities (if not THE foremost authority) on these mysterious structures, he asks the difficult questions about these sites and presents clear evidence that conventional wisdom fails to adequately explain them and is oftentimes obviously incorrect.[15] Mr. Hancock's examinations make it quite clear that many of these structures were built further back in time than modern archeology permits and by unknown civilizations that possessed advanced knowledge.

While the *Ancient Aliens* series offers fascinating insight into the structures and their implications, I do not agree with their conclusion that these amazing features were built by extraterrestrial beings.

…or, do I?

I suppose that, in a sense, they *are* correct. However, I submit that it was not space aliens from other worlds, but fallen, spiritual (i.e., non-terrestrial) beings, as described within the bible and other historical Jewish texts.

Fallen Angels, Giants, and Incredible Accomplishments

The bible occasionally touches upon the fact that there were angels who rebelled against God and descended to live on earth, taking and mating with human wives (Gen 6:2-4), which was against the natural order of things (Matt 22:30). Jude 6-10 (KJV) mentions the fallen angels, stating, "*And the angels which kept not their first estate, but left their own habitation, He hath reserved in everlasting chains under darkness unto the judgement of the great day*." This is supported by 2Peter 2:4, Luke 10:18, Matt 25:41, Isaiah 14:12-15, Ezek 28:13-16, and Rev 12:9. These "fallen" gave in to selfishness and intended to set themselves up as gods on earth, using their superior heavenly knowledge and skills to lord themselves over man. Since being banished from heaven for their sin and realizing their doom, they have since made it their mission to corrupt the rest of humanity (Eph 6:12, 1Peter 5:8, John 8:44 1Tim 4:1, 2Thess 2:9), sometimes subtly (2Cor 11:14, 1John 4:1). I believe that it is these fallen angels and their powerful giant offspring who are responsible for these structures, the "fallen" possessing the knowledge and their offspring possessing the physical strength.

---

[15] Mr. Hancock provides a wealth of information regarding these sites through his website The Official Graham Hancock Website - Graham Hancock Official Website.

According to the Book of Enoch, these "fallen" retained their superior, heavenly knowledge, allowing them to complete these mind-blowing achievements and appear as "gods" to typical earthly inhabitants at the time, to whom such knowledge and abilities would appear as divine and miraculous. This would explain why there is no evidence of "evolution" in the construction process. Whereas modern man has learned over hundreds of years, and through countless successes and failures, how to properly construct a house, the ancient builders of these megalithic sites seem to have known right from the start how to perfectly build these incredibly complex, massive structures.

There is evidence in several cultures that the people who are credited with building these sites, such as the Mayans, Incans, and Aztecs, did not actually build the original structures but worked to repair and inhabit them after the original inhabitants had suddenly and mysteriously disappeared. The repairs and additions to the original structures are obvious and are of inferior quality when compared to the original structures (Appendix G, Figure G9).

Some of these structures were built by these "fallen" with the intent on making a name for themselves. In Gen 11:4, this is one of the stated purposes for the Tower of Babel. Gen 11:4 reads, "*Come, let us build ourselves a city, with a tower that reaches to the heavens, so that we may make a name for ourselves, otherwise we will be scattered over the face of the earth…*" However, this directly contradicted God's instructions that man "…be fruitful and multiply and fill the earth…" Consequently, He saw to it that the completion of the tower was not among their achievements by complicating their speech and forcing them to scatter throughout the earth. He also "blotted out" any remembrance of them, as He has done with other foes (Exod 32:33, Deut 9:14, Deut 25:19, Deut 29:20, Deut 32:26, 2Kings 14:27, Ps 109:13). I suggest that this "blotting out" explains why we do not truly know today anything about these ancient builders. Only God could implement such world-wide amnesia regarding such significant elements of our past.

While there is not a lot of detail within the bible regarding the fallen angels themselves, we can ascertain, through these and other biblical passages (see Appendix H), that the result of their unholy unions with human women were what the bible calls the "nephilim," the "fallen" or "inferior" ones. They are described as being of large stature, possessing great strength, and are commonly referred to in the biblical text as "giants," such as the mighty Goliath who was slain by David (1Sam 17).

At least eleven giants, and possibly as many as fourteen, are identified within the biblical text, including

- King Og of Bashan, King of the Amorites, whose bed was made of iron and measured 9 cubits by 4 cubits (13.5 ft long by 6 ft wide)
- Goliath and his brother Lahmi of the city of Gath (Philistines)
- Saph (a Philistine from the city of Gob)
- Ishbibenob (a Philistine)
- Sippai (a Philistine)
- Anak, of the city of Hebron, and his sons Ahiman, Sheshai, Talmai. The Anakim dwelt in Gaza, Gath, and Ashdod.
- Arba, the father of Anak, also of Hebron; referred to as the forefather of Anak (Jos 15:13, Jos 21:11) and the greatest man among the Anakites (Jos 14:15)

A twelfth unnamed giant of the city of Gath is described as having six fingers on each hand and 6 toes on each foot (2Sam 21:20 and 1 Chron 20:6) and a thirteenth giant, an unnamed Egyptian (1 Chron 11:23), had a spear that, like that of Goliath's brother Lahmi, had a staff as large as a weaver's beam. These latter two giants may be the same as some of those already cited above or they may be in addition to them. Regardless, the existence of giants is clearly stated within the biblical text. In addition to the Anakim (i.e., offspring of Anak), the bible refers to the people of the Zuzim (also referred to as the Zamzummim), Emim, and possibly the Avims and Horims as giants. Most likely, Sihon, of the city of Heshbon, was also a giant due to his identification as a King of the Amorites, concurrent with King Og.

There are 4 verses in scripture that equate the size of a spear being used by a giant to a weaver's beam (1Sam 17:7, 2Sam 21:19, 1 Chron 11:23, and 1 Chron 20:5). Two of these refer to Goliath's spear, one refers to the spear of Goliath's brother's, who was most likely close to Goliath's size, and the fourth refers to a giant size Egyptian in that day who would measure over 7 foot 6 in tall. The weight of just the iron point of Goliath's spear in 1Sam 17:7 is stated to have been six hundred shekels, which is approximately 16 pounds. Overall, the spear is estimated to have been about 12' 7" in length, 2" in diameter, and weighed a staggering 33 lbs.! That's a pretty hefty weapon to be slinging around.

One website (14) describes the spear thusly, "For the physics of our Goliath's spear beam to work properly with a 16lb 11oz spear head and the height of Goliath, we choose a 10' length 2" diameter pole, including a 6lb 1.2oz counterweight, giving our spear a total length of 12' 7". This is not to say the spear could not have been even longer. The Bible doesn't give us the exact length. However, the length we calculated for our replica would allow Goliath to have a center of balance to hold the spear easily with one hand about 62" from the tip. This would allow him to thrust it directly at the enemy to achieve the best leverage and killing force. A spear of much longer length would cause the weight of the head to become overwhelming to wield and bend the shaft making it too flexible and cumbersome for effective hand to hand battle."

There is a fascinating, accompanying YouTube video (15) that shows a replica of the spear and its scale in the hands of a typical human being, providing an eye-opening perspective.

2Sam 21:15-22 mentions several giants and their attributes, stating, "…and Ishbibenob, which was of the sons of the giant, the weight of whose spear weighed 300 shekels of brass in weight…then Sibbechai the Hushathite slew Saph, which was of the sons of the giant…slew the brother of Goliath the Gittite, the staff of whose spear was like a weaver's beam...and there was yet a battle in Gath, where was a man of great stature, that had on every hand six fingers and on every foot six toes, four and twenty in number, and he also was born to the giant… These four were born to the giant in Gath, and fell by the hand of David." The fact that the features of their weapons are stated so specifically indicates that they were clearly far heavier and larger than the norm.

In Deuteronomy, there are multiple references to "a people great and tall, the children of the Anakims," with the Anakim referred to several times as giants. Num 13:33 states, "*And there we saw giants, the sons of Anak, which come of the giants; and we saw we were in our own sight as grasshoppers; and so were we in their sight…*"

Deut 3:11 describes the bed of King Og of Bashan, a "remnant of the giants", as being made of iron and having a length and width of nine cubits and four cubits (that's approx. 13.5 ft long by 6 ft wide), respectively. The size of the bed and its construction of iron clearly are meant to convey King Og's unusually large size.

The Physical Evidence for Giants

The bible is not the only source of information regarding giants on the earth. Many of the ancient texts, as well as much more recent oral traditions that have been passed down by native American Indians, also describe them, and in much the same way as the biblical texts. Dozens of books, such as "Unearthing the Cloud Eaters" and "When Giants were upon the Earth," to name just a few, document hundreds of instances where gigantic bones have been excavated and/or reported in North America since the early 1800's. (16) However, the evidence routinely evaporates once governmental organizations latch on. After all, "giants" do not fit into the timeline of conventional Darwinian evolution that they are working so hard to sell and their existence would lend support to the bible, which also causes them to cringe.

So, it would seem that giants did once actually exist on the face of this earth. While there is much detail within the bible (as well as through historical reporting) regarding these giant offspring of the fallen angels, the details regarding the fallen angels themselves are sparse by comparison. However, the Book of Enoch, the Book of the Giants, and the Book of Jasher each provide a significant amount of amplifying information regarding these foolish beings. These books focus on the existence of demons, giants, and fallen angels and explain why the flood was morally necessary to wipe them out.

While none of these three books are currently part of the bible itself, fragments of the first two have been found among the Dead Sea Scrolls, attesting to their importance to the Jews. Additionally, the Book of Jasher is referenced twice within the bible (Joshua 10:13 and 2Samuel 1:18) and the prophet Enoch (Enoch 1:9) is mentioned as a faithful prophet (most notably in Gen 5:22-24 and Heb 11:5) and directly quoted at least once within the biblical text (Jude 14-15) in direct connection to the fallen angels (Jude 6-13).

There are, in fact, at least a dozen additional books that are specifically mentioned within the bible but which are not a part of the formal biblical canon, including, the Book of Jasher (Joshua 10:13 and 2Sam 1:18), the Books of the Wars of the Lord (Num 21:14), the Book of Jehu (2Chron 20:34), the Books of Shemaiah and of Iddo the Seer (2Chron 12:15), just to name a few. Clearly, these works held significance to the Jews and should not be so quickly discounted just because they weren't ultimately incorporated into the modern bible.

The Dead Sea Scrolls and the Book of Enoch

The Dead Sea scrolls are a collection of ancient (i.e., from between the third century B.C. and the first century A.D.) Jewish manuscripts that were discovered within the Qumran caves along the northwestern bank of the Dead Sea in modern day Jordan. They comprise a collection of thousands of scrolls and fragments that are written primarily in Hebrew, Aramaic, and Greek. Among the scrolls are copies or fragments of every book of the Hebrew bible, except for the book of Esther, as well as other writings that were deemed by the Jews to be important. The biblical writings found within the Dead Sea Scrolls provide Old Testament manuscripts that are approximately 1,000 years older than any previously known manuscripts and testify to the fact that the Old Testament that we have today is essentially the same today as it was within the first century A.D., just decades after Jesus' departure.

One of the books found amongst the Dead Sea Scrolls is the Book of Enoch. Although it is not included within the biblical canon, its preservation alongside the biblical texts attests to its importance and significance in Jewish culture. There is also at least direct quote from the Book of Enoch within the biblical book of Jude, "*And to also Enoch, the seventh from Adam, prophesied, saying, 'Behold, the Lord came with ten thousands of his holy ones, to execute judgment upon all, and to convict all the ungodly of all their works of ungodliness which they have wrought, and of all the hard things which ungodly sinners have spoken against him*" (Jude 14-15). Enoch's prophesy is directly connected to "those who left their former estate" (i.e., the fallen angels, Jude 6-13).

Enoch was the great-grandfather of Noah and was apparently deemed by God as so righteous that he never tasted death. Instead, God "took" him. He was one of only two people described within the bible who never tasted death (Gen 5:21-24 and Hebrews 11:5-6), the second person being Elijah (2Kings 2:11). The Book of Jasher (Jasher 3:27-26) describes Enoch's departure from earth in greater detail than what is provided in Genesis 5.

The Book of Enoch describes how a band of 200 angels rebelled against God and fell to earth at Mount Hermon in Israel (Enoch 6 1-8, Enoch 8:1-3, Enoch 12:4, Enoch 16:3). The mountain is located at the northeastern boundary of Israel, on the border between Syria and Lebanon. These fallen angels took human wives and created offspring, which are identified in the bible as "nephilim" (Gen 6:4, Enoch 6 1-6, Enoch 7:1-3, Enoch 9:8-9, Enoch 12:4, Enoch 15:3-4). Twenty "leaders of ten," as well as the "heavenly knowledge" that they retained here on earth, are specifically named within the Book of Enoch. These include:

- Azazel taught men to make swords, knives, shields, and breastplates and taught them about the metals of the earth
- Semjaza taught the casting of spells and root cutting (cross-pollination).
- Armaros taught counter-spells
- Baraqijal taught astrology
- Kokabel taught portents (i.e., constellations and how to use them for fortune telling)
- Ezeqeel taught the knowledge of the clouds (weather)
- Araqiel taught the signs of the earth
- Shamsiel taught the signs of the sun
- Sariel taught the course of the moon

With their superior, heavenly knowledge, and in their desire to become supreme rulers, they corrupted not only mankind, but all of nature (Gen 6:11). The bible tells us that through them "all flesh,", including man, beast, creeping things, and the fowls of the air had corrupted God's way (Gen 6:7-12).

You may be wondering how "all flesh" could have corrupted God's ways. What would a bird, a cow, or an insect have done to corrupt things? According to the Book of Enoch, these "fallen" came to earth with the knowledge of cross breeding. Could it be that these fallen beings cross bred creatures, turning them into unnatural beings?

The Book of Jasher expands upon this, stating, "…the sons of men in those days took from the cattle of the earth, the beasts of the field and the fowls of the air and taught the mixture of animals of one species with the other…and God saw the whole earth that it was corrupt, for all flesh had corrupted its ways on earth, all men and all animals." (Jasher 4:18). [(17)] There is even one instance within the Book of Jasher where Zepho (a valiant Captain of the Host and son of Eliphaz, the son of Esau) kills a creature that is described as "half-man, half beast" (Jasher 61:15). [(18)]

God's decree to destroy the earth is the result of this world-wide corruption (Jasher 4:19-20). [(17)] The fallen angels and their giant nephilim offspring caused such wickedness that God repented that He had made man on the earth and decided to wipe out all living beings via a flood (Gen 6:4-17, Enoch 15:10).

Fact of Fantasy?

By now, you may be shaking your head in disbelief. It could certainly be understood if you were thinking that this belongs in the realm of fantasy. Yet, there can be no denying the physical evidence, in the form of the unexplained megalithic structures worldwide and the consistent stories within ancient writings from around the world regarding giants of great strength, a global flood, and fantastic half-breed creatures. If there were no seafaring people during this time period, as conventional teaching suggests, and these stories were associated with just a few ancient cultures, they might be readily dismissed as folklore. But they are too similar and widespread among disparate, supposedly unconnected cultures from across the globe to be consigned to myth. These cultures must somehow have been in contact with each other to allow these common ideas, stories, and practices to be spread across them.

For Christians, one must also accept the description of these beings within the bible and their attempts to corrupt mankind. These creatures must once have existed as they have been captured within the biblical text. Either the bible is the unerring Word of God in its entirety or it is not. One cannot pick and choose which biblical verses to accept and which to ignore.

The conventional explanations that are offered by the scientific community for these incredible megalithic structures and archeological sites provide conclusions that are commonly filled with discrepancies, such as the ridiculous 20-year time frame for building the Great Pyramid of Giza and the identification of its purpose (i.e., to serve as a tomb). Clearly, not everything within mankind's past is as we have been taught, or as we have been led to believe. But, if one considers man's history through the lens of the bible, other ancient texts, and historical records, a single, more complete, and unified picture begins to emerge.

The global amnesia when it comes to the vast array of megalithic structures throughout the world is unique and unprecedented. How can it be that the whole world remains in ignorance as to who truly built these magnificent structures, when they were construct, and for what purpose? Only an omnipotent God would have the ability to inflict such wide-spread amnesia.

Resistance Despite Overwhelming Evidence

In the preceding chapters, we have been presented with several distinct scientific methods through which an ancient earth is clearly demonstrated, including the physics of the Big Bang and other observable and measurable indicators (see "The Scientific Evidence for an Ancient Earth," pg. 73). However, those presented herein represent just the tip of the iceberg. There are many other methods available through which scientists can ascertain the age of the earth. Yet, there are those who continue to cast doubt on the ancient nature of the earth despite all indications. They go to great lengths to pooh-pooh scientific claims, twisting the evidence to get it to conform to their point of view or deriding and dismissing it altogether.

For example, in some videos that have been produced by one Christian organization, [(19)(20)] lecturers mock the various scientific hypotheses regarding the process of galaxy and star formation by dogmatically affirming that the various theories can never be proven because "nobody was around to see it happen."

The problem with this assertion is that we currently have well-established and testable laws of physics and innumerable direct observations of currently on-going and past cosmological processes to guide us. These snapshots allow us to accurately reconstruct completed processes and predict future results. We can observe for ourselves innumerable galaxies and stars in various stages of completion. When combined with our current knowledge of the physical laws (i.e., how energy and matter behave), these observations allow us to piece together entire processes and confirm and/or build upon our existing knowledge of the physical laws, enabling us to more clearly comprehend them (i.e., the laws and the processes).

The claim is also made within these videos, without any basis being provided, that the spiral arms of galaxies would no longer exist if these galaxies were, in fact, billions of years old. How do they make this assessment? They also identify anyone who believes in an old-earth scenario as an "evolutionist," which is an absurd leap in logic. One can believe in an old earth without having to accept Darwinian evolution.

Several biblical passages tell us that everything, including the laws of physics, were created by God at the very beginning (see Appendix I). These laws are, at present, sufficiently understood to permit us to learn things about His creation and provide us with many unambiguous clues that reflect His hand in it. Were it not for our correct understanding of these laws, as observed through the natural world, we wouldn't have many of the things that make our lives comfortable and convenient, such as cell phones, computers, GPS, and electrical energy, nor would we be able to perform such amazing feats as placing satellites into orbit or touching down on the surface of the moon, a distant planet, or an asteroid that is traveling through space at tens of thousands of miles per hour.

Christians would do well to more fully study the natural world, embracing its teachings. They should also restrict their challenges to science that is faulty rather than painting all science with the same broad brush of skepticism. Attempting to poke holes in viable scientific theories that have overwhelming supporting evidence, especially when possessing an inadequate understanding of the science, is unreasonable and causes people to turn away. Additionally, when presenting alternative conclusions, it should be done with complete honesty and respect, not with derision and disdain. Disagreement is perfectly acceptable, if it is done respectfully and with a desire to correct or instruct.

Letting the Evidence Speak

On the other side of the argument, scientists must be more open to allowing the scientific data to speak for itself, even if it provides evidence that runs contrary to their beliefs. They should be disciplined and objective, instead of trying to make the data fit within a box of their own making (i.e., one that typically has no room for a Creator). Instead, they too often allow personal anti-God biases to come into play, forcing them to provide implausible explanations or to twist conclusions to ensure that any potential for the existence of a God is eliminated from the conclusion. For example:

Scientists generally agree that the Big Bang marks not only the creation of time, space, and energy/matter, but that it is also responsible for the emergence of the laws of physics that govern their properties. They generally agree that the laws of physics as we know them originated in the earliest moments of the Big Bang (i.e., 10^{-43} seconds after its start) and that these laws did not exist prior to the emergence of the universe. Significant and widespread evidence supports this and it only makes sense. Would the laws of physics, the very laws that govern how matter and energy operate, have existed before the actual appearance of the matter/energy that they were meant to govern? What would have been the purpose of these laws prior to the emergence of matter/energy? Were they just hanging around waiting to be initiated? How would these laws have known what type of matter/energy was going to be created? They would have needed to know this in advance so that they could have equipped themselves to ultimately govern the universe as they now do.

Yet, incredibly, some would suggest that the laws did, in fact, precede the existence of the energy/matter that they currently govern. In one video produced by Discovery UK, the narrator speaks about how quantum mechanics allows for particles such as protons to appear at random, stick around for a while, then vanish again, only to reappear somewhere else. Due to this, the author extrapolates that, "...the universe itself...can simply have popped into existence (i.e., on its own) without violating the known laws of nature." [(21)] This is echoed by another such video, blatantly entitled "The Big Bang Didn't Need God to Start Universe." [(22)] (By the way, these articles, too, can't help but toss in a plug for Darwinian evolution as an established fact.)

The problem with such statements is that physicists also claim (and the evidence supports the fact) that the "laws of nature", that is the laws of physics, did not exist – indeed, could not have even existed – prior to the appearance of the universe.

A quote within another article states, "So it could be that this universe is merely the science fair project of a kid in *another universe* (emphasis added by author). These (physical laws) came into existence around one ten-thousandth of a second after the Big Bang. Before that point, there was really no material in any familiar sense of the word." [(23)] The article goes on to state, "... a plausible hypothesis is that the physical world was made up of a soup of short-lived elementary particles, including quarks, the building blocks of protons and neutrons. ...Quantum field theory tells us that even a vacuum, supposedly corresponding to empty spacetime, is full of physical activity in the form of energy fluctuations. These fluctuations can give rise to particles popping out, only to disappear shortly after."

The common problem with articles such as these is that they do not explain *what causes* these fluctuations and *from where* these particles originate. Indeed, they cannot! Every effect is preceded by a cause. Something must cause the event to happen, so the question of an origin is unavoidable. The laws of physics cannot explain the *origin* of matter and energy. They simply describe how matter and energy behave and interact once they *do* exist.

Statements such as those within the aforementioned articles demonstrate the extreme lengths to which some scientists are willing to contort the science so that it "fits" into a fully natural universe (i.e., one without God).

God & Science

Calling for a Truce

If one closely and objectively scrutinizes the evidence that is on display within both His Word and His World, it is easy to see how the two types of wisdom converge. With a more complete understanding, perceived discrepancies between the two forms of wisdom are eliminated as wisdom brings the facts into sharper focus, revealing the truth and merging them into a single, cohesive story.

In the preceding chapters, the ancient age of the universe has been addressed and a hypothesis has been proffered regarding the builders of, and purpose for, the ancient and mysterious megalithic structures that cover the face of our planet. Next, we'll take a closer look at the six creative days described within Gen 1:3-31 to see how well each of them is supported by the sciences.

CHAPTER FIVE

Preparing the Earth for Habitation

Both science and the bible tell us that the universe has been expanding continually since the first instant of the Big Bang creation event. Each also provides us with a specific sequence of events that turns out to be mutually supportive. Specifically; the bible gives us the following sequence of creation events:

- Creation of the cosmos, with the earth formed but uninhabitable, and the expansion of the universe[16]
- The separation of light and darkness into day and night
- Creation of the sky (i.e., the heavenly firmament)
- The separation on the earth of water from dry land and the emergence of plant life
- The clear, visible appearance of the sun, moon, and stars to serve as markers for day and night, signs, and seasons
- The creation of animal life within the seas and flying creatures
- The creation of animal life, insects (i.e., creeping things) and man on the land, with the latter given dominion to rule over His creation

Within the last century, this very same sequence of events has been verified by the sciences of cosmology, geology, paleontology, and archaeology. Specifically;

[16] Although cosmic expansion is not mentioned within Genesis 1, the process of God's stretching out the universe since its creation is clearly stated in numerous other books of scripture, including Isa 40:22, Isa 42:5, Isa 44:24, Isa 45:12, Isa 51:13, Jer 10:12, Jer 51:15, Ps 104:2, Zec 12:1.

- Cosmology affirms:
  - That there was a singular creation event, with everything arising from nothing, and that the universe has been expanding ever since
  - That shortly after the Big Bang (in terms of cosmological time), light separated from darkness during a period known as Recombination
  - That matter accreted (i.e., collected together), due to gravitational attraction, into stars and galaxies, including our own Milky Way galaxy, solar system, and planet
- Geology affirms:
  - That the earth was initially molten, with iron, as the heaviest of elements, settling into the earth's core and creating the magnetic field that protects the earth from the sun's harmful radiation
  - That the earth was initially covered entirely by seas
  - That land masses arose, due to plate tectonics, to form dry land
- Paleontology affirms:
  - That the first life appeared on planet earth, in the form of simple photosynthetic algae and single celled cyanobacteria, as soon as the earth had cooled enough from its initial molten state to support it
  - That a wide variety of sea life appeared suddenly on the scene billions of years after the first simple forms of life
  - That land animals and homo sapiens appeared equally suddenly millions of years after the eruption of sea life
- Archaeology affirms:
  - The appearance of the first homo sapiens millions of years after the first land animals
  - The sudden appearance of organized agriculture, written texts, and the clustering of people into cities in the Middle East less than 10,000 years ago – the timing of which corresponds quite well with the creation of Adam's soul, according to Genesis 1.

(The bible equates the appearance of Adam with language, organized farming/agriculture, animal husbandry, the use of metallurgy, and sacrificial worship.)

- The prolific existence of mysterious megalithic sites and ancient texts, many dating back more than 10,000 years.

Although not necessarily related to the creation events, archaeological digs have also come to reveal that many of the stories and places that are related in the bible – places and events that were once thought by many to be myth – actually did exist. A few examples include:

- The city of Troy
- The cities of Sodom and Gomorrah
- The existence of Goliath, the giant
- The battle of Jericho
- Inscriptions bearing the name of King David
- The "Pilate Stone" discovered in 1961 at Caesarea Maritima, a coastal Roman city in ancient Judea, with a Latin inscription clearly naming "Pontius Pilate, Prefect of Judea," matching perfectly with New Testament accounts
- The siege of Tyre and the precise manner of its destruction

In light of these biblical and scientific facts, the following synopsis provides a likely overview of the creation epoch:

PRIOR TO CREATION DAY ONE (Gen 1:1-2)

NOTE: Given the facts that there were acts of creation that occurred prior to Gen 1:3 and after Creation Day Seven, and that actual acts of creation during the six day "creation period" only occurred on days 5 and 6 (as evidenced through God's use of "bara" on those two days, rather than "asah' or "yatsar"), I feel that it is a misnomer to call each of the six days described within Genesis 1 "Creation Days." Most of the events of the Genesis 1 days were filled with God making (asah) or forming (yatsar) things via matter that He had previously created rather than actually creating (bara) new things. It would, in fact, be more accurate to describe the days of Genesis 1 as "Creative Days" rather than "Creation Days." However, I have chosen to refer to them herein as "Creation Days" One through Seven as that is how they are most widely referred to worldwide.

Biblical Perspective: The LORD instantly *created from absolutely nothing* (i.e., bara) all the energy/matter that was ever going to exist within our universe. Based on the grammar of Gen 1:1-2, this was completed prior to God's first formative command of Gen 1:3. This initial creation resulted in the matter and energy through which He would ultimately "make" (i.e., asah) or "form" (yatsar) the physical features of the universe. From the very moment of creation, God set in motion the expansion of the universe and established the physical laws (Isa 40:22, Isa 42:5, Isa 44:24, Isa 45:12, Isa 51:13, Jer 10:12, Jer 51:15, Ps 104:2, Zec 12:1).

At some point during His "making/forming" of things following the initial creation of matter/energy, the earth was formed, albeit in an uninhabitable state (i.e., formless and void), with the Spirit of God moving upon (or hovering over) the face of the waters and darkness covering the earth (Gen 1:2).

Scientific Perspective: All energy/matter, space, and even time itself *came into being from absolutely nothing*, and with no discernable natural cause, via an event that has come to be known as the Big Bang. This actually involved the occurrence of not one, but *two* singularities[17]; the emergence of the universe from nothing during the initial Big Bang itself, and a subsequent period shortly after the Big Bang, known as the Inflationary Epoch, which initiated the expansion of the universe.

[17] Singularity – a point in which all physical laws are indistinguishable from one another, where space and time are no longer interrelated realities, but merge indistinguishably and cease to have any independent meaning. (1) They are essentially events for which science has no explanation.

This period of expansion was extremely brief (from 10^{-36} seconds, or 0.000000000000000000000000000000000001 seconds, to 10^{-32} seconds, or 0.00000000000000000000000000000001 seconds) within the earliest moments of the Big Bang, during which the universe expanded faster than light. (2) In a trillionth of a trillionth of a trillionth of a second, the universe doubled in size at least 90 times, going from subatomic-sized to golf-ball-sized almost instantaneously. (3)

It is difficult for a typical human being to grasp the brevity of a trillionth of a trillionth of a trillionth of a second. We regularly watch Olympic runners finish within tens or hundredths of a second of each other and can only determine the winner with the aid of high-resolution, slow motion camera technology. The action otherwise happens too quickly for the human eye to accurately register. A trillionth of a trillionth of a trillionth is just way too brief a period of time to comprehend.

Similarly, it is difficult to fathom the leap in size from something smaller than an atom to the size of a golf ball. We can't really envision something so tiny as an atom. However, if we use the golf ball as an analogy, it would be like having the golf ball double in size by the same factor (i.e., doubling in size 90 times), growing it from 1.68" to 5,583,290,986.277 light years in size (if my math is correct[18]); filling a volume equal to 6% of the entire visible universe! To put it another way, it would be like a grain of salt (0.012 inches on average) growing to a diameter of over 39,000,000 light years during that same brief period!

Clarification: Both the bible and science describe the sudden appearance of the universe from absolutely nothing and tell us that the universe has been expanding ever since. The biblical Hebrew tells us that God first instantaneously created from nothing (bara) the raw materials (i.e., physical matter) then made (asah) or formed (yatsar) the larger elements of our universe from that initial matter. From the scientific standpoint, the initial creation from nothing is known as the Big Bang.

Approximately ten billion years after the Big Bang creation event, a vast cloud primarily of hydrogen and helium particles, but with trace

---

[18] 1.68 inches doubled 90 times = 2,079,739,265,999,438,800,000,000,000 inches, = 173,311,605,499,953,233,333,333,333.333 ft = 32,824,167,708,324,476,010,101.01 mi = 5,583,290,986.277 l/y. Calculation were performed using the following online large number calculator tools:

Calculate a Repeated Multiplication (https://rechneronline.de/sum/repeated-multiplication.php)

Scientific Notation Converter (https://www.calculatorsoup.com/calculators/math/scientific-notation-converter.php)

Big Number Calculator (https://www.calculator.net/big-number-calculator.html?cx=2079739265999438800000000000&cy=12&cp=3&co=divide)

amounts of heavier elements, collapsed inward in our little corner of the universe due to gravitational attraction. As each particle was drawn to those around it by gravity, the cloud started to spin and flatten into a disk like a pancake. In the center, the material clumped together to form a protostar that would eventually become our sun. However, the formation of the sun didn't consume all of the matter within the gigantic particle cloud from which it was born. The remaining material continued to orbit the star, ultimately forming the planets of our solar system.

Our sun is approximately 4.57 billion years old, with our earth being several hundred million years younger. As the largest object in our solar system, the sun would have formed more rapidly as its greater mass would have resulted in stronger gravity, drawing more of our solar system's base materials into it. The remaining planets in our system would have formed more slowly from any leftover material that was not drawn into the sun.

This same scenario had already played out innumerable times throughout the universe prior to the formation of our sun. This was important because early stars were initially comprised primarily of only hydrogen and helium. Many were also larger and burned through their fuel much more rapidly before erupting as supernovae. However, through their death throes, these dying stars created many of the heavier elements that would eventually be necessary for the emergence of life. As they died, they spewed tremendous amounts of these heavier elements out into the universe. These important elements were ultimately collected by our sun and earth as they formed billions of years later.

It is important that our universe is as old as it is, as it took billions of years for these processes to occur in quantities sufficient enough to seed our little section of the galaxy with the elements that would ultimately be needed to promote and sustain life. It is also important that our universe be of such great size to permit these vast stellar explosions to occur far enough away from our location. Too close, and the cloud of accreted matter would have been doused with lethal radiation and scattered to the point where it would have been too thin to accrete into the elements of our solar system.

Those among you who are chaffing over the fact that it took billions of years for all of this to happen should relax. There is nothing within the biblical text to indicate how long after the initial creation (bara) that God made (asah) the earth, nor how long He took to form it. Although He certainly could have done everything instantaneously, the biblical language tells us that this was not the case. He created (bara), then made (asah). In fact, He *completed* the initial creation *before* – perhaps long before – He began to make things on Creation Day One. It would have taken no more or less effort for Him to have created/made everything over a vast period of time, patiently using the physical laws that He created, than for Him to have done everything instantaneously. God is eternal, unbound by time (Ps 90:4, 2Peter 3:8).

CREATION DAY ONE (Gen 1:3-5)

Biblical Perspective: With the first "...*and God said*," God "turns on the lights," igniting our sun. God commands and separates light from darkness, creating the light that He called "day" (yom) on one side of the earth and the darkness that He called "night" on the other side of the earth, where the sun did not shine. What was in a state of disorder (evening/erev) was arranged into order (morning/boker) and called Day One (i.e., "*And there was evening, and there was morning; the First Day.*")

Scientific Perspective:

Once the temperature and pressure of the material within the protostar that would become our sun had sufficiently increased, hydrogen began to fuse into helium at the rate of 600,000,000 tons *each second*, providing the fusion energy that still powers our sun today.

Clarification: Job 38:9 states that the earth was initially covered in darkness. As His first act in preparing our earth, God ignites our sun, permitting it to provide the right type of light and energy and in just the right amount that would be needed to support all the forms of life that He would ultimately create.

Not all sunlight is beneficial to life. In *The Privileged Planet*, a book that describes in great detail how unique the earth is among the cosmos and how unlikely the existence of similar, earth-like planets is, the authors state, "Life can't just use any type of light from any type of star. Our sun, it turns out, is near optimum for (the existence of) any plausible kind of chemical life." [(4)] Our sun emits just the right type and amount of radiation energy to produce light that is in just the right region of the photosphere, and at just the right temperature, to support us. However, it took a significant amount of time for our sun to begin emitting light in the right spectrum and intensity.

A star must be stable, and at just the right mass, to provide the conditions that are suitable for life. Too small, and gravity will be insufficient to squeeze the core into igniting nuclear reactions. Too large, and the opposite will be true, resulting in a sun that burns through its fuel too rapidly and intensely, creating levels of radiation that are too hazardous to support life. According to the website Space.com, "A star the size of our sun requires about 50 million years to mature to a stable adulthood. Our sun will stay in this mature phase for approximately 10 billion years." [(5)] We know this to be true from the direct observation of stars in various stages of development and through a solid understanding of the laws of physics. Our sun is stable, so it is at least 50 million years old.

CREATION DAY TWO (Gen 1:6-8)

Biblical Perspective: With the second "*…and God said*," the "waters" were separated into a "firmament" that He calls Heaven (i.e., sky) to separate the waters below the firmament (i.e., the seas) from the waters above the firmament (i.e., the clouds and the cosmos). It "…came to pass…" (i.e., a period of time elapsed) and what was in a state of disorder (i.e., evening/*erev*) was arranged into order (i.e., morning/*boker*) and called a Second Day (not *the* Second Day).

Scientific Perspective: The earth's early atmosphere forms. Earth's original atmosphere was comprised primarily of hydrogen sulfide, methane, and a healthy dose of carbon dioxide, the latter of which had a concentration perhaps hundreds of times higher than today. Due to the type and quantity of the gases that were present, the early atmosphere would have been opaque, like a dark, super dense fog.

Clarification: When Earth formed 4.6 billion years ago from a hot mix of gases and solids, it had almost no atmosphere and its surface was molten. The early Earth and its thin atmosphere were both very hot. [(6)] As they cooled, the atmosphere became more dense, mainly from volcanic outgassing. After about half a billion years, Earth's surface cooled and solidified enough for water to collect on it. [(7)] In fact, the latest evidence suggests that the planet was once completely covered in water, although scientists can't fully explain where all of the earth's water came from. [(8)]

In its molten state, iron that existed among the other constituent components of the earth collected and "sank", due to its heavier atomic weight, to form the earth's core. This is important because the rotation of the earth's iron core is responsible for generating the magnetic field that surrounds our planet, protecting its surface from much of the sun's harmful ultraviolet rays.

The formation of this field and the resulting reduction of the harmful UV rays permitted the conditions that would allow subsequent plant life to flourish. As a result, our atmosphere is perfectly balanced, blocking most of the harmful UV energy from the sun while allowing the radiation that is beneficial to us to pass through. (9)

CREATION DAY THREE (Gen 1:9-13)

Biblical Perspective: With the third "...*and God said*," the waters separate from dry land upon the earth and the first plant life appears. The appearance of dry land and the emergence of the first plant life each separately "...came to pass..." (i.e., a period of time elapsed) and what was in a state of disorder (i.e., evening/*erev*) was arranged into order (i.e., morning/*boker*) and called a Third Day (not *the* Third Day).

Scientific Perspective: The earth has cooled, land masses begin to rise from beneath the water due to plate tectonics, and the first life forms appear almost immediately in the form of single celled cyanobacteria and photosynthetic algae. The fossil record unambiguously demonstrates that simple life appeared on the earth as soon as the planet had cooled enough for life to survive. (10) These very simple life forms lived on energy from the sun and carbon dioxide in the water, producing oxygen as a byproduct. The level of oxygen steadily increases due to photosynthetic reactions and the degeneration of water vapor. The latter is separated by ultraviolet light into hydrogen and oxygen, with the former escaping earth from the atmosphere, thus preventing the gasses from recombining.

As the oxygen in our atmosphere increased and the levels of carbon dioxide decreased, the atmosphere grew less and less opaque, allowing more and more sunlight to penetrate through to the earth's surface. (6)

Clarification: According to Dr Gerald Shroeder and others, this marks the *beginning* of plant life, which actually developed over an extended period of time and not solely on this day. (11) It is important to note that God did not directly create the dry land or the first plant life, but directed the earth to do so. This started the action of plate tectonics and the growth of plant life in the soil in such a way as to guarantee that both of these processes would continue as a natural course of things; processes that endure to the present day.

CREATION DAY FOUR (Gen 1:14-19)

Biblical Perspective: With the fourth "...*and God said*," the sun, moon, and stars became clearly visible, with the sun designed to rule the daytime and the moon to rule the night. With these heavenly bodies visible, they could now be used reliably for determining seasons, days, and years. This "...came to pass..." (i.e., a period of time elapsed) and what was in a state of disorder (i.e., evening/*erev*) was arranged into order (i.e., morning/*boker*) and called *a* Fourth Day (not *the* Fourth Day).

Scientific Perspective: As previously stated, Earth's original atmosphere lacked free oxygen. Cyanobacteria continued to create free oxygen, eventually producing enough to react with the methane in the atmosphere, transforming it forever. It is likely that hundreds of millions of years separated the first biological production of oxygen by unicellular organisms and its eventual accumulation in the atmosphere to the norm of our present day. (7) About two billion years ago, the methane haze cleared and the sky turned blue.

Between 700-550 million years ago, in the late Proterozoic, oxygen levels in the oceans and atmosphere increased dramatically due to several factors. (12) By 600 million years ago, the oxygen in the atmosphere reached about one-fifth of today's level.

Clarification: Through Gen 1:2 and Job 38:9, God affirms that the earth's atmosphere was initially wrapped in a cloak of thick darkness. Prior to Creation Day Four, some sunlight could penetrate the earth's cloudy atmosphere to facilitate photosynthesis, but the sun itself (nor the moon and stars) could not be clearly seen in the sky. Creation Day Four marks the time when the level of oxygen became sufficient enough to change the atmosphere from translucent to transparent, allowing the heavenly bodies above to become visible and useful as seasonal markers. Our modern atmosphere is comprised of 78% nitrogen and 21% oxygen, among other gases, which enables it to support life as we currently know it. (13)

CREATION DAY FIVE (Gen 1:20-23)

Biblical Perspective: With the fifth "*…and God said,*" God creates (bara) fully-formed living creatures and the waters swarm with life. He also creates (bara) the first flying creatures. What was in a state of disorder (i.e., evening/erev) was arranged into order (i.e., morning/*boker*) and called *a* Fifth Day (not *the* Fifth Day). These were immediate creations so they did not "come to pass."

Scientific Perspective: The fossil record unambiguously demonstrates that the first simple life forms (i.e., cyanobacteria and algae) appeared on the earth as soon as the planet had cooled enough for life to survive (about 3.8 billion years ago), and remained *the only forms of life* on earth until about 530 million years ago. Then, during a period that has come to be known as the Cambrian Explosion of Life, multicellular life forms suddenly burst onto the scene, fully formed and functional, captured as fossils within the Burgess Shale in Canada. (14) (15)

Since their initial finding within the Burgess Shale, the fossil evidence has been affirmed by findings from around the world. (15) There can be no doubt at this point that the fossils bare clear and undeniable evidence of a *sudden explosion of a wide variety of fully functional life* during the Cambrian period.

Clarification: God newly and instantaneously created (bara) these life forms, which is why (I suspect) the phrase "…and it came to pass…" does not appear here. The fact that He created them instantly is affirmed through the fossil record (i.e., the Cambrian explosion).

Note that every single source that is cited here (14) contains an affirming nod to Darwinian evolution, treating it as an established fact.

The first states, "…animals (suddenly) learned how to make hard, mineralized body parts." Even without diving into this statement more deeply, it begs the question, "How, exactly, did animals <u>*learn*</u> to do this?" The construction of hard, mineralized body parts would be dictated by the genetic coding of DNA. It seems quite a stretch to me that animals "learned" how to manipulate their genetic coding to develop mineralized body parts or to physically modify themselves in *any* way to better adapt to their environment.

The second source states, "(the "Cambrian Explosion") marked a dramatic burst of <u>evolutionary</u> changes in life on Earth. Among the animals that <u>evolved</u> during this period were the chordates — animals with a dorsal nerve cord; hard-bodied brachiopods, which resembled clams; and arthropods — ancestors of spiders, insects and crustaceans." (underscoring added by author)

The third source simply speaks to how "phyla *evolved* over time."

The problem with these statements, which are truly representative of nearly all such writings, is that the life forms of which they speak appeared *suddenly* within the fossil record, with no – I mean ZERO – indication that the previous *single-celled forms of life* were about to erupt overnight into multicellular creatures comprised of *billions or trillions of cells*. The sea creatures and winged life forms <u>*did not*</u> evolve over time from the single celled organisms that predated them. <u>*They burst onto the scene literally overnight!*</u>

The complete lack of transitional fossils is another problem for Darwinian evolution and is one aspect of the theory that is typically ignored by articles like these.

Dinosaurs?

As incredible as it may seem, the text of Gen 1:21 could very well be describing the creation of dinosaurs. This verse describes the creation (bara) of several general types of animals, one of which is listed within the King James version of the bible as "great whales" and as "great creatures" within the NIV version.

The Hebrew term for this type of creature is "tanninym gedolim." The second word (i.e., gedolim) means "great, big, large" in any sense of the word, physical or otherwise (i.e., he has a big personality). The first word occurs just this once within the bible, but it is the plural form of "tanniyn" (8577), the meaning of which we can ascertain from other biblical verses.

In Exod 4:3, when God instructs Moses to throw his staff to the ground, it turns into a snake (nachash; 5175). Later, in Exod 7:9, 10, and 12, when Moses and the Egyptian sorcerers each throw their staffs to the ground, each staff in turn becomes a "serpent" (tanniyn; 8577). Finally, in Exod 7:15, God instructs Moses to take the staff that had turned into a snake (nachash; 5175) and approach pharoah again.

The same staff is said to have turned into both a snake and a serpent. As only general animal types are referenced within Gen 1:21, where the plural term "tanninym" is used, the singular version of the term tanniyn must refer to the general category to which snakes belong, which is, of course, reptiles. Consequently, the term "tanninym gedolim" of Gen 1:21 could very well be translated as "great reptiles."

God Himself seems to be describing a dinosaur to Job in Job: 40:15-24; a creature whose tail sways like a cedar and which is ranked "first among the works of God."

We could speculate all day long as to why God would create dinosaurs. Perhaps it was to ultimately provide mankind with the fossil fuels that we would eventually consume daily and in copious amounts. Perhaps it was to provide doubters with the delusion that they needed to deny Him. Or, perhaps He just thought that it would be cool to create such creatures as a T-rex, triceratops, and stegosaurus! After all, they *are* pretty impressive creatures!

Regardless of the reason, the same text could be read and understood thousands of years ago, while ultimately revealing a deeper meaning to us today.

CREATION DAY SIX (Gen 1:24-31)

Biblical Perspective: With the sixth "*…and God said,*" God directs the earth to produce the first land animals. This "…came to pass…" (i.e., a period of time elapsed). God subsequently takes the man that He made and creates (bara) the man in the image of God. No "…it came to pass…" is associated with the creation of man in God's image because this would have been an instantaneous event. Man is first *made, then created.* It is extremely important to realize that man is the only creature that is made in God's image. What was in a state of disorder (i.e., evening/erev) was arranged into order (i.e., morning/boker).

Scientific Perspective: The paleontological record shows the first appearance of aquatic animals approximately 541 million years ago and land animals between 400 – 450 million years ago, with mammals gaining supremacy about 66 million years ago following a great extinction event that killed off the dinosaurs. Hominids arrived last on the scene, about 300,000 to 500,000 years ago (although some estimates are that homo sapiens first appeared millions of years ago). [(16)] [(17)] This is exactly the sequence of events that is described within Creations Days Five and Six in Genesis 1. While these events have been confirmed through science only during the last 200 years, the bible has been saying it for thousands of years.

Clarification: As He did with plant life during Creation Day Three, God directed the earth to bring forth living creatures, including man. It is my belief that this command has a two-fold meaning, one literal and one figurative. The first meaning involved the literal making of human and animal life from the dust of the earth. The second, figurative meaning was God's way of instructing the human and animal inhabitants of the earth to procreate and populate the earth from this time forth (i.e., from their initial creation). Since the time of His initial creation of humans and animals from the dust of the earth, all subsequent human and animal life has originated naturally from a set of male and female creatures.

Ask the question online, "When did homo sapiens first appear on earth?" and you will get a wide variety of answers. The range of "guesses" is all over the map. Between 200,000 and 300,000 years ago, [(18)] [(19)] [(20)] 550,000 to 750,000 years ago, [(21)] [(17)] and from 500,000 to 1,000,000 years ago, [(22)] with predecessors (i.e., non-homo sapiens such as neanderthals) existing on the earth as far back as 6,000,000 years. One thing that *is* clear though from the fossil record is that bipedal hominids have been around for at least tens of thousands of years. For those of you who feel that this doesn't jibe with biblical teachings, let me assure you that you have no reason to worry. If you continue reading you will realize that there is no disconnect here between biblical and scientific teachings.

The Making and Creating of Man

There is ample irrefutable evidence that both Cro-Magnon man and Neanderthals have existed on the earth for quite some time, pre-dating modern man by millennia. Either God placed their fossilized remains within the earth for some reason, which would be duplicitous and against His truthful nature, or they actually existed. Dr. Gerald Schroeder states, "The early fossil record is too complete and too well documented to pretend that it is all a fantasy of some misguided paleontologists. We are not talking of one or two fossils…Fossil finds from 6,000 to 40,000 years fill museums." [(23)]

However, while hominids have existed for quite some time, the archeological record chronicles a dramatic *qualitative* change in man about 6,000 to 10,000 years ago, as evidenced by the beginning of farming, the advent of pottery and metallurgy, and the first written texts. I believe that it was at this time that God transitioned pre-existing man into His own (i.e., God's) image.

"Pre-existing man?!" To many Christians, this would seem blasphemous. But, is it? Again, let's examine the evidence.

The bible teaches that plant life preceded aquatic life, which preceded land animals, which preceded mankind. We have already learned that God initially created (bara) the heavens and the earth, then made (asah) all subsequent physical things from the materials of His initial creation. The universe was first created (Gen 1:1), then made (Exod 20:11, Exod 31:17). However, when reviewing the biblical account of the creation of man, we find that this sequence was reversed.

In the case of man, God first instructs the earth to bring forth land animals and man (Gen 1:24). It is only after God *formed* man from the dust of the ground (i.e., it "came to pass," meaning that some time had elapsed) that God *creates* (bara) man in His own image. The sequence of the wording strongly suggests that man existed as hominids before (perhaps *long* before) God breathed into his nostrils the breath/spirit (Neshama) of life, making man a new, spiritual creation.

Gen 1:26-27 tell us that God made (asah) man *then* created him in His own image. Similarly, Gen 2:7 tells us that God formed man from the dust of the ground *then* breathed into his nostrils the breath (Neshama) of life, at which time man *became* a *living soul*. The sequence of events is consistent, with the vessel of man first formed from the dust of the earth, *then* transformed into the image of God when God provided man with the breath of life (i.e., the Neshama) after forming him. The bible is mute on how much time elapsed between the "making" and the "creating" here, so it is entirely possible that man existed as non-spiritual hominids long before God infused Adam with spirituality and intellect. If we combine the biblical and scientific facts, the following facts emerge:

- Hominids have existed on the earth for at least 100,000 years, based on the fossil record.
- According to the biblical text, man was physically *made prior to* God *creating* man in His own image, with no time frame specified between the two events. In fact, *some time must has elapsed* between the two events based on the use of "*...it came to pass...*" between the "making" and the "creating" of man (Gen 1:24-27).
- Archeology affirms a qualitative change in man around 6,500 years ago, with the advent of farming, use of pottery and metallurgy, people gathering into cities, and the first written texts. This coincides quite nicely with the timing of God breathing the spirit of life and intellect (Neshama) into man, if one were to use biblical lineages as a basis for the timeline.

According to Gen 1:24-27, God first made land animals, then He created man. Both were made (asah) from the dust of the earth (Gen 2;7 and 2:19) and given a "nephesh"; a spirit of vitality or life. Subsequently, God infuses man with a second spirit; His breath/spirit (i.e., the Neshama), which is a unique connection between God and man. This is not something that was provided to animal life. Dr. Schroeder makes a number of significant points regarding the difference between the forming and creating of man and animals. I quote him extensively here because I feel that his description is far superior to anything that I might write on the subject. His insights include:

- There are two Hebrew words for "soul", one being the nefesh (Strong's 5315) and the other being the Neshama (Strong's 5397). All animals, including humans, have a nefesh, which is the soul of animal life – the will to survive. Only human beings have been infused by God with the Neshama (i.e., spirituality and intellect). (24)

- "The Hebrew word for formed, *ya-tsar*, when used for the forming of mankind is spelled with two Hebrew letters *yud*. ...when used for the formation of animals, ya-tsar is spelled with one letter *yud*. Every Torah scroll...is written in this way.

  Yud is the abbreviation of God's explicit name, best translated as the Eternal. ...by doubling the *yud* for mankind, the bible is telling us that, although mankind and animals may share a common physical origin, there is an extra spiritual input into humanity. The Neshama, the intellect and spiritual soul of mankind, is a crucial factor that distinguishes man from beast." (24)

- Dr. Schroeder further states, "The closing of Gen 2:7 has a subtlety lost in the English. It is usually translated as, "...and (God) breathed into his (i.e., man's) nostrils the breath (Neshama) of life and the adam (i.e., man) became a living soul." The Hebrew text actually states, "...and the adam became <u>*to*</u> a living soul." Nahmanides, seven hundred years ago, wrote that the "to" (the Hebrew letter lamed prefixed to the word "soul" in the verse) is superfluous from a grammatical stance and so must be there to teach something.

  Lamed, he noted, indicates a change in form. Upon receiving the Neshama, the soulless bipedal creature that already existed became a human (being). He (i.e., Nahmanides) concludes his commentary on the implications of this *lamed* as, "...or it may be that the verse is stating that (prior to receiving the Neshama) it was a completely living being and (by the Neshama) it was transformed into *another* (i.e., spiritual) man." (24)

Based on these facts, it seems that man was among the "animals" that were created in Gen 1:24 before one representative of man (i.e., Adam) was chosen and subsequently transitioned to a spiritual being through the infusion of the Neshama. There is nothing within the biblical text that says that these two events happened in rapid succession, so Adam may well have existed as a non-spiritual hominid for years before being infused with God's spirit. This could be likened to the situation in Genesis 1 with the creation of the universe and the earth in Gen 1:1-2 at some time before the subsequent preparation of the earth that follows in Gen 1:3.

The creation of man in God's image is hugely important as it distinguishes man from all of the other living creatures that God created. Dr. Hugh Ross states, "…the quality that makes people unique…is…the "spirit" (Neshama) that has been breathed into them by God. None of the rest of earth's creatures…possess it. The "Neshama" spirit supplies (an) awareness of God, awareness of self, intellect, and the capacity to form a relationship with the Creator." (25) This is something given to mankind that creatures of the animal world lack.

One dies a physical death when the "nefesh" spirit ceases. Consequently, animals can suffer only a physical death. Man, however, can also die spiritually.

Physical Versus Spiritual Death

Many believe that when Romans 5:12 says "*sin entered the world through one man, and death through sin*," it is saying that death did not exist prior to Adam's transgression. Yet when God told Adam that he would die by eating from the Tree of Knowledge, Adam clearly comprehended what God was saying. How could this be so, if he had never seen death of any sort before?

Adam and Eve were not created as immortal beings. Only by eating of the Tree of Life could they have *obtained* eternal life (Gen 3:22), something that God ensured *did not happen* by placing Cherubim to guard the Tree of Life after driving Adam and Eve from the Garden (Gen 3:24).[19]

The mere presence of the Tree of Life within the Garden of Eden indicates that physical death was, from the outset, an expected part of life. There would have been no need for this tree to have been in the Garden if man were already immortal. Moreover, if man needed to eat from the Tree of Life in order to obtain eternal life, it goes without saying that the same would have been true for animal and insect life. After all, it is only "man", amongst all of God's creatures, that is made in His image.

---

[19] It is interesting to me that Adam could easily have eaten of the Tree of Life at any time prior to his fall, but elected not to do so. After all, it was only the Tree of Knowledge of Good and Evil that was forbidden. Perhaps the reason for this is that Satan focused his attention on getting man to eat from the one tree that was expressly forbidden by God, knowing that this sin would separate man from God.

No man ever ate from the Tree of Life. And, if man is higher in the hierarchy than animals, and since there are at present no animals in the world that possess eternal life, it stands to reason that no animal ever did either. So, it would seem that physical death was a planned part of the circle of life from the very beginning. Jesus Himself alludes to this in John 12:24 when He said, "Unless a kernel of wheat falls to the ground *and dies*, it remains only a single seed. But if it dies, it produces many seeds." It seems that this would have been a familiar concept to Adam, as keeper of the Garden.

Physical death must have existed prior to man's fall in order for Adam to fully comprehend the meaning of "death" as a consequence of his disobedience, should he choose to ignore God's warning. Otherwise, the threat of death would not have meant anything to Adam. How could it, if he had never before observed it?

Gen 3:7 instructs us that Adam and Eve suddenly gained understanding, such as awareness of the impropriety and immodesty of their nakedness, as soon as they had transgressed God's command. Yet, God's admonition to Adam came *before* they ate of the Tree of Knowledge of Good and Evil, so Adam would have had to gain any knowledge of death *prior to* his sinful act. He clearly understood the meaning of death before his eyes were "opened" by his act of disobedience. He must, therefore, have been exposed to the finality of, and perhaps to the suffering often associated with death prior to having received the gift of God's Neshama.

According to Gen 2:7-15, God created Adam *before* He planted the Garden of Eden, then subsequently placed this newly created man within the Garden once it had been planted. Adam was initially created *outside* of the Garden, then later placed (i.e., put) into the Garden by God. The Hebrew word used for "put" in Gen 2:15 is "yanach" (Strong's 3240), which means "to deposit." Hence, Adam was physically deposited or relocated from outside of the Garden into its interior.

The bible also tells us that man was *first* formed from the dust of the ground *then* created as a spiritual being when God subsequently "*...breathed into his nostrils the breath of life*" (Gen 2:7). However, the bible does not say that both of these events (i.e., the making, then creating of man) occurred close together chronologically. In fact, there is good reason to believe that the two events were separated in time by a long gap (see "The Making and Creating of Man", pg. 113). This would explain why Adam first existed outside of the Garden of Eden. It was only when he became a *created, spiritual* soul – through the infusing of the Neshama that God breathed into him – that God placed him into the Garden to dress and keep it. It seems that man was not worthy of the honor until he became a spiritual creation. Perhaps this is because man was no different from animals prior to receiving the Neshama.

The Garden had some special, supernatural features and was clearly different from the rest of the world as we know it. It was the only place where the Tree of Knowledge of Good and Evil and the Tree of Life existed. As Adam had once already existed for a period of time outside of the Garden, he would have had the opportunity to observe nature without the Garden's supernatural elements. It seems probable that he had the opportunity to observe death in the natural world before being "relocated." Consequently, he would have understood the consequences when God warned him that he would die.

When God warns Adam against eating from the Tree of the Knowledge of Good and Evil, the consequences of disobedience were that Adam would "surely die" on that very day. To emphasize that He meant business, God didn't just say that Adam would *die*, but that, "*…on the day that thou eatest thereof, thou shalt surely die*" (Gen 2:16-17) So, what did happen after Adam and Eve partook of the forbidden fruit? They became aware of and felt shame at their nakedness, the earth was cursed, and they were expelled from the Garden. Yet, despite being warned that he would surely die on the day that he ate of the forbidden tree, Adam lives *several hundred more years*. How could this be in light of God's warning?

In Rom 5:12, we are informed of the following, "*Therefore, just as sin entered the world through one man, and death through sin, and in this way, death came to all people, because all sinned…*" Note here that the bible specifically tells us that death came "to all people," not to all living things. It also states that the cause of this death was because "all sinned." Animals are incapable of sinning as they lack the moral reasoning that has been instilled in man through the infusion of a spiritual soul (i.e., the Neshama). Consequently, animals would not have incurred death as a penalty. Yet, animals did, and still do, physically die.

Given that this statement (i.e., Rom 5:12) is directed at mankind as a result of man's disobedience, and the fact that Adam did not physically die on *the day* that he ate the forbidden fruit (which a literal translation of Gen 2:17 would demand), it seems that we are to take this as spiritual vice physical death. We cannot directly tell from the biblical text if Adam was aware of the distinction between physical or spiritual death, but he clearly knew that death was undesirable.

There is actually no biblical text that directly says or implies that physical death did not exist prior to man's fall. However, the bible *does* indicate that pain and suffering *were* a part of life before man's fall. In Gen 3:16, as God is banishing the first couple from the Garden of Eden, He tells Eve that He will "greatly *increase*" her sorrow during childbirth. He does not say that He will *introduce* pain, but that He will *increase* it, indicating that pain was already an expected part of the process. Additionally, manual labor was also an expected part of life, as God puts Adam in the Garden of Eden to "dress it and keep it" (Gen 2:15). If pain, and toil existed prior to the fall of man, then it is not unreasonable to assume that the same was true of physical death.

Finally, there is also abundant physical evidence within the fossil record that millions of animals died before man even arrived on the scene. In some instances, entire species went extinct before man's arrival. So, it seems clear that physical death was part of God's plan from the beginning.

In light of all of this evidence, it is clear that the "death" that is meant in Gen 2:16-17 and Romans 5:12 is referring to man's spiritual rather than physical death.

CREATION DAY SEVEN

Biblical Perspective: The bible informs us that God "rested" on this day, ending His work of creating and making (Gen 2:1-3). From this point, we are provided with additional details regarding the state of the earth, the development of Adam and Eve, and God's direction to Adam to be fruitful and multiply, filling the earth.

Scientific Perspective: The paleontological record demonstrates that no new animal phyla (i.e., classes of animals) have appeared on the scene following the explosion of sea life during the Cambrian period and land animals during the Devonian period. In both cases, animals appeared fully formed and functional with no transitional fossils in evidence, as Darwinian evolution would suggest.

Clarification: The phrase "*...and there was evening, and there was morning...*" is not mentioned for Creation Day Seven.[20] This makes perfect sense if we accept the idea, as proposed by Nahmanides (see Bringing Order to a Disorderly World, pg. 22), that the "evening" and "morning" references within Genesis 1 are meant to indicate God's efforts to turn disorder into order, as He did during creations days one through six. God did no creating or making on Creation Day Seven, which means that He did not create further order (boker) out of disorder (erev).

The paleontological record tells us that no new animal phyla have emerged in the millions of years since the initial explosions of aquatic and land animals. The emergence of new forms of life has ceased. This jibes quite well with the bible's claim that God rested from His creative acts on Creation Day Seven, forming no further new creatures.

There is, however, one final instance that occurs either on, or following Creation Day Seven, where God is said to "make" something. At first glance, this would seem to contradict the claim that God ended His creative work (Gen 2:1-2) and requires an explanation. I am speaking here about the creation of Eve.

The "Building" or "Bearing" of Eve

In Gen 2:1-3, we are told that God "ended His work" and "rested" on Creation Day Seven. Gen 2:3 specifically says, "*And God blessed the seventh day and sanctified it; because that **in it** He rested from **all** his work which He created and made.*" It seems pretty clear from this that God was done creating by Creation Day Seven. The bible clearly teaches that God rested *for the duration* of Creation Day Seven (i.e., ...because that *in it,* He rested...). It specifically states that God "ended His (creative) work" and "rested" on Day 7 (Gen 2:1-3)[21]. Yet, in Gen 2:22, we are told that God made a woman with flesh that was taken from Adam, seemingly on the very same day. How can it be that God "ended all of His creative work" on Creation Day Seven, yet also made a woman from

[20] Again, this is a sticky point for Young Earthers. If they insist that the phrase, "...and there was evening, and there was morning, the nth day..." marks a 24-hour day, then why is this phrase missing from Creation Day Seven? The fact that this phrase is missing here, plus the fact that the bible teaches that, even now, we may enter into God's rest today (Heb 4:1-9) leads some to believe that we are still in (Creation) Day Seven; the period of God's rest.

[21] Although His creating days may be done for the time being, the bible clearly states that God continues to actively sustain His creation (Neh 9:6, 2Peter 3:5 and Col 1:17). We are told in Nehemiah that God "preserves" the heavens, the earth, the seas, and all that is within them, using the term "chayah; (Strongs 2421), which means to revive or keep alive. In 2Peter and Colossians, the word "sunistao" is used to describe the same thing.

Adam? Isn't this an act of making or creating? I believe the explanation lies in the unique manner in which Eve is brought into being.

Gen 2:21-22 states, "*And the LORD God caused a deep sleep to fall upon Adam, and he slept. And He took one of his ribs and closed up the flesh instead thereof. And the rib, which the LORD God had taken from man, made He a woman and brought her unto the man.*"

Here, the term used in Gen 2:22 for "made" is unique and is used in no other instance when it comes to the creation of human life. In all other instances, God created (bara), made (asah), or formed (yatsar) living creatures. But, when it comes to making Eve, the word used is "banah" (Strong's 1129), which means "to build" or "to obtain or bear children."

The term "banah" appears 375 times throughout the bible, most often to describe the building of physical things, such as altars, houses, fortifications, and cities, although it is also occasionally used to illustrate the building of a family. The creation of Eve is the sole instance of the term being used for the formation of an individual human being. Unlike all other created, living creatures, the "first woman" was not formed directly from the dust of the earth, but was extracted and constructed from Adam's existing flesh.

Gen 2:22 is the only place within the bible where "banah" is used in this manner. Unfortunately, there is insufficient detail within the biblical text to inform us more specifically as to how God did this. *Still, the making of Eve was clearly done in a manner that was unique among all living creatures.* God must also have "breathed His Spirit" (i.e., the Neshama) into her, as He did with Adam, to make her in His image in accordance with Gen 1:27. This seems like a creative act to me, which seems to contradict Gen 2:1-3 (where we are informed very clearly that God ceased all of His creative work on Creation Day Seven). How do we reconcile this?

Perhaps the answer lies in the fact that Adam and Eve, although two separate entities, were also "one." Gen 2:23-24 reads, "*And Adam said, This (at last) is now bone of my bones and flesh of my flesh; she shall be called Woman* (ishshah) *because she was taken out of Man* (ish). *Therefore shall a man leave his father and mother and shall cleave to his wife, and they shall be one flesh.*" By taking a piece of Adam's flesh, God was making Eve an equal partner with Adam. As further testament to this, Gen 1:27 states, "God created man in His own image; in the image of God, He created him; *male and female He created them.*" Maimonides comments on this, stating, "The unity of the two is proven by the fact that both (i.e., man and woman) share the same name, for she is called "ishshah" (woman), because she was taken out of "ish" (man). (26) Perhaps this is meant to inform us that Eve, being extracted from Adam, was not a totally new physical creation, but was in essence a modified version of the already-created man.

It is also very likely that other things have since been newly created by God following the burst of creation that is described in Genesis 1. Indeed, based on the biblical text, it seems that when God rested from "all His work of creating and making," as detailed within Gen 2:1-3, the bible is referring to "all His work of creating and making" *so far* (i.e., up to that point, as it pertains to the creation of the universe). There are over two dozen passages within the bible that indicate that God did, indeed, create other new things much later in the biblical narrative. For example:

- When God is speaking to the stubborn nation of Israel in Isa 48:6-7, He says, "*...from now on I will tell you of new things, of hidden things unknown to you. They are created now, and not long ago; you have not heard of them before today.*" This verse states unambiguously that it is referring to newly created things and not to things that have already been created in the past.
- In speaking of all of God's creatures (including man), Ps 104:29-30 states, "*...when You take away your breath, (Your created beings) die and return to the dust. When You send Your Spirit, they are created.*" The verse says that creatures <u>are</u> created – not <u>were</u> created – and seems to be speaking of the perennial process of life and death, with new souls continually being created and placed on this earth.
- In Isa 45:5-8, God says, "*I form the light and create darkness, I make peace and create evil. I, the LORD, do all of these things.*" As in the verse above, the creation of evil is being stated as a continuing rather than as a completed process. Incidentally, the word for "evil" here is "ra" (Strong's 7451) and generally means "adversity", "affliction", or "calamity". It does not carry the meaning of "morally corrupt," which is typically associated with Satan or evil spirits.
- Other verses that speak to God's creation of new things after the original creation events of Genesis 1 include Num 16:30, Ps 102:16-18, Isa 4:5, Isa 43:1, Isa 54:16, Isa 65:17-18, Jer 31:22, 2Cor 5:17, Eph 2:10, Eph 2:15, Eph 4:24, and Gal 6:15.

The creation of Eve must have occurred on a day that followed Creation Day Seven, rather than on Creation Day Seven itself. Otherwise, Gen 2:22 would contradict Gen 2:1-3, which clearly states that God rested "*from all His work of creating and making*" on Creation Day Seven. The use of the phrase "happa'am" (Strongs 1945 and 6471) by Adam within Gen 2:23, upon seeing Eve for the first time, is further evidence of this as it indicates that some time had passed since Adam's creation. In Gen 2:23, Adam states, "*This is now* (happa'am, meaning "finally" or "at last") *bone of my bones and flesh of my flesh...*" As previously discussed, this phrase carries the connotation of "at last" or "finally", which strongly suggest that a lengthy period of time had elapsed between the creation of Adam and the creation of his mate. [(27)] [(28)]

If this is correct, then the making of Eve would mark a second creative period that God accomplishes *outside of* the 7-day week of creation (the first occurring in Gen 1:1-2), lending further credence to the notion that not all of God's creative acts were contained within the 7-day creation period of Gen 1:3-31. I propose that the days continued to roll by unabated but were no longer being "counted" within the bible as the individual days themselves were no longer relevant to the narrative. It was no longer necessary to count them because the creation epoch was over.

Whatever the case may be, it is clear that the creation of Eve was a truly special event that was completed in a very unique way among all of God's creatures.

Is There More?

So far, we have seen that there is ample biblical evidence for an ancient earth and that the scientific observations are in perfect accord with the creation events of Genesis 1. Table 1 provides a high-level, side-by-side comparison of the Genesis 1 creation events and what we have learned through prolonged and concerted study of the natural world. When viewed together, the sequence of events is amazingly consistent and far too compelling to be consigned to coincidence. Yet, the bible described these events thousands of years before they were ultimately confirmed through the sciences. It is science that has come to agree with the biblical narrative, not the other way around.

It has also been demonstrated that both man and woman were created very differently from other forms of life, with God gifting His spirit (Neshama – Strong's 5397) solely to mankind and giving man dominion over the beasts of the earth (Gen 1:26-28). These facts attest to the special status that God has gifted to mankind. The bible makes this quite clear.

You may be surprised to learn that nature also makes man's special status quite clear. God's other instruction manual – nature – also offers a wealth of evidence that speaks to God's hand in preparing not only the earth, but the entire universe for our arrival. This evidence will be the subject of the next chapter.

Table 1: Comparison of Biblical and Scientific Sequences of Creation Events		
Scripture	**Biblical Description**	**Scientific Description**
Gen 1:1-2, Job 38:9	Prior to Creation Day 1 Creation of the entire physical universe (matter, energy, space, and time) from nothing and the beginning of cosmic expansion. The earth has been created, but is uninhabitable; covered by water and cloaked in darkness. The bible details a one-time event where the "Spirit of God moved upon the face of the waters". **(see NOTES 1 and 2 below)**	Cosmology affirms the following: • that there was a singular creation event, with space, time, and matter/energy emerging simultaneously from nothing and a period of rapid cosmic inflation that ultimately settled into the current rate of expansion. • that light separated from darkness as CBR shortly (in terms of cosmological time) after the Big Bang, during a period known as Recombination. • that matter, which formerly existed as a hot plasma, cooled and accreted (i.e., collected together due to gravitational attraction) into stars and galaxies, including our own Milky Way galaxy and solar system. Geology confirms that the earth was once completely covered by water, which the bible has been saying for millennia. [8]
Gen 1:3-5	Creation Day 1 God turns on the sun, separating light (which He called "day") from darkness (which He called "night") **(see NOTE 3)**	The sun ignites, creating the day/night cycle on the earth. Without the sun's light, the earth was previously covered in darkness (as stated in Gen 1:2).
Gen 1: 6-8	Creation Day 2 Division of the "waters" into seas, cloud-filled skies, and the outer atmosphere **(see NOTE 4)**	Earth's atmosphere begins to develop; a process that continues over a lengthy period of time.

Table 1 (cont.): Comparison of Biblical and Scientific Sequences of Creation Events		
Scripture	**Biblical Description**	**Scientific Description**
Gen 1: 9-13	<u>Creation Day 3</u> The separation on the earth of water from dry land and the emergence of plant life **(see NOTE 5)**	Dry land appears on the earth, which was once covered by water. (8) Paleontology affirms that the first life appeared on planet earth, in the form of simple photosynthetic algae and single celled cyanobacteria, as soon as the earth was cool enough to support it. Algae begin using the sun's light to scrub carbon dioxide from the air, replacing it with oxygen.
Gen 1:14-19	<u>Creation Day 4</u> The sun, moon, and stars become visible, to serve as markers for day and night, signs, and seasons **(see NOTE 7)**	Paleontology affirms that the earth's atmosphere, once opaque due to hot noxious gases, became translucent and ultimately transparent as the level of oxygen (created over time by algae through photosynthesis) sufficiently saturated the air.
Gen 1:20-23	<u>Creation Day 5</u> The creation of animal life within the seas and flying creatures	Paleontology affirms that a wide variety of sea life and winged insects appeared suddenly on the scene during the Cambrian Explosion of Life approximately 530 million years ago
Gen 1:24-31	<u>Creation Day 6</u> The creation of animal life on the land and the creation of human beings to rule over the earth	Paleontology affirms the sudden appearance of land animals 400 million years ago, followed by homo sapiens **(see NOTE 6)**. Archeology affirms a sudden qualitative change in man through the sudden emergence of writing and the formation of cities approximately 6,000 years ago.
Gen 2:1-3	<u>Creation Day 7</u> God rests from creating and making.	Paleontology affirms that no new animal phyla have been created since the initial appearance of land animals.

Table 1 (cont.): Comparison of Biblical and Scientific Sequences of Creation Events	
NOTE 1:	The Hebrew phrase "the heavens and the earth" (i.e., shamayim erets") is a euphemism within the biblical Hebrew that is meant to indicate the physical universe in its entirety. [29] Although cosmic expansion is not mentioned within Genesis 1, the process of God's "stretching out the universe" since its creation is clearly stated in numerous other books of scripture.
NOTE 2:	The earth is described here as being "formless and void," indicating either that it did not yet exist or that it existed in a chaotic, uninhabitable condition. The Hebrew wording used here to describe this state is "tohuw and bohuw." Use of this phrasing in Jeremiah 4 and Isaiah 34 strongly supports the latter meaning of "uninhabitable", rather than "non-existent."
NOTE 3:	This marks the first of God's formative commands; the first "…and God said", where He begins to prepare the earth for habitation. Igniting the sun was a necessary first step, as it permitted the processes of photosynthesis and water vapor degeneration through UV light that would ultimately make earth's atmosphere breathable. Prior to this, Gen 1:2 and Job 38:9 state that the earth was initially covered in darkness.
NOTE 4:	Here God makes earth's atmosphere (i.e., the firmament = sky), separating the "waters below the firmament" (i.e., the seas) from the "waters above the firmament" (i.e., the clouds and the cosmos). Use of the term "waters" here can be confusing as it is being used to describe three separate things; namely, the seas, the atmosphere, and the cosmos. Scientists remain puzzled as to why there is so much water on the earth.
NOTE 5:	God does not give a specific command for the creation of the earth from nothing. The biblical text does not ever state nor infer that He instantaneously created (i.e., bara) earth from nothing. Instead, He "formed" (asah) it from the materials that He initially *did* create from nothing at the very beginning.
NOTE 6:	The fossil record demonstrates that hominids appeared on the scene tens of thousands of years ago. (While this may *seem* at first glance to contradict the bible's account of the creation of man, the evidence affirms that this is not so.) There is an inexplicable (by scientific reasoning) *qualitative* change in man that occurs exactly at the time (by biblical reckoning) that God created Adam "in His image".

Table 1 (cont.): Comparison of Biblical and Scientific Sequences of Creation Events	
NOTE 7:	The evidence suggests that God "formed/made" (asah) these heavenly bodies over a period of time with the matter/energy that He created (from nothing) at the very beginning and that they ultimately *became visible* during this time. Due to the opaque nature of earth's early atmosphere, these heavenly features were not initially visible from the earth's surface. Light from the sun did penetrate the atmosphere to a certain degree, allowing algae to produce oxygen and debonding water vapor, ultimately resulting in a transparent atmosphere. God does not speak the sun, moon, and stars into immediate existence through a new creation (bara), but makes them (asah) and directs them to "appear" on this Creation Day. Our sun had to have been in existence prior to this point to allow the first plant life to flourish, creating oxygen in our atmosphere and cleansing it of noxious carbon dioxide. Once the level of oxygen rose to a certain point, the atmosphere, which was initially translucent due to the concentration of noxious gases, became transparent, allowing the sun, moon, and stars to become visible. While it is certainly possible that God could have sustained the first plant life that He created on the previous day through some other means until the sun made its appearance, this is not indicated anywhere within the biblical text. Additionally, this would not appear to us as a natural process and would contradict the physical evidence that He has provided to us. As He tells us that He reveals Himself through nature, the physical evidence must be reliable or it would be misleading, which would go against God's truthful nature.

CHAPTER SIX

The Fine Tuning of the Universe

It is my hope that, by this point in your reading, you have become convinced of the fact that biblical and scientific wisdom are not contradictory, but provide a unified, cohesive picture of the nature of God and our universe, as He reveals Himself through His creation. I personally find this revelation to be extremely exciting! Accepting this has caused me to scrutinize His Word more carefully, giving me deeper and more meaningful understanding.

Although I won't present most of them here, there are certainly reasons other than what I have already presented herein to accept the fact that the bible is the unerring Word of God and that it is supported by what we can observe within His natural World. (These will be the subject of a future book.) However, there is one other significant scientific aspect of His creation that bears pervasive and unambiguous witness to the existence of our Creator that I do wish to discuss herein. I am speaking here of the fine-tuning of the universe.

The Cosmological Evidence of God

Psalms 19 and 97, as well as Heb 11:3, attest to the fact that thc heavens declare the glory of God and that the skies proclaim the work of His hands. At no other time since the creation of man has this been as abundantly evident as it is today. Through the gift of His Neshama, God has given us the ability to scrutinize nature to exquisite detail and to *comprehend* its inner workings and hidden implications (Job 32:8, James 1:5, Prov 1:7, Prov 2:6, Prov 28:5, Ps 119:104 and 130, Col 2:3, Prov 4:7 and many others).

Hundreds of books, such as *A Fortunate Universe*, [(1)] and *The Goldilocks Enigma*, [(2)] have already been written on the subject of the universe's fine-tuning, covering the subject quite comprehensively. It is, therefore, not my intent herein to fully cover the subject. My goal is to provide the reader with a snapshot of how God has revealed Himself through the most minutely detailed aspects of our universe. I hope to offer enough though-provoking details to ignite an interest in the subject within those who have not yet realized the depths of God's hand in nature, as He has revealed it, and our ability to see and understand it.

Scientific discoveries are increasingly providing evidence that our universe is not the result of random chance, but required a Creative Force. While scientists generally won't go so far as to say "God" or "Creator," many are willing to concede, or at least to entertain the possibility, that the universe is the product of "Intelligent Design." This revolution in scientific thinking has been brought about in large part by recent observations regarding the complexity of language within DNA, the irreducible complexity of biological cells, and the realization that the physical laws of our universe are incredibly fine-tuned. In fact, they seem to have been designed specifically with us in mind. In all three areas, it has become abundantly clear that the odds of their self-development under naturalistic processes are remote to the extreme.

With respect to the physical laws, scientists began to consider the fine-tuning argument as early as the early 1900's, when Joseph Henderson initially suggested it in his 1913 book, *The Fitness of the Environment.* [(3)] Since then, the physical laws have been the subject of intense scrutiny and many scientists now admit, albeit ofttimes reluctantly, that many of them are perfectly balanced to allow for the existence of our universe as it presently is and for the emergence of complex life. Although there is no affirmed consensus as to the number of universal parameters that are so finely tuned, the evidence of design is, nonetheless, everywhere. Prominent scientists who admit (though sometimes reluctantly) to the fine-tuning phenomenon include:

- English Philosopher Anthony Flew who, after decades of staunchly touting atheism through dozens of books, such as The *Presumption of Atheism* (1976), changed his mind and became a believer based solely on the scientific evidence, such as the fine-tuning of the universe and the incredible complexity of genetic coding within DNA. In a subsequent book, entitled *There is a God* (2007), Mr. Flew states, "The philosophical question that has not been answered in origin-of-life studies is this: How can a universe of mindless matter produce beings with intrinsic ends, self-replication capabilities, and 'coded chemistry'?" (4)

- English astronomer Sir Fred Hoyle, who wrote in his 1983 book *The Intelligent Universe*, "The list of anthropic properties[22], apparent accidents of a non-biological nature without which carbon-based and hence human life could not exist, is large and impressive". (5) And, "A common sense interpretation of the facts suggests that a super intellect has monkeyed with physics, as well as with chemistry and biology, and that there are no blind forces worth speaking about in nature. The numbers one calculates from the facts seem to me so overwhelming as to put this conclusion almost beyond question." (6) Finally, he states, ""Some super-calculating intellect must have designed the properties of the carbon atom, otherwise the chance of my finding such an atom through the blind forces of nature would be less than 1 in 10^{40000}." (7)
- Physicist Paul Davies, who admits: "There is now broad agreement among physicists and cosmologists that the Universe is in several respects 'fine-tuned' for life. There is for me powerful evidence that there is something going on behind it all." (8) It seems as though somebody has fine-tuned nature's numbers to make the Universe....The impression of design is overwhelming." (9)
- Theoretical physicist and astronomer Stephen Hawking, who stated, "The laws of science, as we know them at present, contain many fundamental numbers, like the size of the electric charge of the electron and the ratio of the masses of the proton and the electron. The remarkable fact is that the values of these numbers seem to have been very finely adjusted to make possible the development of life." (10) (6)

[22] The term "anthropic properties" relates to human beings or their span of existence on earth

- British astronomer Sir Arthur Eddington, who estimated in 1931, "The picture of the world, as drawn in existing physical theories, shows arrangement of the individual elements for which the odds are multillions to 1 against an origin by chance." Eddington defined multillions as a general term for numbers of the order of 10 to the 100th power "or larger".(9)

- NASA astronomer John O'Keefe said, "If the Universe had not been made with the most exacting precision, we could never have come into existence. It is my view that these circumstances indicate the universe was created for man to live in." (9)

- In discussing Stephen Hawking's claim that, "With gravity in place, the cosmos-as-we-know-it was just a matter of hanging out for a few billion years," Famed astronomer Seth Shostak asks, "Who or what built the universe?" Shostak then observes: "...this approach inevitably begs the question, "who designed gravity?" Isn't it remarkable that this gentle force seems so perfectly suited to the job of assembling a grand and habitable universe? ...If, for instance, the charge on the electron were of a slightly different value, stars wouldn't work adequately, and you would be spared both this blog and your existence. Depending on your personal philosophies, you can either credit this custom fitting to the intentions of God, or go for Plan B. The latter posits a multiverse... (11)

- Physicist Robert H. Dicke, who argued that certain forces in physics, such as gravity and electromagnetism, must be perfectly fine-tuned for life to exist in the universe. (12)

- British cosmologist, astrophysicist, and Astronomer Royal, Martin Rees, who provided amplification of the subject in 1999 within his book, *Just Six Numbers*. Rees described the consequences of tweaking any one of six key physical constants, noting that, "These six numbers constitute a 'recipe' for a universe. Moreover, the outcome is sensitive to their values: *if any (single) one of them* were to be 'untuned', there would be no stars and no life" (emphasis and parenthetical text added by author). (13)

If the parameters of any one of the factors covered by Mr. Rees were tweaked in either direction (i.e., were they to be made stronger or weaker) by the tiniest fraction, life as we know it could not possibly exist within our universe. The six parameters Rees discusses at length and the repercussions of their tweaking include:

- The strength of gravity – If this were slightly stronger (for example, 10^{30} rather than 10^{36}), the major components of our universe, including the sizes for galaxies, suns, and planets, would be scaled down to the point where planetary systems could be unstable and unsuitable for life. Stars would also burn through their fuel far more quickly, lasting only tens of thousands rather than billions of years. Sir Rees states, "All we know is that nothing as complex as humankind could have emerged if N (i.e., the strength of gravity) were much less than 10^{36} (i.e., 1,000,000,000,000,000,000,000,000,000,000,000,000). (14)
- The strength of the force that binds atomic nuclei together (i.e., protons and neutrons). "If the nuclear glue were weaker (i.e., if it were 0.006 rather than 0.007), a proton could not be bonded to a neutron and deuterium would be unstable. Then, the path to helium formation would be closed off. We would have a simple universe comprised of hydrogen, whose atoms consist of one proton orbited by a single electron, and (there would be) no chemistry. We also couldn't have existed if it (i.e., the strength of the nuclear glue) were 0.008, because no hydrogen would have survived from the Big Bang." (15)
- The initial tuning of the expansion energy of our universe – If any stronger, the universe would have collapsed into itself long ago. If any weaker, the universe would have expanded too fast and stars and galaxies would not have been able to form, "…the required precision (of the initial expansion rate) is astonishing: at one second after the Big Bang, it (i.e., the rate of expansion) cannot have differed from unity by more than one part in a million billion (i.e., 10^{15}) in order that the universe should now, after ten billion years, be still expanding and with a value that has certainly not departed wildly from unity." (16)
- The ratio of the actual density of our universe to its critical density, both of which need to be very closely balanced. Any gap that may have existed between these two factors would grow wider as the

universe expanded. If the ratio had started off slightly less than unity, kinetic energy would eventually dominate and the universe would expand too rapidly, resulting in a universe where galaxies and stars would not have been able to form. If it had been greater than unity, then gravity would have soon brought expansion to a halt, causing the universe to collapse back in on itself in a big crunch. In either scenario, life would have had no chance to develop and thrive. (17)

- The fabric (i.e., rest to mass energy) of our universe – Any stronger, and the universe would be a turbulent and violent place, one dominated by black holes and intense radiation, incapable of sustaining life. Any weaker, and our universe would be structureless, with primordial gas clouds being unable to condense into gravitationally bound structures. (18)
- The number of spatial and temporal dimensions. One consequence of three-dimensions is that forces such as gravity and electricity are obliged to obey an inverse-square law, which creates stability among planetary bodies and orbits. (19)

The list of scientists is certainly far more extensive than what has been presented here, but the gist is clear. Eminent scientists generally accept that *the physical laws of our universe are incredibly fine-tuned to the point that it/we couldn't exist if any one of them were tweaked by the slightest degree*. Some of their reasoning and conclusions may be difficult, at first, for a layperson to understand, but they are not beyond comprehension. It may take a little more effort to develop an appreciation of them, but it is achievable.

The fact that the fine-tuning of the universe is so widely accepted across differing fields (i.e., cosmology, astrophysics, mathematics, etc.) in itself speaks volumes as to its validity. While they may be reluctant to admit it, more and more scientists are concluding that such fine-tuning cannot be attributed to chance. Yet, with such remarkable evidence for design, many of them remain reluctant, or simply blatantly refuse to accept the idea of a Designer or Creator.

Theoretical physicists Michio Kaku is so impressed by the level of fine tuning that he states, "…our universe really is special. It is fine-tuned, *perhaps fine-tuned by luck*, but it is fine-tuned nonetheless. …Our universe, in some sense, knew we were coming." (20) (emphasis added by author) Incredibly, even knowing the dramatic extent of the universe's fine tuning and the impossibility of life if any of these parameters were altered even slightly, he stubbornly clings to the notion that it is all due to luck or a series of cosmic accidents. He is also a proponent of the multiverse theory, a hypothesis that will forever remain unprovable simply because, even if they did exist, these other universes will never be observable. Here, again, is an example of a scientist speaking of a pet theory as though it has been established as fact, stating, "…it is no accident that our universe has these conditions (i.e., the DNA of life) because it was a spinoff of another universe." (20)

Mr. Kaku is by no means the only well-educated mind that attributes the existence of the universe to blind luck. Paul Davies states, "Somehow, the universe has engineered not just its own awareness, but also its own comprehension. *Mindless, blundering atoms have conspired* to make not just life, not just mind, but understanding." (21) (emphasis added by author) Sir Fred Hoyle attributes the existence of the universe to "apparent accidents." (5) Despite the "overwhelming appearance of design," Stephen Hawking remained an atheist until he took his last breath. (22) And Richard Dawkins stated, "Biology is the study of complicated things *that give the appearance* of having been designed for a purpose." (23) (emphasis added by author) He further states, "(living things) overwhelmingly impress us *with the appearance of design* as if by a master watchmaker." (24)

God truly does confound the wisdom of the wise (1Cor 1:19, 27).

Fortunately, there are plenty of scientists who are willing to follow the evidence and accept the conclusion that it speaks to a Creator. Among the list of candid proponents of intelligent design are such prominent names as Drs. Stephen Meyer, Douglas Axe, John Lennox, Gerald Schroeder, Hugh Ross, Michael Denton, James Tour, and Michael Behe. These brave scientists have been quite vocal in voicing their support of the existence of a Creator, which has brought them much criticism and rebuke within their respective fields from those who cannot seem to look at the facts objectively.

By themselves, the astonishing precision of just the six numbers that are detailed by Mr. Rees attest to the incredible level of the universe's fine tuning. Tweak any one of them by the merest fraction – in some cases, we are talking about a few billionths of one degree – and we simply could not exist. However, since the publication of "*Just Six Numbers*", many more physical laws have revealed themselves to be just as incredibly fine-tuned.

Dr. Ross, founder of Reasons to Believe.org, specified during an interview in May of 2014, that "…there are 850 individual characteristics of the universe and that the chances of them all coming together naturalistically are too astronomical to even consider." He continues, "There is less than 1 chance in $10^{1,050}$ that all 850 characteristics of the universe happened without Divine miraculous intervention." (25) To put this into perspective, Dr. Ross states that the odds of these finely tuned laws happening by chance would be the same as a person winning the lottery 150 consecutive times, buying a single lottery ticket each time. (25)

The odds of winning the MegaMillions jackpot are 1 in 302,600,000 and the odds of winning it twice in a row are 1 in 14,907,351,000,000,000!! (26) So, while the odds of winning it just once are long enough, the odds of winning it twice in a row are 49 million times longer, making it 49 million times less likely to happen. And the odds grow exponentially larger with each consecutive win. So, the odds of winning it 150 times in a row (and, by analogy, the odds of these physical laws happening together by chance) are astronomical (no pun intended).

Renowned mathematician and winner of a Nobel Prize in physics, Sir Roger Penrose, has calculated the precision needed within nature for the conditions and energy distribution at the moment of the Big Bang to have eventually produced an environment suitable for life. Sir Penrose states, "The likelihood, *or better the unlikelihood*, that those initial conditions might produce such a universe is less than one chance out of 10 to the power of 10 to the power of 123 (i.e., $10^{10\ 123}$). That is one out of a billion billion billion etc., repeated more than a billion billion times." (27) (emphasis added by author)

To say that this number greatly surpasses the total number of atoms in the universe (i.e., 10^{80}) would be a dramatic understatement. It's difficult to envision such a vast number so I'll use an analogy that is closer to home.

There are an estimated 400 quintillion grains of sand on all the beaches in the world.[23] That's the number 400 followed by 19 zeroes. (28) Four-hundred quintillion is a huge number, but it is still only the tiniest fraction

---

[23] That's about 1,000,000,000 grains per cubic foot of sand. That means that there are about 12,000,000,000 grains beneath a typical 2' by 6' beach towel – and that's just to the depth of 12".

The estimates for the numbers of grains of sand and stars in the universe can vary widely. Another site claims that there are between 10 and 200 sextillion stars in the universe (10,000,000,000,000,000,000,000 to 200,000,000,000,000,000,000,000 stars) and between 2.5 and 10 sextillion grains of sand on the earth. (29) The difference may be that this estimate tries to account for all the grains of sand on the earth, including deserts etc., while the previously cited estimate accounts only for those grains of sand that lie on the earth's beaches. Regardless of which number we use, it is a mere fraction of $10^{10\ 123}$.

of $10^{10^{123}}$. If expressed as actual numbers, a comparison of these numbers looks something like this:

<u>400 x 10^{19}</u> quintillion grains of sand
(or, 4,000,000,000,000,000,000,000)

<u>10^{80}</u> (atoms in the universe)
(or,100,000,000,000,000,000,000,000,000,000,000,000,000,000,000,
000,000,000,000,000,000,000,000,000,000,000,000)

<u>$10^{10^{123}}$</u>
(10,000,000,000,000,000,000,000,000,000,000,000,000,000,000,000,
000,000,000,000,000,000,000,000,000,000,000,000,000,000,000,
000,000,000,000,000,000,000,000,000,000,000,000,000,000,000,
000,000,000,000,000,000,000,000,000,000,000,000,000,000,000,
000,000,000,000,000,000,000,000,000,000,000,000,000,000,000,
000,000,000,000,000,000,000,000,000,000,000,000,000,000,000,
000,000,000,000,000,000,000,000,000,000,000,000,000,000,000,
000,000,000,000,000,000,000,000,000,000,000,000,000,000,000,
000,000,000,000,000,000,000,000,000,000,000,000,000,000,000,
000,000,000,000,000,000,000,000,000,000,000,000,000,000,000,
000,000,000,000,000,000,000,000,000,000,000,000,000,000,000,
000,000,000,000,000,000,000,000,000,000,000,000,000,000,000,
000,000,000,000,000,000,000,000,000,000,000,000,000,000,000,
000,000,000,000,000,000,000,000,000,000,000,000,000,000,000,
000,000,000,000,000,000,000,000,000,000,000,000,000,000,000,
000,000,000,000,000,000,000,000,000,000,000,000,000,000,000,
000,000,000,000,000,000,000,000,000,000,000,000,000,000,000,
000,000,000,000,000,000,000,000,000,000,000,000,000,000,000,
000,000,000,000,000,000,000,000,000,000,000,000,000,000,000,
000,000,000,000,000,000,000,000,000,000,000,000,000,000,000,
000,000,000,000,000,000,000,000,000,000,000,000,000,000,000,
000,000,000,000,000,000,000,000,000,000,000,000,000,000,000,
000,000,000,000,000,000,000,000,000,000,000,000,000,000,000,
000,000,000,000,000,000,000,000,000,000,000,000,000,000,000,
000,000,000,000,000,000,000,000,000,000,000,000,000,000,000,
000,000,000,000,000,000,000,000,000,000,000,000,000,000,000,
000,000,000,000,000,000,000,000,000,000,000,000,000,000,000,
000,000,000,000,000,000,000,000,000,000,000,000

Depending upon where you look, you'll find varying lists of the universe's finely tuned parameters. The Discovery Institute (www.Discovery.org) provides a partial list of 22 such constraints. [(30)] Another blog cites over 400 of them, as attributed to Dr. Ross. [(31)]

The fine-tuning of these physical laws balances the existence of the universe, and life as we know it, on a razor's edge. Although the list of specific parameters varies in number quite a bit depending upon the source, it is clear that there are at least several dozen key physical laws that scientists view as being tuned with astonishing precision. An abbreviated list, as assembled by the organization Cold and Lonely Truth, using information originally provided by Dr. Hugh Ross, includes the following: [(31)]

- Strong nuclear force constant (binds protons and neutrons in atomic nuclei):
- Weak nuclear force constant (responsible for processes like beta decay in radioactive materials and the stability of atoms)
- Gravitational force constant
- Electromagnetic force constant
- Ratio of electromagnetic force constant to gravitational force constant
- Ratio of proton to electron mass
- Ratio of number of protons to number of electrons
- Ratio of proton to electron charge
- Expansion rate of the universe
- Mass density of the universe
- Baryon (proton and neutron) density of the universe
- Space energy or dark energy density of the universe
- Ratio of space energy density to mass density
- Entropy level of the universe
- Velocity of light
- Uniformity of radiation
- Homogeneity of the universe
- Average distance between galaxies
- Average distance between stars
- Density of giant galaxies during early cosmic history
- Electromagnetic fine structure constant
- Gravitational fine-structure constant
- Decay rate of protons
- Ratio of neutron mass to proton mass

- Initial excess of nucleons over antinucleons
- Ratio of exotic matter to ordinary matter
- Number of effective dimensions in the early universe
- Number of effective dimensions in the present universe
- Mass values for active neutrinos
- Number of different species of active neutrinos
- Number of active neutrinos in the universe
- Magnitude of the temperature ripples in cosmic background radiation
- Flatness of universe's geometry
- Strength of primordial cosmic magnetic field
- Strength of the cosmic primordial magnetic field
- Constancy of the velocity of light
- Constancy of the electron-to-proton mass ratio
- Constancy of the gravitational constant

Even if the list of finely tuned parameters required for the existence of our universe was narrowed down to only a handful, such as only those that are covered in *Just Six Numbers*, it would still be remarkable that each of them are so 'magically' aligned and tuned with such precision to enable it (and us) to exist. But there is more to this story still…

The Goldilocks Principle

For the universe to exist at all, the four fundamental forces (i.e., gravity, electromagnetism, and the strong and weak nuclear forces) had to have been fixed into existence with exceeding precision less than one millionth of a second into the Big Bang event. And, while this itself is an incredible achievement for the universe as a whole, there are also numerous circumstances that must be just right for any given planet to sustain life. There is a whole host of other important factors that must converge in order for a world to be hospitable to life

Based on the following criteria and the unlikelihood of them all converging for any one planet, it is highly improbable that complex life exists anywhere else within our universe. In *The Privileged Planet*, the authors state the following: "Recent discoveries from a variety of fields and from the new discipline of astrobiology have undermined this sanguine enthusiasm of (finding) extraterrestrials. Mounting evidence suggests that the conditions necessary for complex life are exceedingly rare, and that the probability of them all converging at the same place and time is minute." (32) They further state, "…taken individually, each of these examples of fine-tuning is impressive. But in the real universe, *the values of all the constants and force strengths must be satisfied simultaneously* to have a universe hospitable for life. …The range for each of these parameters is narrow. The range within which all of them are satisfied simultaneously is much smaller…"(emphasis added by author) (33)

There are lists of these life-sustaining properties all over the internet but they generally include the following elements:

- The existence of liquid water. If a planet is too close to its sun, temperatures soar and liquid water boils into gas. Too far away, and almost everything freezes.

  As reported by New Scientist, (34) "Water's life-giving properties exist on a knife-edge. It turns out that life as we know it relies on a fortuitous, but incredibly delicate, balance of quantum forces. ... We are used to the idea that the cosmos' physical constraints are fine-tuned for life. Now it seems water's quantum forces can be added to this 'just right' list."

- A surface gravity strong enough to prevent the loss of water to space through the atmosphere
- A protective ozone layer to filter out harmful ultraviolet radiation and stabilize temperature swings
- A rotation rate on its axis that provides for daytime and nighttime temperatures that do not wildly deviate
- An atmosphere with a chemical composition (20% oxygen, etc.) that supports life's high-energy requirements.
- An atmospheric pressure that enables water to evaporate at an optimal rate to support life
- An atmosphere that is transparent enough to allow an optimal, life-supporting range of solar radiation to reach the surface
- An atmosphere having the capacity to hold water vapor in a suitable hydrologic cycle, facilitating stable temperature and rainfall ranges
- Being suited with a stable sun that provides heat and light in just the right spectrums

- The planet's position within the galaxy so that it does not exist in an active region of stellar development, which would douse it with lethal radiation
- Possessing an axial tilt (i.e., the amount that a planet is angled relative to the sun it orbits) such that regions closer to the northern and southern poles develop distinct seasons
- Having a degree of axial precession (i.e., the amount that it wobbles on its axis) that advantageously moderates the intensity of the seasons
- Holding a low degree of orbital eccentricity (i.e., how much a planet's orbit deviates from a perfect circle). Planets with more eccentric orbits can have huge differences in temperature as they get closer to and further away from the sun
- Possessing a molten core and plate tectonics that ensure that the planet is surrounded by a protective magnetic shield that deflects harmful solar winds and cosmic rays
- Being surrounded by larger planets, which draw asteroids and meteors into themselves, protecting the life-giving planet from devastating collisions
- Possessing a moon or moons, which stabilize the planet's rotation

In *The Privileged Planet*, the authors further state, "Not only are numerous factors about our universe incredibly fine-tuned, but the conditions for intelligent life on earth also make our planet strangely well-suited for viewing and analyzing the universe. The fact that our atmosphere is clear, that our moon is just the right size and distance from the earth and that its gravity stabilizes earth's rotation, that our position in the galaxy is just so, that our sun is its precise mass and composition – all these facts and many more not only are necessary for earth's habitability, but also have been surprisingly crucial to the discovery and measurement of the universe by scientists. Earth offers surprisingly good views of both distant and nearby universes while providing an effective platform for discovering the laws of physics." [(35)] In addition to providing a viable viewing platform, our moon also stabilizes the rotation axis of earth, preventing it from varying over a large range, which would cause more dramatic climate fluctuations.

Eric Metaxas, award-winning author and host of the talk show Socrates in the City, which specializes in merging biblical and scientific matters, underscores the impossibility of the universe's existence through natural forces in the following manner, "…there are over 200 known parameters necessary for a planet to support life, *every single one of which must be perfectly met, or the whole thing falls apart.* By altering *any single one* of these forces ever so slightly, our universe could not exist. When *all* factors are considered, the odds that the universe just happened by chance are equivalent to tossing a coin into the air and having it come up "heads" 10 quintillion (10,000,000,000,000,000,000) times in a row!" (emphasis added by author) (36)

In *The Science of God*, Dr. Gerald Schroeder makes a very interesting observation regarding the position of the earth within our solar system, pointing out that the Earth isn't where it should be. He states, "The distances of the planets from the sun fall on an exponential distribution. Each planet is approximately two times farther from the sun than the preceding planet, except for the earth. The earth is not where is should be. …earth, at 150 million kilometers from the sun, does not fit on the exponential distribution." (27) To illustrate his point, he provides the following:

In millions of kilometers from the sun, the distances are:

58	Mercury
110	Venus
150	Earth (should be closer to Mars' current location)
230	Mars
440	Asteroid belt
780	Jupiter
1430	Saturn
2880	Uranus

It is intriguing that earth's present position places it inside the sun's habitable zone (a.k.a. the Goldilocks Zone); the range where conditions are just right for life to thrive. The habitable zone is defined as "the region around a star where a planet could potentially have liquid water (a key ingredient for life) on its surface." The habitable zone for our sun is between 0.9 – 1.5 astronomical units, (37) which is the average distance between the earth and the sun (i.e., 92,955,807.3 mi.). This equates to between 83,660,226.6 and 139,433,711 miles (or between 133,856,363 and 223,093,938 km). If earth were to exist along the exponential curve, as it *should*, it would lie at the extreme outer edge of this zone and would likely be unsuitable for life.

So how did earth end up in its present orbit? Nobody really knows the answer to that question. However, it is generally thought that, at some point in the distant past, another planetary body collided with earth, causing material to be ejected from our planet that would ultimately form our moon. This is known as the Giant Impact Hypothesis. Such a collision could have nudged the earth into its present orbit. Not only would this have placed the earth within the habitable zone, but it would have resulted in the creation of our moon, which is incredibly important for the development and sustainment of life on the earth.

Final Thoughts

There can be no denying that there are, at a minimum, dozens of physical laws and conditions that have been perfectly established to permit the existence of our universe and the development and maintenance of life on planet earth. It may be easy to look at any one factor, or even a number of them collectively, and dismiss them as coincidence. But to dismiss the totality of the overwhelming evidence that attests to the universe's fine-tuning and the extremely unlikely convergence of factors that make our planet hospitable for life, or to chalk these things up to chance or accident, truly stretches the bounds of credibility.

Yet, denial of the scientific facts seems to be the norm within many scientific circles, as evidenced by the examples provided at the beginning of this chapter. Add to that an extreme reluctance to objectively consider any biblical teachings that are pertinent to the natural world and the result is a jaded and incomplete view of our existence.

On the other side, theologians are also in denial; routinely dismissing scientific evidence that, if looked at objectively and in the light of what the bible *actually* says rather than what *they think* is says, would serve to not only affirm their own belief but aid them in strengthening the case for their God for non-believers. Denying the science through which our God says that He reveals Himself (Rom 1:19-20, Ps 19:1-4, Isa 45:18-21, and Heb 11:3) is unwise and detrimental to the Christian desire to spread the Good News.

My own experience in delving deeply into both the bible and the sciences has taught me that the two are not only completely compatible but mutually supportive in ways that boggle the mind. I once prided myself on how well I "knew" the bible. But I have found that the more closely and objectively that I view it in concert with the scientific evidence, the more deeply I understand the bible's less obvious teachings and the more clearly I see how He has chosen to reveal Himself through both. I can't help but think that the same would be true for any scientist or theologian who openly and objectively studies the evidence in the same way.

The Christian bible is filled with deep meaning that has served people well across the ages. It provides mankind with a moral compass and direction on how to live our lives meaningfully and with limited angst, should we choose to follow its guidance. It has also been written in such a way as to make sense to people thousands of years ago while holding within the very same text information that could be revealed more fully through modern scientific insight (e.g., Dinosaurs, pg. 113). Through the ages, millions of people have studied its text with both awe and skepticism. In these latter days, fresh scientific discoveries are serving more and more to affirm the biblical text, just as God foretold in Daniel 12. In His infinite wisdom, God has seen to it that time and science have served to vindicate Genesis.

****

Bibliography

CHAPTER ONE

1. Neo-Darwinism | Evolutionary Theory, Natural Selection & Genetics | Britannica
2. 'Bouncing' universe theory still can't explain what came first | Space, Robert Lea, August 12, 2022; The Universe Began with a Bang, Not a Bounce, New Studies Find | Scientific American, James Riordon, May 24, 2023
3. What is multiverse theory? | Live Science, Paul Sutter, August 23, 2021
4. Rees, Martin, *Just Six Numbers: The Deep Forces That Shape the Universe*, New York: Basic Books, 2001, pg.12
5. Bill Gates, Nathan Myhrvold, Peter Rinearson, *"The Road Ahead"*, (1996)
6. Tim Barnett, Building a Protein by Chance, Stands to Reason, September 15, 2015
7. Can something be statistically impossible?, December 8, 2016; edited July 18, 2018
8. Dr. Gerald Schroeder, *The Science of God*; Simon & Schuster, 1997, pg. 102
9. Martin Rees *Just Six Numbers, The Deep Forces That Shape the Universe*; Basic Books, 1999, pg. 22
10. Stephen C. Meyer, *Darwin's Doubt*, HarperOne books, 2013, pgs. 172-176
11. Geraint F. Lewis and Luke A Barnes, *A Fortunate Universe, Life in a Finely Tuned Cosmos*; pg. 17
12. Martin Rees *Just Six Numbers, The Deep Forces That Shape the Universe*; pgs. 8-9
13. Darren Orf, Popular Mechanics, Scientists Have Observed Evidence of Evolution in Real Time, last accessed 8/25/2025
14. R. Laird Harris, Gleason L. Archer, and Bruce K Waltke, *Theological Wordbook of the Old Testament*, Chicago; Moody, 1980, 1:127
15. Rodney Whitefield, Ph.D., *Genesis One and the Age of the Earth*, 2011, pg. 19

16. Jacob Newman M.A, D.Litt Leiden, E.J. Brill, The Commentary of Nahmanides, Genesis Chapters 1-6. 1960, pgs. 33- 36
17. Moses Maimonides, Guide for the Perplexed, Second Edition; 1904, Chapter XXX; as translated by M. Friedlander Ph.D.
18. List of Scientific Insights in the Bible – The Breath of God (godsbreath.net)
19. Grand Canyon: Exposing the Flood | The Institute for Creation Research; Tim Clarey, Ph.D., and Brian Thomas, Ph.D., December 30, 2020; A meteor may have led to the formation of the Grand Canyon, new study says | The Independent, Rachel Dobkin, July 15, 2025; America's Largest Crater Has Surprise Link to Grand Canyon, Study Finds : ScienceAlert, Ivan Farkas, July 23, 2025; Giant meteor impact may have triggered massive Grand Canyon landslide 56,000 years ago | Live Science, Sasha Pare, July 17, 2025; all last accessed 8/25/2025
20. https://www.universetoday.com/84147/singularity/, Matthew Williams, February 16, 2011

CHAPTER TWO

1. NASA defines the Big Bang as, "…the idea that the universe began as just a single point, then expanded and stretched to grow to its current size." What Is the Big Bang? | NASA Space Place
2. What Is the Big Bang? The Beginning of the Universe, Explained
3. Answers in Genesis: This Video DISMANTLES The Big Bang Theory (youtube.com)
4. Answers in Genesis: EXPLODING the Big Bang Myth (youtube.com)

CHAPTER THREE

1. Hugh Ross, A Matter of Days, rtb Press, 2015, pgs. 47 – 64, 327 – 331
2. Christianity Stack Exchange; A Historical Sketch of Young-Earth Creationism – Proclaim & Defend, July 11, 2018; The Origins of Young Earth Creationism, April 11, 2022

3. Moses Maimonides, Guide for the Perplexed, Second Edition; 1904, Chapter XXX; as translated by M. Friedlander Ph.D.
4. Rodney Whitefield, Ph.D., *Reading Genesis One*, 2011, pgs. 24-27 and Genesis One and the Age of the Earth, 2011, pgs. 10-11
5. Genesis 1 1 3 Michael Heiser PhD NEW (youtube.com)
6. Chuck Missler, Ph.D., An Expositional Commentary on The Book of Genesis, Session 02, 2023; The Book of Genesis - Session 2 of 24 - A Remastered Commentary by Chuck Missler (youtube.com)
7. Rodney Whitefield, Ph.D., *Genesis One and the Age of the Earth*, 2011, pg. 13
8. John Lennox, *Seven Days that Divide the World*, Zondervan, 2011, pg. 52
9. *Strong's Exhaustive Concordance of the Bible*, forty-eight printing, 1993: see tohuw (8414) and bohuw (922)
10. Rodney Whitefield, Ph.D., *Reading Genesis One*, 2011, pgs. 24-27 and *Genesis One and the Age of the Earth*, 2011, pg. 47
11. Rodney Whitefield, Ph.D., *Reading Genesis One*, 2011, pg. 48; Chuck Missler, Ph.D., An Expositional Commentary on The Book of Genesis, Sessions 03 and 05, 2023; The Book of Genesis - Session 3 of 24 - A Remastered Commentary by Chuck Missler (youtube.com) and The Book of Genesis - Session 5 of 24 - A Remastered Commentary by Chuck Missler (youtube.com); and Michael Heiser, Ph.D., Genesis 1 1 3
12. Rodney Whitefield, Ph.D., *Reading Genesis One*, 2011, pgs. 24-27, 60-73 and *Genesis One and the Age of the Earth*, 2011, pgs. 58-73 and 81-85
13. Rodney Whitefield, Ph.D., *Reading Genesis One*, 2011, pg. 84
14. Gleason L. Archer, *Encyclopedia of Bible Difficulties*, Baker 1982, pgs. 60-61
15. John Lennox, *Seven Days that Divide the World*, Zondervan, 2011, pg. 53-54
16. Dictionary.com; DAY Definition & Usage Examples | Dictionary.com
17. Jacob Newman M.A. D.Litt, *The Commentary of Nahmanides*, Genesis Chapters 1-6, Leiden E.J. Brill, 1960
18. Rodney Whitefield, Ph.D., *Reading Genesis One*, 2011, pg. 95

19. Robert C. Newman, Perry G Phillips, and Herman J. Eckelmann, *Genesis One and the Origin of the Earth*, Interdisciplinary Biblical Research Institute, 2007, Location 1187 ("location" is used in lieu of page numbers); David Snoke, *A Biblical Case for an Old Earth*, BakerBooks, 2006, pg. 101; Hugh Ross, *A Matter of Days*, rtb Press, 2015, pg. 90
20. Bad Love | Hebrew Word Study | Skip Moen, Skip Moen, April 7, 2016
21. Does the Bible Affirm Young-Earth Creationism? - Reasons to Believe, Hugh Ross, March 6, 2023
22. Rodney Whitefield, Ph.D., *Reading Genesis One*, 2011, pg. 28-29
23. Paul Davies, *The Goldilocks Enigma; Why the Universe is Just Right for Life*, A Mariner Book, 2006, pg. 50
24. Hugh Ross, *A Matter of Days*, rtb Press, 2015, pgs. 246-250
25. How Do Stars Die and How Long Do Stars Live? | Sky & Telescope, Maria Temming, July 15, 2014
26. Robert C. Newman, Perry G Phillips, and Herman J. Eckelmann, *Genesis One and the Origin of the Earth*, Interdisciplinary Biblical Research Institute, 2007, Location 687 ("location" is used in lieu of page numbers)
27. Hugh Ross, *A Matter of Days*, rtb Press, 2015, pg. 234
28. Guillermo Gonzalez and Jay W. Richards, *The Privileged Planet*, Regnery Publishing, 2004, pg. 25

CHAPTER FOUR

1. Egyptian People | Khufu, Khufu | Biography, Reign, Pyramid, Tomb, History, & Facts | Britannica, October 29, 2024
2. BBC - History - Khufu, 2014
3. Ancient Egypt's Use of the Wheel Explored – Egypt Insights; Evidence of Ancient Advanced Technology: The Great Pyramid of Giza - The Ancient Code; Scientists Have an Answer to How the Egyptian Pyramids Were Built - JSTOR Daily (These sites are representative of the subject and barely scratch the surface.)
4. A Look into the Secret Behind The Great Pyramid's Stumping Alignment — Curiosmos, Ivan Petricevic, April 16, 2020
5. L. Clerc, 'The accurate construction of the right angles of the Great Pyramid's ground plan', JAEA 4, 2020, pp. 97-115

6. Evidence of Ancient Advanced Technology: The Great Pyramid of Giza - The Ancient Code, Ancient Code Team, February 26, 2025
7. Wikipedia; Also featured in Job and the Great Pyramid | ArmstrongInstitute.org, Christopher Eames, June 18, 2022
8. Christopher Dunn, *The Giza Power Plant*, Bear & Company, 1998; pg. 121
9. UNESCO World Heritage Centre - World Heritage List, used with permission
10. Pyramids around the World | A Map & List of Every Pyramid, TheBrainChamber, 12/24/2024
11. Enigma of the Missing Pyramid Bodies - Ancient Egyptian Mystery Remains Unsolved - Ancient Pages, December 10, 2018
12. Valley of the Kings: The Burial Place of the Pharaohs of Egypt | History Cooperative, Maup van der Kerkhof, August 12, 2024
13. Christopher Dunn, *The Giza Power Plant*, Bear & Company, 1998; Evidence of Ancient Advanced Technology: The Great Pyramid of Giza - The Ancient Code, Ancient Code Team, 2/26/2025
14. What is a weaver's beam? — Goliath's Spear
15. Goliath's Spear: Ever wonder what size and kind of weapon the Giant Goliath used?, John Adolphi, YouTube
16. Stephen Quayle & Dr. Thomas Horn, *Unearthing the Cloud Eaters*, Defender Publishing, 2017; Brian Godwa, *When Giants were upon the Earth*, Embedded Pictures Publishing, 2014; Douglas Van Dorn, *Giants, Sons of the Gods*, Waters of Creation Publishing, 2013
17. Ken Johnson, *Ancient Book of Jasher*, Biblefacts Edition, 2013, location 547
18. Ken Johnson, *Ancient Book of Jasher*, Biblefacts Edition, 2013, pg. 222
19. Answers in Genesis: This Video DISMANTLES The Big Bang Theory (youtube.com)
20. Answers in Genesis: EXPLODING the Big Bang Myth (youtube.com)
21. The Most Mind-Blowing Space Discoveries https://www.youtube.com/watch?v=ga3A0vWXwnU

22. The Big Bang Didn't Need God to Start Universe, Researchers Say https://www.space.com/16281-big-bang-god-intervention-science.html
23. What existed before the Big Bang? (bbc.com), Alastair Wilson, 5 January 2022

CHAPTER FIVE

1. https://www.universetoday.com/84147/singularity/, Matt Williams, Universe Today, February 16, 2011
2. Cosmic inflation | New Scientist
3. Our expanding universe: Age, history & other facts | Space, Ailsa Harvey, Charles Q. Choi, January 18, 2022
4. Guillermo Gonzalez and Jay W. Richards, *The Privileged Planet*, Regnery Publishing, 2004, pg. 67
5. How Was the Sun Formed? | Space, Nola Taylor Tillman, June 9, 2021
6. **How did Earth's atmosphere form? | NOAA SciJinks – All About Weather; How did Earth's atmosphere form?**
7. The Earliest Atmosphere; **Smithsonian Environmental Research Center;** Patrick Neale, Barbara Stauffer, Siobhan Starrs, Marsha Rehns, and Katherine Lenard
8. 1.5 billion-year-old Earth had water everywhere, but not one continent, study suggests | Live Science; Mindy Weisberger, March 2, 2020; and Was ancient Earth a water world? | Earth | EarthSky; Paul Scott Anderson, March 17, 2021
9. Guillermo Gonzalez and Jay W. Richards, *The Privileged Planet*, Regnery Publishing, 2004, pg. 66
10. New Findings of Early Life on Earth Date Back 3.77 Billion Years | News | Astrobiology, Miki Huynh, March 3, 2017
11. Dr. Gerald Schroeder, *The Science of God*; 2009, pg. 68; Rodney Whitefield, *Reading Genesis One*, 1997, pg. 97
12. Proterozoic Eon | Oxygen Crisis, Animals, & Facts | Britannica, Brian Frederick Windley
13. Formation of Earth; National Geographic.org

14. Life Through Time - Visual Timeline | Natural History Museum, Richard Paselk, Cambrian Period & Cambrian Explosion: Facts & Information | Live Science, Mary Bagley, May 27, 2016; Cambrian explosion | Evolution, Paleontology & Geology | Britannica, Timothy Fridtj, November 6, 2024; History of Life on Earth | Smithsonian National Museum of Natural History, March 14, 2025; all sites last accessed July 31, 2025
15. The Qingjiang biota—A Burgess Shale–type fossil Lagerstätte from the early Cambrian of South China | Science, Dongjing Fu, Guanghui Tong, Tao Dai, Wei Liu, Yuning Yang, Yuan Zhang, Linhao Cui, Luoyang Li, Hao Yun, and Xingliang Zhang, March 22, 2019; Chengjiang Maotianshan Shales, Chengjiang fossil site | Cambrian period, Yunnan, China | Britannica, John P. Rafferty; all sites last accessed August 1, 2025
16. An Evolutionary Timeline of Homo Sapiens | Smithsonian, Brian Handwerk, February 2, 2021; Human evolution | History, Stages, Timeline, Tree, Chart, & Facts | Britannica, Russell Howard Tuttle, December 5, 2024; sites last accessed August 1, 2025
17. Timeline of the Evolution of Life on Earth, Muhammad Tuhin, April 7, 2025
18. Where Did Humans First Appear? - WorldAtlas, When did Homo sapiens first appear? | Live Science, Krisina Killgrove, Dec 11, 2023, Human evolution | History, Stages, Timeline, Tree, Chart, & Facts | Britannica, Russell Howard Tuttle, May 16, 2025; sites last accessed August 1, 2025
19. When did Homo sapiens first appear? | Live Science, Krisina Killgrove, Dec 11, 2023
20. Human evolution | History, Stages, Timeline, Tree, Chart, & Facts | Britannica, Russell Howard Tuttle, December 5, 2024
21. An Evolutionary Timeline of Homo Sapiens, Brian Handwerk, February 2, 2021
22. Modern humans, Homo sapiens: When, where and how did we evolve? | Natural History Museum, James Ashworth
23. Dr. Gerald Schroeder, *The Science of God*; Simon & Schuster, 1997, pg. 130
24. Dr. Gerald Schroeder, *The Science of God*; Simon & Schuster, 1997, pgs. 139-142

25. Hugh Ross, A Matter of Days, rtb Press, 2015, pg. 305
26. Moses Maimonides, *Guide for the Perplexed*, Second Edition; Christian Classics Ethereal Library, 1904, Chapter XXX; as translated by M. Friedlander Ph.D.
27. Robert C. Newman, Perry G Phillips, and Herman J. Eckelmann, Genesis One and the Origin of the Earth, Interdisciplinary Biblical Research Institute, 2007, Location 1187 ("location" is used in lieu of page numbers); David Snoke, A Biblical Case for an Old Earth, BakerBooks, 2006, pg. 101; Hugh Ross, A Matter of Days, rtb Press, 2015, pg. 90.
28. Does the Bible Affirm Young-Earth Creationism? - Reasons to Believe, Hugh Ross, March 6, 2023
29. Moses Maimonides, Guide for the Perplexed, Second Edition; 1904, Chapter XXX; as translated by M. Friedlander Ph.D.

CHAPTER SIX

1. Geraint F. Lewis and Luke A Barnes, *A Fortunate Universe, Life in a Finely Tuned Cosmos*; pg. 17
2. Paul Davies, *The Goldilocks Enigma; Why the Universe is Just Right for Life*, A Mariner Book, 2006
3. Henderson, Lawrence Joseph (1913), *The fitness of the environment: an inquiry into the biological significance of the properties of matter*, The Macmillan Company
4. Anthony Flew, Roy Abraham Varghese, *There is a God, How the World's Most Notorious Atheist Changed His Mind*, New York Harper One, 2007, pg. 124
5. Hoyle, F., *The Intelligent Universe* (London: Michael Joseph Ltd, 1983)
6. The Fine-Tuning of the Universe: What Does It Mean? - Richard E. Simmons III, May 3, 2018
7. Fred Hoyle, *The Universe: Past and Present Reflections*, Department of Applied Mathematics and Astronomy, University College, 1981, pg. 26
8. Paul Davies, *The Accidental Universe*, Cambridge University Press, 1993, pgs. 70–71
9. Paul Davies, *The Cosmic Blueprint: New Discoveries in Nature's Creative Ability to Order the Universe*, Simon and Schuster, 1989, pg. 203

10. Stephen Hawking, *A Brief History of Time,* Bantam Books, 1988, pgs. 7, 125
11. Who or What Built the Universe? | HuffPost Life, Seth Shostak, September 5, 2010 (updated May 25, 2011)
12. DICKE, R. *Dirac's Cosmology and Mach's Principle*. *Nature* **192**, 440–441 (1961)
13. Martin Rees, *Just Six Numbers: The Deep Forces That Shape the Universe* New York: Basic Books. (3 May 2001), pg.4
14. Martin Rees, *Just Six Numbers, The Deep Forces That Shape the Universe*; Basic Books, 1999, pg. 35
15. Martin Rees, *Just Six Numbers, The Deep Forces That Shape the Universe*; Basic Books, 1999, pg. 55
16. Martin Rees, *Just Six Numbers, The Deep Forces That Shape the Universe*; Basic Books, 1999, pg. 99
17. Martin Rees, *Just Six Numbers, The Deep Forces That Shape the Universe*; Basic Books, 1999, pgs. 97 – 99
18. Martin Rees, *Just Six Numbers, The Deep Forces That Shape the Universe*; Basic Books, 1999, pgs. 127 – 129
19. Martin Rees, *Just Six Numbers, The Deep Forces That Shape the Universe*; Basic Books, 1999, pgs. 150 – 155
20. Michio Kaku - Is the Universe Fine-Tuned for Consciousness?
21. Paul Davies, *The Goldilocks Enigma; Why the Universe is Just Right for Life*, A Mariner Book, 2006, pg. 4
22. Stephen Hawking Was an Atheist: His Words on Death and God | TIME, Jamie Ducharme, March 14, 2018
23. Richard Dawkins, *The Blind Watchmaker: Why the Evidence of Evolution Reveals a Universe Without Design* (New York; Norton, 1986), pg. 1
24. Richard Dawkins, *The Blind Watchmaker: Why the Evidence of Evolution Reveals a Universe Without Design* (New York; Norton, 1986), pg. 21
25. God's Fine-Tuning of the Universe - YouTube, The John Ankerberg Show, May 23, 2014
26. Your Odds Of Winning The Mega Millions Twice Are Better Than Your Odds Of Winning $1 Billion With A Perfect Bracket, Tony Manfred, March 18, 2014
27. Dr. Gerald Schroeder, *The Science of God*; Simon & Schuster, 1997, pgs. 184-186; Fine Tuning Odds Less than 1 in 10^10^123 Roger Penrose

28. Do Stars Outnumber the Sands of Earth's Beaches? | Scientific American, Phil Plait, March 29, 2024
29. Are There More Grains of Sand Than Stars? - Universe Today, Fraser Cain, Nov 25, 2013
30. https://www.discovery.org/a/fine-tuning-parameters/; Jay W. Richards, January 14. 2015
31. List of Factors of Fine-Tuning of Intelligent Life in the Universe, Cold and Lonely Truth
32. Guillermo Gonzalez and Jay W. Richards, *The Privileged Planet*, Regnery Publishing, 2004, location 118
33. Guillermo Gonzalez and Jay W. Richards, *The Privileged Planet*, Regnery Publishing, 2004, pg. 205
34. http://www.newscientist.com/article/mg21228354.900-waters-quantum-weirdness-makes-life-possible.html, Lisa Grossman, October 19, 2011
35. Guillermo Gonzalez and Jay W. Richards, *The Privileged Planet*, Regnery Publishing, 2004, location 85, location 150
36. Amazing factors that are carefully fine tuned to allow life on Earth, August 3, 2015
37. Habitable zone | Astrobiology, Exoplanets & Habitability | Britannica, Jack J. Lissauer, last updated 9/10/2018
38. Ice age | Definition & Facts | Britannica, Dec 22, 2024, last updated 8/17/2025; Ice Age - Definition & Timeline | HISTORY, March 11, 2015, last updated 5/28/2025; sites last accessed 8/29/2025
39. Gregory Wrightstone, *Inconvenient Facts*, Silver Crown Productions, 2017, pgs. 19 -21
40. Gregory Wrightstone, *Inconvenient Facts*, Silver Crown Productions, 2017, pgs. 30-33
41. Lithium: Not as clean as we thought, Alex Kim, January 14, 2022
42. Latest data shows California will fall far short of power needed to fuel all-EV future – Orange County Register
43. What Is the True Cost of Maintaining an EV? | U.S. News, Cherise Threewitt, September 18, 2024
44. Everything You Need To Know About Insuring An Electric Vehicle | Bankrate, R.E. Hawley, November 1, 2024
45. Chernobyl Aftermath: How Long Will Exclusion Zone Be Uninhabitable? - Newsweek, Robyn White, October 14, 2022

Appendix A – The Four Beasts of Daniel 7

There are five modern nations and one global governing body that are identified within Daniel 7 as being present on the earth when Jesus returns. Daniel 7 describes four beasts, including a lion with eagle's wings, a bear, a four-headed leopard with the wings of a fowl on its back, and a ten-horned beast with great iron teeth. The fourth beast was so unique that Daniel could scarcely describe it. We don't have to wonder about what or who these beasts represent, because the biblical text tells us this precisely. They are specifically identified as representing kings or kingdoms (Dan 7:17).

For hundreds of years, these four kingdoms have been equated to the kingdoms of the Babylonians, Medes, Persians, and Greeks. However, there are at least two major problems with this interpretation:

1. The four beasts of Daniel 7 exist *simultaneously*. This was not so of the Babylonians, Medes, Persians, and Greeks, which rose up in succession – one after the other, with some limited overlap. In fact, their appearance *in succession* is exactly how they are described within a separate vision that occurs in Daniel 2, which describes an image (i.e., statue) with a head of gold, a chest and arms made of silver, a belly and thighs made of brass, legs of iron, and feet made partly of iron and partly of clay.

   In Daniel 2, Daniel tells King Nebuchadnezzar that he (the king) represents the head of gold and that "after his kingdom" would arise another, inferior to his (as silver is considered to be inferior to gold). Other kingdoms would follow, each inferior to the one before it, as represented by the lesser values of the metals that represent them. History records that this is exactly what happened. Nebuchadnezzar's kingdom lasted from 605 B.C. to 539 B.C. Following his kingdom came the Medo-Persian empire (the chest and arms of silver; 539 B.C. – 331 B.C.), the Greek empire (belly and thighs of brass; 331 B.C. – 168 B.C.), and the Roman empire (the legs of iron; 168 B.C. – 476 A.D.).

   As for the feet that were comprised of iron and clay, this kingdom is presently rising and will be on the earth when Christ returns. We know this because this kingdom is destroyed when Jesus returns and establishes His heavenly kingdom, as described in Dan 2:34-35 and Dan 2:44-45). Dan 2:43 further indicates that at least some of those who participate in this iron/clay kingdom are evil *spiritual* beings who "mingle themselves with the seed of men." The fact that they are *mingling* with men tells us that they are *not* men. This seems eerily familiar to what occurred prior to the great flood, when God wiped out civilization due to the intermingling of the "sons of God" with the daughters of men (Gen 6:1-4).

The kingdoms of Dan 2 were clearly successive as Dan 2:39 has Daniel telling the king that "After you, another kingdom will arise, inferior to yours. Next, a third kingdom…Finally, there will be a fourth kingdom…" In contrast, the kingdoms that are described in Daniel 7 exist concurrently, not successively.

2. <u>The kingdoms that are being described by the beasts of Daniel 7 are all on the earth when Christ returns</u>. We know this because Daniel 7:9-12 tells us that *Christ personally dethrones the fourth king upon His return and takes away the dominion of the remaining three kings, although the latter three kingdoms are still allowed to exist (at least for a while).*

   Dan 7:9 states, "*I beheld until the thrones* (of the four beasts) *were cast down and the Ancient of Days did sit.*" Dan 7:11 states that the fourth beast is slain and destroyed but verse 12 states, "*As concerning the rest of the beasts* (meaning the lion with eagle's wings, the leopard with wings of a fowl, and the bear)*, they had their dominion taken away, yet their lives were prolonged for a season and a time.*" For these things to happen, these kings/nations *must all be reigning on the earth at the time of His return.*

Neither of the two criteria described above are met by using the interpretation of these nations as Babylonians, Medes, Persians, and Greeks, so they cannot be the subjects of Dan 7:9-12. These kingdoms did not all exist on the earth simultaneously but appeared sequentially. Additionally, the kingdoms of the Babylonians and Medes no longer exist. While, the Persians and Greeks *do* currently exist on the earth, they are not currently global powers. Furthermore, these two nations are unambiguously equated with other beasts (a ram and a goat, respectively) within Daniel 8.

In Daniel 8, the Medes and Persians are described as a "ram with two horns" and the kingdom of Greece as a "rough goat" (Dan 8:20 – 21). If one clings to the conventional wisdom regarding the identification of the Dan 7 beasts, then the Medes and Persians would have already been identified (jointly) as a bear, and the Greeks as a four-headed leopard. While it is certainly possible that God could refer to these same nations as different beasts between Daniel 7 and Daniel 8, this is not supported by the biblical evidence and would be inconsistent with how nations are identified throughout the bible.

The fact that the kings/kingdoms of Daniel 7 must be reigning on the earth during Christ's return is bolstered by Dan 7:16-22, which indicates that the "four kings" shall be dethroned by the "saints of the Most High" when Jesus establishes His kingdom (Dan 7:9). This verse specifically states that the thrones of these kings/kingdoms were cast down and the Ancient of Days did sit. These scriptures tell us that the four kings/kingdoms are supplanted by Christ's heavenly kingdom, which is established after He gathers up the saints and defeats Satan's forces through the battle of Armageddon (Dan 7:21-27).

God revealed to Daniel *over 2,500 years ago* the symbols of various kingdoms/nations that would exist concurrently on this earth when Christ returns (Dan 7). There are currently five nations on the face of this earth that have incorporated *these very same symbols* into their national identities. Additionally, this is the first time in recorded human history that all of these nations/symbols have existed concurrently as global powers. The bible tells us that Christ supplants these nations upon His return, when He begins to reign.

So…which kingdoms are being represented in Daniel 7? Based on the following, I am convinced that they include the United Kingdom, the United States of America, Russia, Germany, and France[24]:

- The Lion with Eagles Wings equates to the United Kingdom and to the United States, respectively.

  The national symbols for the U.K. and the U.S. are the lion and the eagle, respectively. While these symbols were initially merged into a single creature, the eagle's wings were ultimately plucked from the lion, lifted from the earth, made to stand upon the feet as a man, and a man's heart was given unto

[24] I was originally introduced to the identification of these nations in this manner through the works of Rev. Irvin Baxter of Endtime Ministries (Endtime.com) several years ago. Although I do not agree with some of his other teachings, my own studies have convinced me that he got this one correct.

it (Dan 7:4). This describes the separation of the U.S. (the eagle's wings) from the U.K. (the lion), with the goal of establishing the U.S. as a sovereign nation.

Once plucked from the lion, the "eagle's wings" were "made to stand upon the feet as a man and a man's heart was given to it." It is interesting that the second symbol of the U.S. is a man, known affectionately as "Uncle Sam." Both of these (i.e., the eagle and Uncle Sam) remain in use today by America as national symbols.

- The Bear with three ribs in its mouth equates to Russia

  The national symbol of Russia is the bear. This bear was instructed to "arise and devour much flesh" (Dan 7:5). During the era of the Soviet Union, tens of millions of people died as a result of imprisonment in the gulags, executions (i.e., political purges), and disastrous government-controlled agricultural reforms. Although I cannot state dogmatically the meaning of the three ribs in the bear's mouth, I believe that they may stand for the nations of Latvia, Lithuania, and Estonia, which were illegally annexed by the Soviet Union just prior to WWII.

- The Leopard with four heads and wings of a fowl on its back equates to Germany and France

  The leopard is one of the national symbols of Germany while France uses the gallic rooster. In Daniel 7, the leopard had four heads. In biblical prophecy, "heads" represent the number of times a king or kingdom will rise. This is based on Rev 17, which describes a beast having seven heads and ten horns. Rev 17:10 says that these represent seven kings, five of which have fallen, one that is, and another that is yet to come. Based on this, we can reasonably conclude that the four heads of the leopard represent the four German "Reichs", three of which have fallen and the last of which is now in ascension.

  The First Reich was that of Charlemagne, the first emperor to rule the holy Roman empire. The Second Reich began in 1871 under the leadership of Kaiser Wilhelm I and Otto Von Bismark. Hitler's infamous Third Reich arose during WWII, and the fourth and final (if biblical prophecy is to be believed) German Reich is currently rising.

The wings of the fowl on the leopard's back represent France through the Franco-German alliance that remains in place since the end of WWII.

- The fourth beast represents the European Union, a conglomeration of nations that has been forming for the last several decades and from which the antichrist (the Little Horn among the ten horns) ultimately rises (Dan 7: 8 – 11).

The convergence of all of these factors is too astonishing to be relegated to coincidence and stands as pretty powerful evidence that we are truly on the cusp of Christ's return!

By the way, three of these same beasts (minus the eagle's wings/U.S. and the fowl/France) appear on the scene again in Revelation 13. However, whereas the creatures of Daniel 7 were specifically stated to be four *separate* beasts, the beasts of Rev 13 have merged into a single beast to form a one-world government, *which is currently the goal of most world leaders around the globe*. It is from this one-world government that the antichrist ultimately arises (Rev 13: 3 – 8, same as Dan 7: 8 – 11).

It is noteworthy (in my opinion) that neither the U.S. nor France are part of this unholy, one-world alliance.

Appendix B – Godly Inspiration of the Bible		
Scripture	**King James Version**	**New International Version**
Exod 20:1	And God spake all these words saying, (gives the 10 Commandments)	And God spoke all these words (gives the 10 Commandments)
Exod 24:4	And Moses wrote all the words of the LORD	Moses then wrote down everything that the LORD had said.
Deut 29:1	These are the words of the covenant, which the LORD commanded Moses to make with the children of Israel in the land of Moab, beside the covenant that He made with them in Horeb.	These are the terms of the covenant that the LORD commanded Moses to make with the Israelites in Moab, in addition to the covenant He had made with them at Horeb.
Job 23:12	(Job answered…) Neither have I gone back from the commandment of His lips. I have esteemed the words of His mouth more than my necessary food.	(Job answered…) I have not departed from the command of His lips; I have treasured the words of His mouth more than my daily bread.
Ps 119:105	Thy word is a lamp unto my feet and a light unto my path.	Your word is a lamp for my feet, a light on my path.
Jer 1:9	(Jeremiah speaking) Then the LORD put forth His hand and touched my mouth. And the LORD said unto me, Behold, I have put My words in thy mouth.	(Jeremiah speaking) Then the LORD reached out His hand and touched my mouth and said to me, "I have put My words in your mouth.

Godly Inspiration of the Bible (cont.)		
Scripture	**King James Version**	**New International Version**
Jer 36:1-2	And it came to pass in the fourth year of Jehoiakim the son of Josiah king of Judah, that this word came from Jeremiah from the LORD, saying Take thee a roll of a book and write therein all the words that I have spoken unto thee…	In the fourth year of Jehoiakim son of Hosiah the king of Judah, this word came to Jeremiah from the LORD, "Take a scroll and write on it all the words that I have spoken to you…
Ezek 1:3	The word of the LORD came expressly unto Ezekiel the priest…and the hand of the LORD was there upon him.	…the word of the LORD came to Ezekiel the priest…There the hand of the LORD was upon him…
Hab 2:2	And the LORD answered me (the prophet Habbakuk) and said, Write the vision and make it plain upon tables, that he may run that readeth it.	Then the LORD replied, "Write down the revelation and make it plain on tablets so that the herald may run with it.
Zech 7:12	Yea, they made their hearts as an adamant stone, lest they should hear the law and the words which the LORD of hosts hath sent in His spirit by the former prophets…	But they refused to pay attention, stubbornly they turned their backs and covered their ears. They made their hearts as hard as flint and would not listen to the law or to the words that the LORD Almighty had sent by His Spirit through the earlier prophets.

Godly Inspiration of the Bible (cont.)		
Scripture	**King James Version**	**New International Version**
Matt 1:22-23	Now all this was done that it might be fulfilled which was spoken of the LORD by the prophet, saying, Behold a virgin shall be with child, and shall bring forth a son, and they shall call His name Emmanuel, which being interpreted is God with us.	All this took place to fulfill what the Lord had said through the prophet, "The virgin will conceive and give birth to a son, and they will call Him Immanuel (which means "God with us")
Matt 2:14-15	When he (Joseph) arose, he took the young child and his mother by night and departed into Egypt, and was there until the death of Herod; that it might be fulfilled which was spoken of the LORD by the prophet saying, Out of Egypt have I called My son.	So, he (Joseph) got up, took the child and his mother during the night and left for Egypt, where he stayed until the death of Herod. And so was fulfilled what the Lord had said through the prophet, "Out of Egypt I called My Son."
Matt 4:3-4	And when the tempter came to Him, he said, If Thou be the Son of God, command that these stones be made bread. But He answered and said, It is written, Man shall not live by bread alone, but by every word that proceedeth out of the mouth of God.	The tempter came to Him and said, "If you are the Son of God, tell these stones to become bread." Jesus answered, "It is written: Man shall not live by bread alone, but on every word that comes from the mouth of God."

Godly Inspiration of the Bible (cont.)		
Scripture	**King James Version**	**New International Version**
Luke 1:18-19	And Zecharias said unto the angel, Whereby shall I know this? For I am an old man, and my wife well stricken in years. And the angel answered him saying, I am Gabriel, that stand in the presence of God, and am sent to speak to thee, and to shew thee glad tidings.	Zechariah asked the angel, "How can I be sure of this? I am an old man and my wife is well along in years." The angel said to him, "I am Gabriel. I stand in the presence of Gpd and I have been sent to speak to you and to tell you this good news."
John 10:34-35	Jesus answered them (the Jews), Is it not written in your law, I said, Ye are Gods? If he called them gods, unto whom the word of God came, and the scripture cannot be broken, say ye of him, whom the Father has sanctified and sent unto the world, Thou blasphemest, because I said, I am the Son of God?	And Jesus answered them, "Is it not written in your law, 'I have said you are "gods"? If he called them "gods" to whom the word of God came – and scripture cannot be set aside – what about the One whom the Father set apart as His very own and sent into the world? Why, then, do you accuse me of blasphemy because I said, "I am God's Son?
John 16:13	…when He, the Spirit of Truth, is come, He will guide you into all truth; for He shall not speak of himself, but whatsoever He shall hear, that shall He speak…	But when He, the Spirit of Truth, comes He will guide you into all the truth. He will not speak on His own, He will speak only what He hears, and He will tell you what is yet to come.

Godly Inspiration of the Bible (cont.)		
Scripture	**King James Version**	**New International Version**
Acts 1:16	(Peter speaking) Men and brethren, this scripture needs have been fulfilled, which the Holy Ghost, by the mouth of David, spake before concerning Judas, which was guide to them that took Jesus.	…and (Peter) said, "Brothers and sisters, the scripture had to be fulfilled in which the Holy Ghost spoke long ago through David concerning Judas, who served as a guide for those who arrested Jesus."
Acts 2:4	And they were all filled with the Holy Ghost and began to speak with other tongues, as the Spirit gave them utterance.	All of them were filled with the Holy Spirit and began to speak in other tongues, as the Spirit enabled them.
Rom 3:1-2	(Paul speaking) What advantage then hath the Jew? Or what profit is there in circumcision? Much every way, chiefly, because unto them were committed the oracles of God.	Paul, a servant of Christ Jesus, called to be an apostle and set apart for the gospel of God – the gospel that He promised beforehand through His prophets in the holy Scriptures regarding His Son…

Godly Inspiration of the Bible (cont.)		
Scripture	**King James Version**	**New International Version**
1Cor 2:12-14	Now we have received not the spirit of the world, but the Spirit that is of God; that we might know the things that are freely given us of God. Which things we now speak, not in the words that man's wisdom teacheth, but which the Holy Ghost teacheth, comparing spiritual things with spiritual. But the natural man receiveth not the things of the Spirit of God, for they are foolishness unto him. Neither can he know them, because they are spiritually discerned.	What we have received is not the spirit of the world, but the Spirit who is from God, so that we may understand what God has freely given us. This is what we speak, not in words taught by human wisdom but in words taught by the Spirit, explaining spiritual realities in Spirit-taught words. The person without the Spirit does not accept the things that come from the Spirit of God but considers them foolishness, and cannot understand them because they are discerned only through the Spirit.
1Cor 14:37	If any man think himself a prophet, or spiritual, let him acknowledge that the things that I write unto you are the commandments of the LORD.	If anyone thinks they are a prophet or otherwise gifted by the Spirit, let them acknowledge that what I am writing to you is the Lord's command.
1Thess 2:13	For this cause also we thank God without ceasing, because when ye received the word of God which ye heard of us, ye received it not as the word of men, but as it is in truth, the word of God, which effectually worketh also in you that believe.	And we also thank God continually because, when you received the word of God, which you heard from us, you accepted it not as a human word, but as it actually is – the word of God – which is indeed at work in you who believe.

Godly Inspiration of the Bible (cont.)		
Scripture	**King James Version**	**New International Version**
2Tim 3:16-17	All scripture is given by inspiration of God and is profitable for doctrine, for reproof, for correction, for instruction in righteousness. That the man of God may be perfect, thoroughly furnished unto all good works.	All scripture is God-breathed and is useful for teaching, rebuking, correcting, and training in righteousness so that the servant of God may be thoroughly equipped for every good work.

Appendix C – The Natural World / Universe are Instructive		
Scripture	**King James Version**	**New International Version**
2Pet 1:20-21	Knowing this first, that no prophecy of the scripture is of any private interpretation. For the prophecy came not in old time by the will of man, but holy men of God spake as they were moved by the Holy Ghost.	Above all, you must understand that no prophecy of scripture came about by the prophet's own interpretation of things. For prophecy never had its origin in human will, but prophets, though human, spoke from God as they were carried along by the Spirit.
Job 12:7-10	But ask now the beasts and they shall teach thee, and the fowls of the air and they shall tell thee. Or speak to the earth and it shall teach thee, and the fishes of the sea shall declare unto thee. Who knoweth not in all these that the hand of the LORD hath wrought this? In whose hand is the soul of every living thing, and the breath of all mankind?	But ask the animals and they will teach you, or the birds in the sky, and they will tell you; or speak to the earth, and it will teach you, or let the fish in the sea inform you. Which of all these does not know that the hand of the LORD has done this? In His hand is the life of every creature and the breath of all mankind.
Job 35:10-11	But none saith, where is God my maker, Who giveth songs in the night; Who teaches us more than the beasts of the earth and maketh us wiser than the fowls of heaven?	But no one says, "Where is God my Maker, who gives songs in the night, Who teaches us more than He teaches the beasts of the earth and makes us wiser than the birds in the sky?
Job 36:22, 24-25	Behold, God exalteth by His power; who teacheth like Him? Remember that thou magnify His work, which men behold. Every man may see it; man may behold it afar off.	God is exalted in His power, who is a teacher like Him? …Remember to extol His work, which people have praised in song. All humanity has seen it; mortals gaze upon it from afar.

The Natural World / Universe are Instructive (cont.)		
Scripture	**King James Version**	**New International Version**
Ps 19:1-4	The heavens declare the glory of God and the firmament sheweth His handywork. Day unto day (they) uttereth speech and night unto night (they) shewest knowledge. There is no speech nor language where their voice is not heard. Their line is gone out through all the earth, and their words to the end of the world.	The heavens declare the glory of God; the skies proclaim the work of His hands. Day after day they pour forth speech; night after night they reveal knowledge. They have no speech, they use no words; no sound is heard from them. Yet their voice goes out into all the earth, their words to the ends of the world.
Ps 50:6	And the heavens shall declare his righteousness…	And the heavens proclaim His righteousness, for He is a God of justice.
Ps 97:6	The heavens declare his righteousness and all the people see His glory.	The heavens proclaim His righteousness, and all the peoples see His glory.
Ps 104:24-26	O LORD, how manifold are Thy works! In wisdom hast Thou made them all, the earth is full of Thy riches. So is this great and wide sea, wherein are things creeping innumerable, both small and great beasts. There go the ships, there is that leviathan, whom Thou hast made to play therein.	How many are Your works, LORD! In wisdom, You made them all; the earth is full of Your creatures. There is the sea, vast and spacious, teeming with creatures beyond number – living things both large and small. There the ships go to and fro, and leviathan, which You formed to frolic there.

The Natural World / Universe are Instructive (cont.)		
Scripture	**King James Version**	**New International Version**
Isa 45:18-19, 21	Thus saith the LORD that created the heavens; God Himself that formed the earth and made it; He hath established it, He created it not in vain, He formed it to be inhabited. I am the LORD and there is none else. I have not spoken in secret, in a dark place of the earth. …I declare things that are right. …who hath declared this from ancient time? who hath told it from that time? Have not I, the LORD?	For this is what the LORD says – He who created the heavens; He is God; He who fashioned and made the earth, He founded it; He did not create it to be empty but formed it to be inhabited – He says, "I am the LORD and there is no other. I have not spoken in secret from somewhere in a land of darkness. …Who foretold this long ago, who declared it from the distant past? Was it not I, the LORD?
Isa 48:2-3, 6-7	…The LORD of Hosts is His name. I have declared the former things from the beginning, and they went forth out of My mouth and I shewed them. I did them suddenly and they came to pass. …I have shewed thee new things from this time, even hidden things, and thou didst not know them. They are created now, and not from the beginning, even before the day when thou heardest them not…	…the LORD Almighty is His name; I foretold the former things long ago, My mouth announced them and I made them known, then suddenly I acted and they came to pass. …You have heard these things; look at them all. Will you not admit them? From now on I will tell you of new things, of hidden things unknown to you. They are created now, and not long ago, you have not heard of them before today…

The Natural World / Universe are Instructive (cont.)		
Scripture	**King James Version**	**New International Version**
Rom 1:19-20	Because that which may be known of God is manifest in them (i.e., godless and wicked people), for God hath shewed it to them. For the invisible things of Him from the creation of the world are clearly seen, being understood by the things that are made, even His eternal power and Godhead, so that they (i.e., the ungodly) are without excuse.	…since what may be known about God is plain to them (i.e., godless and wicked people), because God has made it plain to them. For since the creation of the world God's invisible qualities – His eternal power and divine nature – have been clearly seen, being understood from what has been made, so that people are without excuse.
Heb 11:3	Through faith we understand that the worlds were framed by the word of God, so that things which are seen were not made of things that do appear.	By faith we understand that the universe was formed at God's command, so that what is seen was not made out of what is visible.

Appendix D – The Fallacy of Human Induced Global Warming (and Man's Shortsighted Remedy)

First, let me be clear that, by referring to global warming as a "fallacy," I do not mean to imply that global warming is not a real thing. I am also not saying that human beings aren't damaging the environment, including our atmosphere. Both of these things are, unfortunately, very real. What I am saying is that global warming is a natural phenomenon that is going to happen regardless of human activities. It is a cycle that has occurred countless times in the past and it will continue to do so for as long as God allows. The problem is that the cause for it is currently being laid solely at the feet of mankind and the countermeasures that are being implemented or recommended often have unintended consequences that not only cannot solve the issue but actually cause greater harm to the environment than the original problem.

Current teachings state that at least five major ice ages have occurred throughout Earth's history, with most transpiring long before man appeared on the scene. (38) The earliest known ice age took place during Precambrian time, dating back more than 570 million years, and the most recent periods of widespread glaciation occurred during the Pleistocene Epoch (2.6 million to 11,700 years ago) (38). It's quite clear that global warming and cooling have long been a natural part of earth's cycle. Consequently, <u>any efforts on the part of man to impact this cycle is pointless</u>.

Global warming <u>*is*</u> going to happen. What very much concerns me is that many of our proposed "solutions" are knee-jerk reactions that are being implemented without any serious forethought as to their long-term consequences, which will ultimately be more damaging to the environment than our carbon emissions are currently thought to be.

So how is it that human beings are presently being touted as the primary cause of global warming?

While human activity is undoubtedly having an impact on the atmosphere, placing the blame solely on the human race ignores the fact that global cooling and warming are natural, cyclical processes that are going to occur regardless of the activities of man. How would we otherwise explain the warming periods at the end of the previous ice ages during the last several million years, when man did not yet exist?!

In "*Inconvenient Facts*" – a book that lists literally dozens of scientific reasons why human induced global warming is a myth – the author states, "In the discussion about greenhouse gases, alarmist organizations and their allies in the media focus solely on man-made gases as the main agents of greenhouse warming.[25] They do not mention the most significant greenhouse gas of all – water vapor…which contributes to between 60% and 95% of the greenhouse effect." (39) Water vapor occurs naturally, with man having very limited impact on the amount of it that appears within the atmosphere.

Global warming alarmists state that man's prolific production of carbon dioxide is a principal cause of the current round of warming. Yet, the warming effect of CO_2 actually *decreases* as the concentration of the gas increases, meaning that man's CO_2 output cannot be a main contributor to the problem. In fact, the level of CO_2 in our atmosphere is at its lowest point in the last 100,000 years and has been significantly higher than present days levels at least seven times during the last several hundred million years. (40) Additionally, while plants use photosynthesis to convert the sun's energy into food, emitting oxygen in the process, they use CO_2 for the same purpose. Consequently, greater levels of CO_2 should result in a thriving plant ecology and a commensurate increase in oxygen, which would serve to balance things out.

As a result of misinformation and an improper understanding and use of science, politicians across the globe are pushing for "cleaner" energy and the elimination of the use of fossil fuels. Unfortunately, they are rushing headlong into unchartered territory without having taken the time to study the potential impact of these new methods of energy production. The rush to replace gasoline driven vehicles with electric vehicles (EV)s is a prime example, with the significant negative impact to the environment caused by the production and use of EVs often ignored. These negative impacts include:

- Production of EV Batteries. Production requires large quantities of water, approximately half a million gallons (i.e., 500,000 gal) per each ton of lithium that is produced. Water and soil pollution are two common side effects of lithium production, with hydrochloric acid commonly being discharged.

[25] "*Inconvenient Facts*" is literally filled with scientific counter-arguments regarding claims of human induced global warming. I recommend it highly for anyone who is interested in understanding the unwarranted present-day hype.

Lithium production, which, in itself, is extremely damaging to local environments, also requires the production of other environment-damaging metals to support the assemblage of lithium batteries, such as cobalt and nickel. The production of these chemicals has more than tripled in the last 10 years, and the percentage of EVs on the road at the moment is currently less than 3%. It is estimated that the carbon dioxide that is produced through Chinese efforts at battery production are 60% higher than those produced by conventional internal combustion engines.

- Disposal of EV Batteries. Discarded EV batteries contain several compounds that are toxic to the environment. This is not an insignificant issue as only a small fraction (of EV batteries) is actually being recycled, meaning that the overwhelming majority of them end up in landfills or "short term" storage areas, awaiting the technologies that don't yet exist to allow for their recycling. A study from Australia found that over 98% of lithium-ion batteries (not exclusively car batteries) end up in landfills. This massive influx of batteries into landfills significantly increases the likelihood of landfill fires that can burn for years. Consequently, fires are becoming increasingly more common, with 21 fires reported on the site in 2018, rising to 47 by 2020. [(41)] One landfill in the Pacific Northwest is reported to have seen 124 fires between June 2017 and Dec. 2020 due to lithium-ion batteries.

- Recycling of EV Batteries. The biggest problem with recycling EV batteries is that nobody has really figured out yet how to do it effectively and efficiently. Lithium is difficult to extract from source material and requires the use of hazardous chemicals such as sulfuric acid. Additionally, in high quantities and using conventional recycling techniques, lithium is prone to spontaneous combustion.

- Increasing use of EVs requires a significantly greater production of electrical power at a time when current demands can barely be met. The use of "green" energy sources, such as solar and wind, will never be able to sufficiently keep up with the rising demand, resulting in even more reliance on fossil fuel burning plants that are said to be responsible for environment-damaging greenhouse gases.

The Biden administration set a goal for half of all new vehicles sold in the U.S. to be electric by 2030. As of July 2025, EVs accounted for only 1.4% of vehicles on the road in the U.S. Yet in states such as California, which is most actively pursuing the replacement of fossil-fueled vehicles with EVs, the headlong rush to implement EV policies is currently doomed to fail due to shortsighted political policies. One recent article states, "California's collision of its electric-vehicle mandate and its legislated transition to a zero-carbon power grid by 2045 isn't going to cause sparks as much as it will bring darkness. Because of increased demand for charging electric vehicles, (a demand that is) fully manufactured by public policy, California will fall 21 percent short of the power needed to meet the demand according to a new Pacific Research Institute report." (42)

Not only must the amount of electrical power be vastly increased, so too must the infrastructure to carry the increased production of electricity. Yet, according to this same report, "...transmission capacity will need to be roughly tripled by 2050, a number of (California) state agencies have said. This won't take years to accomplish; it will take decades and more than just a couple of them." (42)

These issues merely scratch the surface when it comes to problems with EV manufacturing and use. Other negative issues include:

- Safety. EV battery fires are notoriously difficult to extinguish as they burn much hotter and longer than other fires as the electrical current within the battery continuously generates the heat that is causing the conflagration. EV batteries are also stored within a sealed steel case and are not readily accessible to allow for direct firefighting methods, compounding the firefighting problem. Consequently, these fires require way more water than a conventional vehicle fire. Additionally, some of the gases that are created during an EV battery fire are either toxic or flammable themselves, posing additional risks to firefighters and bystanders.

Even when an EV battery fire has been extinguished, the battery packs can spontaneously re-ignite days later. To date, there is a lack of training available to firefighting crews on how to safety and properly extinguish an EV battery fire.

- Cost of Purchasing and Operation. EVs are some of the highest priced vehicles on the market today, making them generally unviable as a purchase option to most mainstream consumers. While the general maintenance costs of an EV are lower than for a fossil fuel vehicle, EV tires must be replaced more frequently due to higher torque and vehicle weight. (43) Additionally, insurance premiums for EVs are between 18% and 30% higher than they are for a similar gas-powered vehicle due to complex repairs and longer claim cycles. (44)

- Use and availability of public chargers. Current chargers are notoriously unreliable and do not exist in numbers great enough to support widespread EV use by the general population

I am certainly not opposed to cleaner energy. However, man has quite simply proven time and again to be irresponsible regarding the care of our environment, with dollar signs commonly overriding environmental concerns. For example, the world rushed headlong into the nuclear power era in the 1960's and 1970's to provide power that was being advertised as "too cheap to meter" despite not having a plan for the long-term storage and disposal of spent fuel rods, many of which will remain extremely hazardous for as long as 24,000 years!

Even today, more than seventy years after the first nuclear power plant began operation (on July 27, 1954), the issue of long-term spent fuel rod disposal remains a serious, unresolved problem, with spent fuel rods still being routinely maintained in vast on-site cooling pools for years before being sent to a more "permanent" storage facility. While it is highly unlikely that such an accident involving spent nuclear fuel would rise to the severity of one involving an operating nuclear power generator, the impact could be equally wide-spread and long-lasting. This was a serious concern during the Fukushima disaster in 2011, when the power outage resulted in an inability to provide cooling water to the thousands of spent fuel rods being "temporarily" stored within its cooling ponds.

Photo by Kato Blackmore U□ on Unsplash

Photo by Mads Eneqvist on Unsplash

Photo by Anzhela Bets on Unsplash

Photo by Romain Chollet on Unsplash

Photo by Viktor Hesse on Unsplash

Abandoned areas of Pripyat city; buildings crumbling and overtaken by vegetation. Areas surrounding the failed Fukushima Daishi plant in Japan are already beginning to look the same.

The accidents at Three Mile Island (March 1979), Chernobyl (April 1986), and Fukushima (March 2011) provide ample evidence that we can never make the generation of nuclear power a completely safe endeavor. The potential for human error, mechanical failure, natural disaster, or even intentional sabotage will always be a part of the equation, with consequences that would be wide-spread and long-term. For example, an area of over 1,000 sq. miles will long be impacted by radiation and the Ukrainian city of Pripyat, which was abandoned following the Chernobyl accident, will be uninhabitable for an estimated 3,000 years. Others feel that this is too optimistic, with the reactor site remaining uninhabitable for at least 20,000 years. [45]

We are deluding ourselves if we seriously think that we can safely store hazardously radioactive spent fuel for thousands of years without incident. Yet, the headlong rush into an era of EVs could be equally as damaging to the environment, given the planned significant increase in their proliferation worldwide, the use of currently destructive manufacturing techniques, and the lack of a plan for long-term disposal or recycling of hazardous EV batteries and other components.

The inability for man to find an ultimate solution for this issue after 70+ years of nuclear power generation does not exactly encourage me that we will ever be able to safely dispose of an ever-growing volume of hazardous EV components.

Appendix E – Use of the Word "Created" in the Bible *(i.e., Strong's 1254, "bara" and 2936, "ktizo")*		
Scripture	**King James Version**	**New International Version**
Gen 1:1	In the beginning, God *created* the heaven and the earth.	In the beginning, God *created* the heavens and the earth.
Gen 1:20-21	And God said, Let the waters bring forth abundantly the moving creature that hath life, and fowl (see NOTE 1) that may fly above the earth in the open firmament of heaven. And God *created* great whales, and every living creature that moveth, which the waters brought forth abundantly, after their kind, and every winged fowl after his kind, and God saw that it was good.	And God said, Let the water teem with living creatures and let birds fly above the earth across the vault of the sky. So God *created* the great creatures of the sea and every living thing with which the water teems and that moves about it, according to their kinds, and every winged bird according to its king. And God saw that it was good.
Gen 1:26-27	And God said, Let us make man in our image…So God *created* man in His own image, in the image of God *created* He him, male and female *created* he them	Then God said, Let us make mankind in our image, in our likeness… So God *created* mankind in His own image, in the image of God He *created* them, male and female, He *created* them.
Gen 2:3-4	And God blessed the seventh day and sanctified it, because that in it He had rested from all His work that God *created* and made. These are the generations of the heavens and of the earth when they were *created* in the day that the LORD God made the earth and the heavens. (see NOTE 1)	Then God blesses the seventh day and made it holy, because on it He rested from all the work of *creating* that He had done. (see NOTE 5)

Use of the Word "Created" in the Bible (cont.)		
Scripture	**King James Version**	**New International Version**
Gen 5:1-2	This is the book of the generations of Adam. In the day that God *created* man, in the likeness of God made He him. Male and female *created* He them, and blessed them, and called their name Adam, in the day when they were *created.* (see NOTE 1)	This is the written account of Adam's family line. When God *created* mankind, He made them in the likeness of God. He *created* them male and female and blessed them. And He called them mankind when they were *created.* (see NOTE 1)
Gen 6:7	And the LORD said, I will destroy man whom I have *created* from the face of the earth, both man and beast and creeping thing and the fowls of the air, for it repenteth me that I have made them. (see NOTE 1)	So the LORD said, I will wipe from the face of the earth the human race that I have *created*, and with them the animals, the birds, and the creatures that move along the ground, for I regret that I made them. (see NOTE 1)
Num 16:30	But if the LORD *make* (create) a new thing, and the earth open her mouth and swallow them (Dathan and Abiram) up…then you shall understand that these men have provoked the LORD.	But if the LORD brings about (*creates*) something totally new, and the earth opens its mouth and swallows them (Dathan and Abiram), …then you will know that these men have treated the LORD with contempt.
Deut 4:32	For ask now of the days that are past, which were before thee, since the day that God *created* man upon the earth, and ask from one side of heaven unto the other, whether there hath been any such thing as this great thing is, or hath been heard like it?	Ask now about the former days, long before your time, from the day God *created* human beings on the earth. Ask from one end of the heavens to the other. Has anything so great as this ever happened, or has anything like it ever been heard of?

Use of the Word "Created" in the Bible (cont.)		
Scripture	**King James Version**	**New International Version**
Ps 51:9-12	Hide Thy face from my sins, and blot out all mine iniquities. *Create* in me a clean heart, O God, and renew a right spirit within me. Cast me not away from Thy presence and take not Thy Holy Spirit from me. Restore unto me the joy of Thy salvation and uphold me with Thy free Spirit.	Hide Your face from my sins and blot out mu iniquity. *Create* in me a pure heart, O God, and renew a steadfast spirit within me. Do not cast me from your presence or take your Holy Spirit from me. Restore to me the joy our Your salvation and grant me a willing spirit to sustain me.
Ps 89:11-12	The heavens are thine (O LORD), the earth also is thine; as for the world and the fullness thereof, thou hast founded them. The north and the south thou hast *created* them…	The heavens are Yours, and Yours also the earth; you founded the world and all that is in it. You *created* the north and the south…
Ps 102:16-18	When the LORD shall build up Zion, He shall appear in His glory…This shall be written for the generation to come, and the people which shall be *created* shall praise the LORD. (see NOTE 2)	For the LORD will rebuild Zion and appear in His glory. …Let this be written for a future generation, that a people not yet *created* may praise the LORD.
Ps 104:29-30	Thou hidest Thy face, they (i.e., God's created beings) are troubled; Thou takest away their breath, they die and return to their dust. Thou sendest forth Thy Spirit, they are *created*, and Thou renewest the face of the earth.	When You hide your face, they are terrified; when You take away their breath, they die and return to the dust. When You send Your Spirit, they are *created*, and You renew the face of the ground.

Use of the Word "Created" in the Bible (cont.)		
Scripture	**King James Version**	**New International Version**
Ps 148:5	Let them (i.e., the angels, sun, moon, stars, heavens, and waters) praise the name of the LORD, for He commanded, and they were *created*.	Let them praise the name of the LORD, for at His command they were *created*.
Isa 4:5	And the LORD will *create* upon every dwelling place of mount Zion, and upon her assemblies, a cloud and smoke by day and the shining of a flaming fire by night, for upon all the glory shall be a defense.	Then the LORD will *create* over all of Mount Zion and over those who assemble there a cloud of smoke by day and a glow of flaming fire by night, over everything the glory will be a canopy.
Isa 40:25-26	To whom then will ye liken Me, or shall I be equal? saith the Holy One. Lift up your eyes on high and behold who hath *created* these things (i.e., the earth and its inhabitants), that bringest out their host by number; He calleth them all by names by the greatness of His might, for that He is strong in power, not one faileth.	To whom will you compare Me? Of who is My equal? says the Holy One. Lift up your eyes and look to the heavens; Who *created* all these?
Isa 41:20	(The LORD speaking) That they may see and know and consider and understand together, that the hand of the LORD hath done this, and the Holy One of Israel hath *created* it (i.e., the waters and the trees).	…so that the people may see and know, may consider and understand, that the hand of the LORD has done this, that the Holy One of Israel has *created* it.

Use of the Word "Created" in the Bible (cont.)		
Scripture	**King James Version**	**New International Version**
Isa 42:5	Thus saith God the LORD, He that *created* the heavens and stretched them out, He that spread forth the earth and that which cometh out of it, he that giveth breath unto the people upon it and spirit to them that walk therein.	This is what God the LORD says – the *Creator* of the heavens, Who stretches them out, Who spreads out the earth will all that springs from it, Who gives breath to its people and life to those who walk on it.
Isa 43:1	But now thus saith the LORD that *created* thee, O Jacob, and He that formed thee, O Israel. Fear not, for I have redeemed thee, I have called thee by name, thou art Mine.	But now, this is what the LORD says – He who created you, Jacob, He who formed you Israel. Do not fear, for I have redeemed you, I have summoned you by name, you are Mine.
Isa 43:6-7	…bring My sons from afar and my daughters from the ends of the earth, even every one that is called by My name, for I have *created* him for My glory, I have formed him, yea, I have made him. (see NOTE 1)	…bring My sons from afar and My daughters from the ends of the earth – everyone who is called by My name, whom I *created* for my glory. Whom I formed and made.

Use of the Word "Created" in the Bible (cont.)		
Scripture	**King James Version**	**New International Version**
Isa 45:5-8	I am the LORD, and there is none else. There is no God beside Me. I have girded thee, though thou hast not known Me. That they may know from the rising of the sun, and from the west that there is none beside me. I am the LORD and there is none else. I form (yatsar – Strong's 3335) the light and *create* darkness, I make peace and *create* evil (see NOTE 3), I the LORD do all these things. Drop down, ye heavens, from above and let the skies pour down righteousness, let the earth open and let them bring forth salvation, and let the righteousness spring together, I the LORD have *created* it.	I am the LORD and there is no other; apart from Me, there is no God. I will strengthen you, though you have not acknowledged Me, so that from the rising of the sun to the place of its setting people may know that there is none beside Me. I am the LORD and there is no other. I form light and *create* darkness, I bring prosperity and *create* disaster; I, the LORD, do all these things. You heavens above, rain down My righteousness, let the clouds shower it down. Let the earth open wide, let salvation spring up, let righteousness flourish with it. I, the LORD have created it.
Isa 45:12	(Thus saith the LORD) I have made the earth and *created* man upon it. I, even My hands, have stretched out the heavens and all their host have I commanded.	It is I who made the earth and *created* mankind on it. My own hands have stretched out the heavens, I marshalled their starry hosts.
Isa 45:18	For thus saith the LORD that *created* the heavens, God Himself that formed the earth and made it, He hath established it, He *created* it now in vain, he formed it to be inhabited. I am the LORD and there is none else.	For this is what the LORD says – He who *created* the heavens, He is God, He who fashioned and made the earth, He founded it; He did not *create* it to be empty but formed it to be inhabited – He says "I am the LORD and there is no other.

Use of the Word "Created" in the Bible (cont.)		
Scripture	**King James Version**	**New International Version**
Isa 48:2-3, 6-7	…The LORD of Hosts is His name. I have declared the former things from the beginning, and they went forth out of My mouth and I shewed them. I did them suddenly and they came to pass. …I have shewed thee *new things* from this time, even hidden things, and thou didst not know them. They are *created* now, and not from the beginning, even before the day when thou heardest them not…	…you who call yourselves citizens of the holy city and claim to rely on the God of Israel – the LORD Almighty is His name; I foretold the former things long ago, My mouth announced (*created*) them and I made them known; then suddenly I acted and they came to pass.
Isa 54:16	Behold, I have *created* the smith that bloweth the coals in the fire and bringeth forth an instrument for his work, and I have *created* the waster to destroy.	See, it is I who created the blacksmith who fans the coal into flame and forges a weapon for its work. And it is I who have *created* the destroyer to wreak havoc…
Isa 57:19	I *create* the fruit of the lips; peace, peace to him that is far off.	…creating praise on their lips. Peace, peace, to those far and near…
Isa 65:17-18	For behold, I *create* new heavens and a new earth, and the former shall not be remembered, nor come to mind. But be ye glad and rejoice in that which I *create*, for behold, I *create* Jerusalem a rejoicing and her people a joy.	See, I will *create* new heavens and a new earth. The former things will not be remembered, nor will they come to mind. But be glad and rejoice forever in what I will *create*, for I will create Jerusalem to be a delight and its people a joy.

Use of the Word "Created" in the Bible (cont.)		
Scripture	**King James Version**	**New International Version**
Jer 31:22	…for the LORD hath *created* a new thing in the earth, a woman shall compass a man.	…the LORD will create a new thing on earth – the woman will return to the man…
Ezek 21:19	Also, thou Son of Man, appoint Thee two ways…and choose (*create*) a place, choose (*create*) it at the head of the way to the city.	Son of Man, mark out (*create*) two roads for the sword of the king of Babylon to take, both starting at the same country.
Ezek 21:30	…I will judge thee in the place where thou wast *created*, in the land of thy nativity.	…in the place where you were *created*, in the land of your ancestry, I will judge you.
Ezek 28:12-13, 15	…thus saith the LORD God (to the king of Tyrus)… thou hast been in Eden the garden of God, every precious stone was thy covering…the workmanship of thy tabrets and of thy pipes was prepared in thee in the day that thou wast *created*. …Thou wast perfect in thy ways from the day that thou wast *created*, till iniquity was found in thee. (see NOTE 4)	This is what the Sovereign LORD says, You were the seal of perfection, full of wisdom and perfect in beauty, you were in Eden the garden of God; every precious stone adorned you…Your settings and mountings were made of gold; on the day you were *created* they were prepared. …you were blameless in your ways from the day you were *created*, till wickedness was found in you.

Use of the Word "Created" in the Bible (cont.)		
Scripture	**King James Version**	**New International Version**
Amos 4:13	For lo, He that formeth the mountains and *createth* the wind, and declareth unto man what is His thought, that maketh the morning darkness and treadeth upon the high places of the earth. The LORD, the God of Hosts is His name.	He who forms the mountains, who *creates* the wind, and who reveals His thoughts to mankind. Who turns dawn to darkness and treads on the heights of the earth, the LORD God Almighty is His name.
Mal 2:10	Have we not all one Father? Hath not one God *created* us?	Do we not all have one Father? Did not one God *create* us?
Matt 19:4	And He (Jesus) answered and said unto them, Have ye not read, that He which made (*created*) them at the beginning made them male and female.	Haven't you read, He (Jesus) replied, that at the beginning the Creator made (*created*) them male and female…
Mark 13:19	For in those days (i.e., the end times) shall be affliction, such as was not from the beginning of the creation which God *created* unto this time, neither shall be.	…those will be days of distress unequaled from the beginning, when God *created* the world, until now – and never to be equaled again.
Rom 1:25	Who changed the truth of God into a lie, and worshipped and served the *creature* more than the Creator, who is blessed forever.	They exchanged the truth about God for a lie, and worshipped and served *created* things rather than the Creator, Who is forever praised.

Use of the Word "Created" in the Bible (cont.)		
Scripture	**King James Version**	**New International Version**
Rom 8:19-22	For the earnest expectation of the *creature* waiteth for the manifestation of the sons of God. For the *creature* was made subject to vanity, not willingly, but by reason of him who hath subjected the same in hope. Because the *creature* itself also shall be delivered from the bondage of corruption into the glorious liberty of the children of God. For we know that the whole *creation* groaneth and travaileth in pain together until now.	For the *creation* waits in eager expectation for the children of God to be revealed. For the *creation* was subjected to frustration, not by its own choice, but by the will of the one who subjected it, in hope that the *creation* itself will be liberated from its bondage to decay and brought into the freedom and glory of the children of God. We know that the whole *creation* has been groaning as in the pains of childbirth right up to the present time.
Rom 8:39	Nor height, nor depth, nor any other *creature*, shall be able to separate us from the love of God, which is in Christ Jesus our Lord.	…neither height, nor depth, nor anything else in all *creation*, will be able to separate us from the love of God what is in Christ Jesus our Lord.
1Cor 11:9	…neither was man *created* for the woman, but the woman of the man.	…neither was man *created* for woman, but woman for man.
2Cor 5:17	Therefore, if any man be in Christ, he is a new *creature*, old things are passed away. Behold, all things are become new.	Therefore, if anyone is in Christ, the new *creation* has come. The old has gone, the new is here.

Use of the Word "Created" in the Bible (cont.)		
Scripture	**King James Version**	**New International Version**
Eph 2:10	For we are His workmanship, *created* in Christ Jesus unto good works, which God hath ordained that we should walk in them.	For we are all God's handiwork, *created* in Christ Jesus to do good works, which God prepared in advance for us to do.
Eph 2:15	Having abolished in His flesh the enmity, even the law of commandments contained in ordinances, for to *make* in Himself of twain one new man, so making peace.	…by setting aside in His flesh the law with its commands and regulations. His purpose was to *create* in Himself one new humanity out of the two, thus making peace…
Eph 3:9	…to make all men see what is the fellowship of the mystery, which from the beginning of the world hath been hid in God, who *created* all things by Jesus Christ.	…to make plain to everyone the administration of this mystery, which for ages past was kept hidden in God, who *created* all things.
Eph 4:24	…that ye put on the new man, which after God is *created* in righteousness and true holiness.	…put on the new self, *created* to be like God in true righteousness and holiness.
Gal 6:15	For in Christ neither circumcision availeth anything, nor uncircumcision, but a new *creature*.	…neither circumcision nor uncircumcision means anything; what counts is the new *creation*.

Use of the Word "Created" in the Bible (cont.)		
Scripture	**King James Version**	**New International Version**
Col 1:15-16	Who (i.e., Jesus) is the image of the invisible God, the firstborn of every creature. For by Him were all things *created*, that are in heaven, and that are in earth, visible and invisible…all things were *created* by Him and for Him.	The Son is the image of the invisible God, the firstborn of all *creation*. For in Him all things were *created*; things in heaven and on earth, visible and invisible…all things were *created* though Him and for Him. He is before all things, and in Him all things hold together.
Col 1:23	…the hope of the gospel, which ye have heard, and which was preached to every *creature* which is under heaven…	…this is the gospel that you heard and that has been proclaimed to every *creature* under heaven…
Col 3:10	…and have put on a new man, which is renewed in knowledge after the image of Him who *created* him.	…put on the new self, which is being renewed in knowledge in the image of its *Creator*.
2Pet 3:3-4	…that there shall come in the last days scoffers, walking after their own lusts, and saying "where is the promise of His coming? For since the fathers fell asleep, all things continue as they were from the beginning of the *creation*.	…in the last days, scoffers will come, scoffing and following their own evil desires. They will say "where is His coming He promised? Ever since our ancestors died, everything goes on as it has since the beginning of *creation*.

Use of the Word "Created" in the Bible (cont.)		
Scripture	**King James Version**	**New International Version**
1Tim 4:1-4	Now the Sprit speaketh expressly, that in the latter times some shall depart from the faith, giving heed to seducing spirits and doctrines of the devils. Speaking lies in hypocrisy, having their conscience seared with a hot iron, forbidding to marry and commanding to abstain from meats, which God hath *created* to be received with thanksgiving…	The Spirit clearly says that in the later times some will abandon the faith and follow deceiving spirits and things taught by demons. Such teachings come through hypocritical liars, whose consciences have been seared as with a hot iron. They forbid people to marry and order them to abstain from certain foods, which God *created* to be received with thanksgiving…
Heb 4:13	Neither is there any *creature* that is not manifest in His sight, but all things are naked and open to Him with whom we have to do.	Nothing in all *creation* is hidden from God's sight. Everything is uncovered and laid bare before the eyes of Him to whom we must give account.
Heb 9:11-12	But Christ being an high priest of good things to come by a greater and more perfect tabernacle, *made* not with hands, that is to say not of this building, neither by the blood of goats and calves but by His own blood He entered into the holy place, having obtained eternal redemption for us.	But when Christ came as high priest of the good things that are now already here, He went through the greater and more perfect tabernacle that is not made with human hands, that is to say, is not part of this *creation*. He did not enter by means of the blood of goats and calves, but He entered the Most Holy Place once and for all by His own blood, thus obtaining eternal redemption.

Use of the Word "Created" in the Bible (cont.)		
Scripture	**King James Version**	**New International Version**
Rev 4:11	Thou art worthy O Lord to receive glory and honor and power, for Thou hast *created* all things, for Thy pleasure they are and were *created.*	You are worthy, our Lord and our God, to receive glory and honor and power, for you *created* all things, and by your will they were *created* and have their being.
Rev 10:5-6	…and swear by Him that lived for ever and ever, Who *created* heaven and the things that are therein, and the earth and the things that therein are, and the sea and the things that are therein…	And the angel I had seen standing on the sea ad on the land raised his right hand to heaven, And he swore by Him who lives for ever and ever, who *created* the heavens and all that is in them…
NOTE 1:	In this passage, the terms "created" and "made" are both used to describe the creative process, indicating that He first created the materials that He needed, then made (or fashioned) them from the materials that He previously created.	
NOTE 2:	This verse is speaking of the ultimate re-creation of God's people after the tribulation of the latter days.	
NOTE 3:	The word that is translated as "evil" here is "ra" (Strong's 7451), and generally means adversity, affliction, or calamity. It does not carry the meaning of "morally corrupt," which is typically associated with Satan and evil spirits. God is good and would not intentionally create something that is immoral, dishonest, or wicked.	
NOTE 4:	This passage is speaking about the fall of Satan and affirms that the devil, too, was created by God.	
NOTE 5:	In an effort to render the text into modern English, the NIV loses a little something in the translation here; whereas the coincident use of both "created" and "made" within this text is missing, depriving the reader of the hint that there is a distinct difference between the two words.	

Appendix F – The Laws of Nature are Fixed and Unchanging		
Scripture	**King James Version**	**New International Version**
Gen 8:21-22	...the LORD said in His heart, I will not again curse the ground anymore for man's sake, for the imagination of his heart is evil from his youth. Neither will I again smite any more every living thing as I have done. While the earth remaineth, seedtime and harvest, and cold and heat, and summer and winter, and day and night shall not cease.	…the LORD said in His heart, never again will I curse the ground because of humans, even though every inclination of the human heart is evil from childhood. And never again will I destroy all living creatures, as I have done. As long as the earth endures, seedtime and harvest, cold and heat, summer and winter, day and night will never cease.
Job 26: 7-8, 10	He stretcheth out the north over the empty place and hangeth the earth upon nothing. He bindeth the waters up in thick clouds and the cloud is not rent under them. …He hath encompassed the waters with bounds until the day and night come to an end.	He spreads out the northern skies over empty space; He suspends the earth over nothing. He wraps up the water in His clouds, yet the clouds do not burst under their weight. He marks out the horizon on the face of the waters for a boundary between light and darkness.
Ps 104:5	(Bless the LORD, oh my soul…) Who laid the foundations of the earth, that it should not be removed forever.	He sets the earth on its foundations; it can never be moved.

The Laws of Nature are Fixed and Unchanging (cont.)		
Scripture	**King James Version**	**New International Version**
Ps 104: 19-20	...He appointed the moon for seasons, the sun knoweth His going down. Thou makest darkness and it is night...	He made the moon to mark the seasons, and the sun knows when to go down. You bring darkness, it becomes night…
Eccl 1:9-10	The thing that hath been, it is that which shall be, and that which is done is that which shall be done, and there is no new thing under the sun. Is there anything whereof it may be said, See, this is new? It hath been already of old time, which was before us.	What has been will be again, what has been done will be done again; there is nothing new under the sun. Is there anything of which one can say, "Look! This is something new"? It was here already long ago; it was here before our time.
Eccl 3:1	To everything there is a season, and a time to every purpose under the heaven.	There is a time for everything and a season for every activity under the heavens.
Eccl 8:6	…to every purpose, there is time and judgement…	…there is a proper time and procedure (process) for every matter.

The Laws of Nature are Fixed and Unchanging (cont.)		
Scripture	**King James Version**	**New International Version**
Jere 33:20,25	Thus saith the LORD, If ye can break My covenant of the day and My covenant of the night, that there should not be day and night in their season…Thus saith the LORD, If My covenant be not with day and night, and if I have not appointed the ordinances of the heaven and earth…	This is what the LORD says, "If you can break My covenant with the day and My covenant with the night, so that day and night no longer come at their appointed time… This is what the LORD says, "If I have not made my covenant with day and night and established the laws of heaven and earth…
Rom 8:19-22	For the earnest expectation of the creature waiteth for the manifestation of the sons of God. For the creature was made subject to vanity, not willingly, but by reason of Him who hath subjected the same in hope, because the creature itself also shall be delivered from the bondage of corruption into the glorious liberty of the children of God. For we know that the whole creation groaneth and travaileth in pain together until now.	For the creation waits in eager expectation for the children of God to be revealed. For the creation was subjected to frustration, not by its own choice, but by the will of The One who subjected it, in hope that the creation itself will be liberated from its bondage to decay and brought to the freedom and the glory of the children of God. We know that the whole creation has been groaning as in the pains of childbirth right up to the present time.

The Laws of Nature are Fixed and Unchanging (cont.)		
Scripture	**King James Version**	**New International Version**
Col 1:14-17	In whom we have redemption through His (Jesus') blood, even the forgiveness of sins; Who is the image of the invisible God, the firstborn of every creature. For by Him were all things created, that are in heaven, and that are in the earth, visible and invisible…all things were created by Him and for Him. And He is before all things, and by Him all things consist.	…in whom (Jesus) we have redemption, the forgiveness of sins. The Son is the image of the invisible God, the firstborn over all creation. For in Him all things were created, things in heaven and on earth, visible and invisible… all things have been created through Him and for Him. He is before all things, and in Him all things hold together.
John 17:24	...Thou lovest me before the foundation of the world	…You loved me before the creation of the world…
Eph 1:4	According as He hath chosen us in Him before the foundation of the world…	For He chose us in Him before the creation of the world…
2Tim 1:9	Who hath saved us and called us with an holy calling, not according to our works, but according to His own purpose and grace, which was given us in Christ Jesus before the world began.	He has saved us and called us to a holy life, not because anything that we have done but because of His own purpose and grace. This grace was given us in Christ Jesus before the beginning of time.

The Laws of Nature are Fixed and Unchanging (cont.)		
Scripture	**King James Version**	**New International Version**
Titus 1:2	…in hope of eternal life, which God, who cannot lie, promised before the world began.	…in the hope of eternal life, which God, who does not lie, promised before the beginning of time.
1Pet 1:19-20	(we were redeemed) with the precious blood of Christ, as of a lamb without blemish and without spot, who verify was foreordained before the foundation of the world, but was made manifest in these last times for you.	(we were redeemed) with the precious blood of Christ, a lamb without blemish or defect. He was chosen before the creation of the world but was revealed in these last times for your sakes.

Appendix G – Megalithic Structure Architecture

All photos were obtained from Unsplash.com, providing free-access, royalty-free images, videos, audio and other media.

Figure G1: Gate of the Sun near Lake Titicaca, Bolivia, carved from a single piece of andesite stone (which has a hardness of between 6 and 7 on the Mohs Hardness scale)
(by Matheus Oliveira via Unsplash.com

Figure G2: The 1,200-ton Stone of the Pregnant Woman (a.k.a. Stone of the South), Baalbek, Lebanon
Photo by Ralph Ellis via Wikipedia

Figure G3: Stone of the Pregnant Woman. Note the size in comparison to the human workers
(By Oregon State University Archives - Colossal Hewn Block, Ancient Quarries BaalbekUploaded by PDTillman, No restrictions, https://commons.wikimedia.org/w/index.php?curid=14006292)

Figure G4: Foundation stones of the Temple of Jupiter, Baalbek; the largest weighing in at 1,000 tons.
(By Brattarb - Own work, CC BY-SA 3.0, https://commons.wikimedia.org/w/index.php?curid=46933789 Wikipedia)

Figure G5: Six Massive Stones at Ollantaytambo, the largest weighing approximately 50 tons (100,000 lbs. / 50802 kg)
(Photo by Ruben Hanssen on Unsplash)

Figure G6: The Terraces of Ollantaytambo, Peru showing puzzle-piece like construction. Note how the stones each contain multiple angles that fit together as though each was made to fit uniquely with its neighboring stones. Similar construction can be seen at Sacsayhuaman
(Photo by Ruben Hanssen on Unsplash)

Figure G7: Size and interlocking nature of some stones at Sacsayhuaman. The prominent large stone at the center is approximately 12 feet high (3.6 m)
(Photo by Ruben Hanssen on Unsplash)

Figure G8: Size and interlocking nature of some stones at Sacsayhuaman. The prominent large stone at the center is approximately 15 feet high (4.6 m). Some stones are over 23 feet (7 m) in height (Photo by Ruben Hanssen on Unsplash)

Figure G9: Segment of a wall at Sacsayhuaman. Note the distinct difference in construction methods, as evidence by the attempt to fill in one segment of the wall with smaller stones. (By Diego Delso, CC BY-SA 4.0, https://commons.wikimedia.org/w/index.php?curid=43175184)

Figure G10: Close-up of a wall segment at Sacsayhuaman, showing seamless, puzzle-piece like construction (By McKay Savage from London, UK, CC BY 2.0, https://commons.wikimedia.org/w/index.php?curid=23462672)

Figure G11: Sacsayhuaman, showing the scale of the walls compared to human beings.
(Photo by Apollo https://www.flickr.com/photos/39185776@N02/51188929810/, CC BY 2.0, https://commons.wikimedia.org/w/index.php?curid=151175452)

Figure G12: Sacsayhuaman. Note the rounded edges at the corners. (Photo by Ruben Hanssen on Unsplash)

Figure G13: Intricately carved stones of Puma Punku, Bolivia (Photo by Matheus Oliveira on Unsplash)

Figure G14: Evidence of precision machining, Puma Punku, Bolivia (By Brattarb - Own work, CC BY-SA 3.0, https://commons.wikimedia.org/w/index.php?curid=15148737)

Figure G15: Intricately carved stone blocks at Puma Punka, Bolivia (By Janikorpi - Own work, CC BY-SA 3.0, https://commons.wikimedia.org/w/index.php?curid=18763693)

Appendix H – Fallen Angels and Giants	
Scripture	**Passage Text and/or Explanation**
There were 3 separate words used within the bible to describe the giants, including: * n'yphil (Strong's 5303, meaning feller, bully, or tyrant; from the root word naphal, which means "to fall") * gibbor (Strong's 1368, meaning "powerful, warrior, tyrant"; from the root word geber = valiant man or warrior); and * rapha (Strong's 7497, meaning 1. Invigorating; used as a root = heal or mend. 2. A giant).	
Gen 6:1-4	And it came to pass, when men began to multiply on the face of the earth, and daughters were born unto them, that the sons of God saw the daughters of men, that they were fair, and they took them wives of all which they chose. …There were giants (n'yphilim) in the earth in those days, and also after that, when the sons of God came in unto the daughters of men, and they bare children to them, the same became 'mighty men' (gibbowr), which were of old, men of renown.
Gen 14:1-7	Talks about an uprising in which the giants (i.e., Rephaites) in Ashteroth Karnaim, the Zuzites in Ham, the Emites in Shaveh Kiriathiam, and the Horites in the hill country of Seir are defeated. The Zuzites and Emites are identified as giants in subsequent versus, so it is entirely possible that the same can be said of the Horites.
Num 13:22	Israelite spies went into Hebron, where Ahiman, Sheshai, and Talmai, the children of Anak, were. Anak is confirmed as a giant in subsequent verses.
Num 13:33	During the exodus, Israelite spies are sent into Canaan from Kadesh-barnea. The spies come back with a report about how the Israelite would be unable to dwell in Canaan because of the "sons of Anak, which come of the giants Here, as in Gen 6:1-4, gibbowr is used in conjunction with n'yphil in such a way as to indicate that the n'yphilim were 'sons of the gibbowr.

Fallen Angels and Giants (cont.)	
Scripture	**Passage Text and/or Explanation**
Num 28-29, 32-33	The Israelite spies report that they saw the sons of Anak there and that the land was possessed by cannibalistic men of giant stature. They report, "And there we saw giants (n'phiyl), the sons of Anak, which come of the giants (gibbowr); and we saw we were in our own sight as grasshoppers; and so were we in their sight."
Deut 1:28	Moses is rebuking Israel, talking about when the spies went out to scout the land of Canaan, who reported, "The people is greater and taller than we, the cities are great and walled up to heaven and moreover we have seen the sons of the Anakims there."
Deut 2:9-11	Moses is reviewing what happened at Kadesh-barnea in Deut 1:19-33 saying that the people of Canaan were 'greater and taller than we.' When speaking of the land of the Moabites, Moses says, "The Emims dwelt therein in times past, a people great and many and tall as the Anakims, which also were accounted giants as the Anakims, but the Moabites call them Emim.
Deut 2:18-23	Moses describes the land that was given to Lot for a possession as land, "that also was accounted a land of giants, giants dwelt therein in old time, and the Ammonites call them Zamzummims. A people great and many and tall as the Anakims, but the Lord destroyed them (the Zamzummin) before them (the Ammonites) and they (the Ammonites) succeeded them (Zamzummin) and dwelt in their stead.

Fallen Angels and Giants (cont.)	
Scripture	**Passage Text and/or Explanation**
Deut 3:11	For only Og, king of Bashan, remained of the remnant of the giants; behold his bedstead was a bedstead of iron; is it not in Rabbath of the children of Ammon? Nine cubits was the length thereof and four cubits the breadth of it, after the cubit of a man (a cubit is approx 18" so this bedstead measured 13.5" feet by 6 feet)
Deut 3:13	Same as above
Deut 3:13	The region of Argob, with all Bashan, is called land of the giants.
Deut 9:1-2	(God is talking to Israel) Hear, O Israel, thou art pass over Jordan this day to go in to possess nations greater and mightier than thyself, cities great and fenced up to heaven. A people great and tall, the children of the Anakims, whom thou knowest and of whom thou hast heard said, "Who can stand against the children of Anak?"
Jos 12:4-8	Mentions king Og of Bashan as a remnant of the giants.
Jos 13:12	Same as above
Jos 14:12-15	Moses requests of the Lord that He "give me this mountain…for thou heardest in the day how the Anakims were there and that the cities were great and fenced" Hebron given to Caleb as an inheritance. Hebron was known before as Kirjatharba, which Arba was a great man among the Anakims."
Jos 15:8	The border of the land that was given to the tribe of Judah "went up to the top of the mountain that lieth before the valley of Hinnom westward, this is at the end of the valley of the giants northward."

Fallen Angels and Giants (cont.)	
Scripture	**Passage Text and/or Explanation**
Jos 15:13-14	When dividing the promised lands among Israel, Joshua gives unto Caleb, the son of Jephunneh, "… a part among the children of Judah, according to the commandment of the Lord to Joshua, even the city of Arba the father of Anak, which city is Hebron. And Caleb drove thence the three sons of Anak, Sheshai and Ahiman and Talmai, the children of Anak."
Jos 17:15	Joshua admonishes the children of Manasseh (who are not happy with their inheritance of land) to "get thee up to the wood country, and cut down for thyself there in the land of the Perizzites and of the giants, if Mount Ephraim be too narrow for thee."
Jos 18:16	The border (of Benjamin's territory) came down to the end of the mountain that lieth before the valley of the son of Hinnom, and which is in the valley of the giants on the north.
Jos 21:10-13	The children of Aaron were given "the city of Arba the father of Anak, which city is Hebron, in the hill country of Judah."
Jug 1:10	Mentions the slaughter of Sheshai, Ahiman, and Talmai at Hebron.
Judges 1:20	Caleb is said to have expelled from Hebron the three sons of Anak.

Fallen Angels and Giants (cont.)	
Scripture	**Passage Text and/or Explanation**
2Sam 21:15-22	Talks about the war against the Philistines, "and Ishbibenob, which was of the sons of the giant, the weight of whose spear weighed 300 shekels of brass in weight (3,300 grams or 7 lbs.) …then Sibbechai the Hushathite slew Saph, which was of the sons of the giant… slew the brother of Goliath the Gittite, the staff of whose spear was like a weaver's beam. ...and there was yet a battle in Gath, where was a man of great stature, that had on every hand six fingers and on every foot six toes, four and twenty in number, and he also was born to the giant… These four were born to the giant in Gath, and fell by the hand of David.
1Chron 20:4-8	There arose war at Gezer with the Philistines, at which time Sibbechai the Hushathite slew Sippai, that was of the children of the giant
Jude 5-16	Talks about the imprisonment of the angels who did not keep their positions of authority and abandoned their proper dwelling. It likens the wickedness of Sodom and Gomorrah to the behavior of these fallen angels and quotes a prophecy of Enoch regarding their coming judgement.

Appendix I – God Created Everything		
Scripture	**King James Version**	**New International Version**
Gen 1	(The entire chapter)	
Gen 2:7	And the LORD God formed man from the dust of the ground, and breathed into his nostrils the breath of life, and man became a living soul.	Then the LORD God formed man from the dust of the ground and breathed into his nostrils the breath of life, and man became a living being.
Ex 20:11	For in six days the LORD made the heaven and the earth, the sea, and all that is in them…	For in six days the LORD made the heavens and the earth, the sea, and all that is in them…
Ex 31:17	…for in six days the LORD made heaven and earth…	…for in six days the LORD made the heavens and the earth…
Deut 4:32	For ask now of the days that are past, which were before thee, since the day that God created man upon the earth…	Ask now about the former days, long before your time, from the day that God created human beings on the earth…
Neh 9:6	Thou, even thou, art LORD alone. Thou hast made heaven and the heaven of heavens, with all their host; the earth, and all things that are therein; the seas, and all that is therein; and thou preservest them all, and the host of heaven worshipeth thee.	You alone are the LORD. You made the heavens, even the highest heavens, and all their starry host, and the earth and all that is on it, and the seas and all that is in them. You give life to everything, and the multitudes of heaven worship You.
Job 9:8-9	(God…) alone spreadeth out the heavens and treadeth upon the waves of the sea. He maketh Arcturus, Orion, and Pleiades…	He alone stretches out the heavens and treads on the waves of the sea. He alone is the Maker of the Bear and Orion, the Pleiades and the constellations of the south.

God Created Everything (Including the Physical Laws) (cont.)		
Scripture	**King James Version**	**New International Version**
Job 10:8,10-11	Thine hands have made me and fashioned me together… Thou hast clothed me with skin and flesh and hast fenced me with bone and sinew.	Your hands shaped me and made me… Did you not…clothe me with skin and flesh and knit me together with bones and sinews?
Job 26: 7-8, 10	He stretcheth out the north over the empty place and hangeth the earth upon nothing. He bindeth the waters up in thick clouds and the cloud is not rent under them. …He hath encompassed the waters with bounds until the day and night come to an end.	He spreads out the northern skies over empty space; He suspends the earth over nothing. He wraps up the water in His clouds, yet the clouds do not burst under their weight. He marks out the horizon on the face of the waters for a boundary between light and darkness.
Job 34:12-15	Yea, surely God will not do wickedly, neither will the Almighty pervert judgement. Who hath given Him a charge over the earth? Or who hath disposed the whole world? If He set His heart upon man, if He gather unto Himself His spirit and His breath, all flesh shall perish together and man shall turn again unto dust.	It is unthinkable that God would do wrong, that the Almighty would pervert justice. Who appointed Him over the earth? Who put Him in charge of the whole world? If it were His intention and He withdrew His spirit and breath, all humanity would perish together and mankind would return to the dust.
Job 36:26-28	Behold, God is great and we know Him not, neither can the number of His years be searched out. For He maketh small the drops of water; they pour down rain according to the vapor thereof, which the clouds do drop and distil upon man abundantly.	How great is God – beyond our understanding! The number of His years is past finding out. He draws up the drops of water which distill as rain to the streams, and the clouds pour down their moisture and abundant showers fall on mankind.

God Created Everything (Including the Physical Laws) (cont.)		
Scripture	**King James Version**	**New International Version**
Job 37:5-6	God thundereth marvelously with His voice; great things doeth He, which we cannot comprehend. For He saith to the snow, Be thou on the earth, likewise to the small rain and to the great rain of His strength.	God's voice thunders in marvelous ways; He does great things beyond our understanding. He says to the snow, "Fall on the earth," and to the rain shower, "Be a mighty downpour."
Job 37:10-13	By the breath of God frost is given and the breadth of the waters is straitened. Also by watering, He wearieth the thick cloud, He scattereth His bright cloud, and it is turned round about by His counsels that they may do whatsoever He commandeth them upon the face of the world in the earth. He causeth it to come…	The breath of God produces ice, and the broad waters become frozen. He loads the clouds with moisture, He scatters his lightning through them. At His direction they swirl around over the face of the whole earth to do whatever He commands them. He brings the clouds to punish people or to water His earth and show His love.
Job 38: 4-11 (excerpts)	(The LORD answered Job and said…), Where wast thou when I laid the foundations of the earth? Who hath laid the measure thereof, if thou knowest? Or, who hath stretched the line upon it? …who laid the cornerstone thereof; when the morning stars sang together and all the sons of God shouted for joy? Who shut up the sea with doors, when it brake forth…? When I made the cloud the garment thereof and thick darkness a swaddlingband for it, and brake up for it My decreed place, and set doors and bars, and said, Hitherto shalt thou come, but no further, and here shall thy proud waves be stayed?	(Then the LORD spoke to Job out of the storm, and said…) "Where were you when I laid the earth's foundation? Who marked off its dimensions? Surely you know! Who stretched a measuring line across it? …who laid its cornerstone – while the morning stars sang together and all the angels shouted for joy? Who shut up the seas behind doors when it burst forth from the womb, when I made the clouds its garment and wrapped it in thick darkness, …when I said "This far you may come and no farther; here is where your proud waves halt?

God Created Everything (Including the Physical Laws) (cont.)		
Scripture	**King James Version**	**New International Version**
Job 38: 25-26	Who hath divided a watercourse for the overflowing of waters or a way for the lightning of thunder, to cause it to rain on the earth where no man is…	Who cuts a channel for the torrents of rain, and a path for the windstorm to water a land where no one lives…
Job 40:15	(Then answered the LORD…) Behold now behemoth, which I made with thee; he eateth grass as an ox.	Look at behemoth, which I made along with you and which feeds on grass like an ox.
Ps 8:3-6	When I consider Thy heavens, the work of Thy fingers; the moon and the stars, which Thou hast ordained. What is man that Thou art mindful of him, and the son of man that Thou visitest him? For Thou hast made him a littler lower than the angels and has crowned him with glory and honor. Thou hast madest him to have dominion over the works of Thy hands; Thou hast put all things under his feet.	When I consider Your heavens, the work of Your fingers, the moon and the stars, which You have set in place, what is mankind that You are mindful of them, human beings that You care for them? You have made them a little lower than the angels and crowned them with glory and honor, You made them rulers over the works of Your hands and put everything under their feet…
Ps 33:6-9	By the word of the LORD were the heavens made, and all the host of them by the breath of His mouth. He gathereth the waters of the sea together as an heap; He layeth up the depth in storehouses. Let all the earth fear the LORD, let all inhabitants of the world stand in awe of Him. For He spake, and it was done. He commanded and it stood fast.	By the word of the LORD the heavens were made, their starry host by the breath of His mouth. He gathers the waters of the sea into jars, He puts the deep into storehouses. Let all the earth fear the LORD; let all people of the world revere Him. For He spoke, and it came to be; He commanded, and it stood firm.
Ps 50:1	The Mighty God, even the LORD, hath spoken, and called the earth from the rising of the sun unto the doing down thereof.	The Mighty One, God, the LORD, speaks and summons the earth from the rising of the sun to where it sets.

God Created Everything (Including the Physical Laws) (cont.)		
Scripture	**King James Version**	**New International Version**
Ps 102:25	Of old hast Thou laid the foundation of the earth and the heavens are the work of Thy hands.	In the beginning You laid the foundations of the earth, and the heavens are the work of Your hands.
Ps 104:5	(Bless the LORD, oh my soul…) Who laid the foundations of the earth, that it should not be removed forever.	He sets the earth on its foundations; it can never be moved.
Ps 104: 19-20	…He appointed the moon for seasons, the sun knoweth His going down. Thou makest darkness and it is night...	He made the moon to mark the seasons, and the sun knows when to go down. You bring darkness, it becomes night…
Ps 139:14	I will praise Thee, for I am fearfully and wonderfully made! Marvelous are Thy works…	I praise You because I am fearfully and wonderfully made, Your works are wonderful…
Prov 8:26-28	While as yet He had not made the earth, nor the fields, nor the highest part of the dust of the world; when He prepared the heavens, I (i.e., wisdom) was there; when He set a compass upon the face of the depth. When He established the clouds above and strengthened the fountains of the deep.	…I (wisdom) was given birth, before He made the world or its fields or any of the dust of the earth. I was there when He set the heavens in place, when He marked out the horizon on the face of the deep, when He established clouds above and fixed securely the fountains of the deep, when He gave the sea its boundary so the waters would not overstep His command, and when He marked out the foundations of the earth.

God Created Everything (Including the Physical Laws) (cont.)		
Scripture	**King James Version**	**New International Version**
Eccl 3:11	He hath made everything beautiful in His time, also He hath set the world in their heart, so that no man can find out the work that God maketh from the beginning to the end.	He has made everything beautiful in its time. He has also set eternity in the human heart, yet no one can fathom what God has done from beginning to end.
Jere 33:20,25	Thus saith the LORD, If ye can break My covenant of the day and My covenant of the night, that there should not be day and night in their season…Thus saith the LORD, If My covenant be not with day and night, and if I have not appointed the ordinances of the heaven and earth…	This is what the LORD says, "If you can break My covenant with the day and My covenant with the night, so that day and night no longer come at their appointed time… This is what the LORD says, "If I have not made my covenant with day and night and established the laws of heaven and earth…
Isa 40:25-26, 28	To whom then will ye liken Me, or shall I be equal? saith the Holy One. Lift up your eyes on high, and behold Who hath created these things, that bringeth out their host by number, He calleth them all by names by the greatness of His might, for He is strong in power, not one faileth. …Hast thou not known, hast thou not heard, that the everlasting God, the LORD, the Creator of the ends of the earth, fainteth not neither is weary? There is no searching of His understanding.	To whom will you compare Me? Or who is My equal" says the Holy One. Lift up your eyes and look to the heavens; Who created all these? He who brings out the starry host one by one and calls forth each of them by name. Because of His great power and mighty strength, not one of them is missing. …The LORD is the everlasting God, the Creator of the ends of the earth.

God Created Everything (Including the Physical Laws) (cont.)		
Scripture	**King James Version**	**New International Version**
Isa 42:5	(Thus saith the LORD…) I have made the earth and created man upon it. I, even My hands, have stretched out the heavens and all their host have I commanded. …Thus saith God the LORD, He that created the heavens and stretched them out, He that spread forth the earth and that which cometh out of it, He that giveth breath unto the people upon it, and the spirit to them that walk therein.	This is what God the LORD says – the Creator of the heavens, Who stretches them out, Who spreads out the earth with all that springs from it, Who gives breath to its people, and life to those who walk upon it.
Isa 43:7 All three forms of create/made are used here	(The LORD speaking says) Even every one that is called by My name; for I have created (bara) him for my glory, I have formed (yatsar) him; yea, I have made (asah) him.	(The LORD speaking says) everyone who is called by My name, whom I created for my glory, whom I formed and made.
Isa 45:12	I have made the earth and created man upon it. I, even My hands, have stretched out the heavens and all their host have I commanded.	It is I who made the earth and created mankind on it. My own hands stretched out the heavens; I marshaled their starry hosts.
Isa 45:18-19, 21	I have made the earth and created man upon it. I, even My hands, have stretched out the heavens and all their host have I commanded. …Thus saith the LORD that created the heavens; He hath established it, He created it not in vain, He formed it to be inhabited. I am the LORD and there is none else. I have not spoken in secret, in a dark place of the earth. …I declare things that are right. …who hath declared this from ancient time? who hath told it from that time? Have not I, the LORD?	For this is what the LORD says – He who created the heavens, He is God; He who fashioned and made the earth, He founded it; He did not create it to be empty but formed it to be inhabited – He says, "I am the LORD, and there is no other. I have not spoken in secret, from somewhere in a land of darkness… …Who foretold this long ago, who declared it from the distant past? Was it not I, the LORD?

God Created Everything (Including the Physical Laws) (cont.)		
Scripture	**King James Version**	**King James Version**
Isa 48:2-3	…The LORD of Hosts is His name. I have declared the former things from the beginning, and they went forth out of My mouth and I shewed them. I did them suddenly and they came to pass.	…the LORD Almighty is His name; I foretold the former things of long ago, My mouth announced them and I made them known, then suddenly I acted and they came to pass
Jer 10:12-13	He hath made the earth by His power, He hath established the world by His wisdom and hath stretched out the heavens by His discretion. When He uttereth His voice…he maketh lightnings with rain and bringeth forth the wind.	But God made the earth by His power; He founded the world by His wisdom and stretched out the heavens by His understanding. When He thunders, the waters in the heavens roar; He makes the clouds rise from the ends of the earth. He sends lightning with the rain and brings out the wind from His storehouses.

God Created Everything (Including the Physical Laws) (cont.)		
Scripture	**King James Version**	**King James Version**
John 1:1-3, 10, 14	In the beginning was the Word, and the Word was with God, and the Word was God. The same was in the beginning with God. All things were made by Him, and without Him was not anything made that was made. …He was in the world and the world was made by Him, and the world knew Him not. …and the Word was made flesh and dwelt among us and we beheld His glory, the glory of the only begotten of the Father, full of grace and truth.	In the beginning was the Word, and the Word was with God, and the Word was God. He was with God in the beginning. Through Him all things were made, without Him nothing was made that has been made. …He was in the world, and though the world was made through Him, the world did not recognize Him. …The Word became flesh and made His dwelling among us. We have seen His glory, the glory of the one and only Son, who came from the Father, full of grace and truth.
Acts 17:24-25, 28	God that made the world and all things therein, seeing that He is Lord of heaven and earth, dwelleth not in temples made with hands. Neither is worshipped with men's hands as though He needed anything, seeing as He giveth to all life and breath, and all things. For in Him we live and move and have our being…for we are also His offspring.	The God who made the world and everything in it is the Lord of heaven and earth and does not live in temples built by human hands. And He is not served by human hands, as if He needed anything. …For in Him we live and move and have our being…we are His offspring.

God Created Everything (Including the Physical Laws) (cont.)		
Scripture	**King James Version**	**King James Version**
Rom 8:19-22	For the earnest expectation of the creature waiteth for the manifestation of the sons of God. For the creature was made subject to vanity, not willingly, but by reason of Him who hath subjected the same in hope, because the creature itself also shall be delivered from the bondage of corruption into the glorious liberty of the children of God. For we know that the whole creation groaneth and travaileth in pain together until now.	For the creation waits in eager expectation for the children of God to be revealed. For the creation was subjected to frustration, not by its own choice, but by the will of The One who subjected it, in hope that the creation itself will be liberated from its bondage to decay and brought to the freedom and the glory of the children of God. We know that the whole creation has been groaning as in the pains of childbirth right up to the present time.
Col 1:14-17	In whom we have redemption through His (Jesus') blood, even the forgiveness of sins; Who is the image of the invisible God, the firstborn of every creature. For by Him were all things created, that are in heaven, and that are in the earth, visible and invisible…all things were created by Him and for Him. And He is before all things, and by Him all things consist.	…in whom (Jesus) we have redemption, the forgiveness of sins. The Son is the image of the invisible God, the firstborn over all creation. For in Him all things were created, things in heaven and on earth, visible and invisible… all things have been created through Him and for Him. He is before all things, and in Him all things hold together.
Heb 11:3	Through faith we understand that the worlds were framed by the word of God, so that things which are seen were not made of things that do appear.	By faith we understand that the universe was formed at God's command, so that what is seen was not made out of what was visible.

ABOUT THE AUTHOR

Thomas G. Fournier is certified as a Professional Researcher and Writer by the National Security Agency (NSA) and served for over 25 years as an intelligence analyst, researcher, and reporter within the NSA, the Central Intelligence Agency, and the United States Marine Corp. He currently lives in eastern Connecticut.

For another great read by this author, see "Ishtaq; The Second Vial".

Made in United States
North Haven, CT
31 January 2026

87666454R00134